The Curious Cook at Home

To the three who share my daily bread —
Jeff, Darl and Dailyn.

You are what it's all about, guys.

dee Hobsbawn–Smith

The Curious Cook
at home

whitecap

Edited by Elaine Jones
Proofread by Patryce Kidd
Design by Janine Vangool
Photography by Maggie Lennon
Food styling by dee Hobsbawn-Smith

Printed and bound in Canada

NATIONAL LIBRARY OF CANADA CATALOGUING IN PUBLICATION

Hobsbawn-Smith, Dee

The curious cook at home / Dee Hobsbawn-Smith.

Includes index.
ISBN 1-55285-602-X

1. Cookery. I. Title.
TX714.H618 2004   641.5   C2004-904630-6

The publisher acknowledges the financial support of the Government of Canada through the Book Publishing Industry Development Program for our publishing activities.

Table of Contents

Thank You

I am honoured and amazed when I think about the village of loving and supportive people that surrounds me.

To the Whitecap team, for producing another lovely book for me! To Robert McCullough, for hanging in and waiting for the really clear idea to percolate and emerge; to Elaine Jones, for her gentle insistence on syntax and clarity; to photographer Maggie Lennon, for her wonderful and evocative images of my food; and to Janine Vangool, for an elegant design.

To my dear friends, Phyllis McCord and Sarah Newman, who feed me grilled cheese sandwiches and tuna surprise with unflinching élan, share tales of growing kids over countless bottles of wine and hug me when I need it or not.

To my son Darl, for his company in the kitchen and for singing while he stirs and chops. To my youngest son, Dailyn, for his hugs, empathy ("Mom, stop flappin' the bird!") and unequivocal teenage honesty ("Tasty...not!").

To my colleagues and dining companions extraordinaire — Las Chicas, Les Chiquettes, The Chixx — for friendship, blunt honesty, fashion tips that I occasionally heed ("No more pink, dee, ever!") and conviviality.

To my colleagues in Slow Food Calgary, for friendship, shared beliefs and all that great food and wine!

To my longtime pal Janet Webb, for her tasteful wine pairing. Even though volleyball games are often the only spot we meet at recently, a friend is true to the end. And to Richard Harvey and Heidi Wechselberger of Metrovino, for continuing my education in wine.

To my dear friend Susan Hopkins, adventurous soul and *bon vivant*, co-owner of Red Tree Kitchen, for testing recipes, using recipes, cooking recipes and cheering me on.

To the women in my writing group, for being the wonderful women they are and for their support, love and well-tuned ears.

To the gifted restaurateurs, chefs, growers and producers who generously share their passions and their lives with me across the kitchen table.

To my Mom and Dad and Grandma Sarah, because. And to my sister Lee, for listening; to my bro Blaine, for his mad-genius art; and to my other brother Brad, for his mad-genius art.

To Phil Holcomb, coach extraordinaire, for knowing what questions to ask and what goals to set.

To Susi Hately Aldous, for the yoga, and to Daphne Bashford, for the massages. To Annette Bossert, for her care and concern in a trying year. As "witch doctors" go, you really cook.

To the people who read my work, and who take the time to call, e-mail or stop me in the street to talk about what they are cooking. Every artist needs to believe that her work is heeded and isn't falling silently into a void. The wonderful cooks who share their thoughts and their cookies with me have refuelled my belief in the importance of home food.

To my spouse, Jeff, for loving me unconditionally, for gracefully enduring my manic alternating between the kitchen and the computer screen, for cooking me meals he swears keep me grounded in the real world and for restoring my belief in happily-ever-after. *Te queiro.*

In our home, we say a blessing at the dinner table. Some nights, Jeff says a Catholic one, remnant from his Newfoundland childhood; some days, my sons chant a New Age mantra, left over from their Waldorf education. The intention is always the same. We are guests and guardians of the planet, and we appreciate the earth's generosity. Thank you, *merci, gracias.*

dee Hobsbawn-Smith

Foreword
by Catherine Ford

For the past 20 years, dee Hobsbawn-Smith has been a noted and respected public figure in the "food scene" in Calgary. And yes, she does insist her first name is lowercase. And if you ask, she'll say her hyphenated last name is backwards — that Smith-Hobsbawn doesn't quite ring with the same authority. And she has a secret personal passion for multi-coloured toenails, each one painted a different Crayola candy shade. But don't let any of those idiosyncrasies get in the way of understanding that dee might be eccentric, but in the way all artistic people are somewhat off-plumb. It's what makes dee and her fellow professional chefs curious and experimental in their kitchens — which are to them what easels and oils are to painters. In turn, they deliver to us, their waiting public, the best food that can be produced under any circumstances.

Dead of winter in Alberta? Root vegetables and dried fruit. Middle of June? Strawberries and asparagus. Dee is the kind of chef who believes you cook with what nature gives you, not with exotic ingredients that require a trip to New York for the supplies.

Dee's interests are never far from food — writing about it, experimenting with it, cooking it, serving it and loving it. She ran her own restaurant and catering company for years and is one of the directors of Calgary's Slow Food movement. (After all, eating is more than just gathering calories, it's a process requiring care, and it's a matter of love. Dee believes that, like love, it shouldn't be rushed.)

It is a pleasure to be counted among dee's friends — those lucky people who have been in her kitchen and sampled what curiosity, talent and interest can produce from ingredients that are available to all of us. What dee's explorations in her own home can teach the rest of us is that one doesn't have to be a professional chef to be curious and brave.

Dee trained in Canada, France and Ireland, and she shares her culinary passion and curiosity weekly with readers of the *Calgary Herald* and in publications such as *City Palate* and *Canadian Living*. Her first book, *Skinny Feasts*, published in 1997, proved you didn't need a lot of fat to get the flavour into (shhh, don't tell) healthier and lower-calorie dishes. She followed that with *The Quick Gourmet* and has contributed to both *Dishing* and *Double Dishing*.

Just knowing dee has made me a more adventuresome cook, although the day I decided to add grapefruit to mashed turnips was not one of my more glorious moments at the stove. Curiosity isn't always successful, but the home cook always learns something by experimenting.

And that is actually what dee intends in her writing — she doesn't expect you to be a professional chef, but just a curious one. Try something new. Add an ingredient you've never used before; a spice with which you're unfamiliar. Somebody, after all, was the first to figure out chicken livers were the food of the gods. Someone ate the first oyster.

Your kitchen is there for three reasons: you need a place for friends to gather; occasionally your family wants dinner; and it's an opportunity to be creative and curious with the bounty of nature.

Call this new book of dee's your guide to that bounty.

CATHERINE FORD

Catherine Ford has been a journalist and columnist for 40 years. She is a wannabe cook whose talents lie more in the sampling than in the preparing.

Preface
by John Gilchrist

Chefs are an interesting lot. There are those who chop and sizzle with flair and gusto. There are others who are meticulous and painstaking in their creations. And there are some who lovingly describe every detail of their work with flowery prose.

But seldom are all the talents combined in one person. The flamboyant chef may be too difficult to follow, the meticulous one too shy to convey the message to others, and the flowery one may be, well, too flowery.

In dee Hobsbawn-Smith we see the rare embodiment of all the above qualities. She's a skilled chef in the kitchen, schooled in the classics yet willing to stretch the boundaries of creativity. Her attention to detail is admirable; she can put up a peach jam with the best of them and braise a leg of lamb that can bring tears to one's eyes. And she can teach. She loves spreading the culinary word by educating adults, children, awkward single men and savvy kitchen semi-pros in everything from proper knife handling to delicate dessert constructions.

So who is this demi-goddess of the kitchen?

She's a Saskatchewan farm girl raised on the natural goodness of the prairies. She's someone who understands root vegetables and dill weed and the basic foundations of food. She's also the proud mother of two young men who have the kind of kitchen acumen that future mothers-in-law will drool over. They have learned well from her. She's a relentless chef, the kind of annoying person who always has a larder full of the latest preserves and a freezer packed with trays of tasty treats. And she's easily as relentless a writer, crafting stories on food, its creators and its delights.

I knew dee before I met her. It was sometime around 1990 when Canadian chefs were still an oddity in the professional kitchen. Especially young, outspoken, Canadian female chefs. It was at a time when Canadian cuisine was starting to gain recognition as unique and worthwhile. I was made aware of this young chef who was using fresh, organic, Canadian ingredients in her upstart catering business. I sampled; I liked. The gentle blends of flavours, the assured balance of textures and the pride in the food were all front and centre.

When dee opened her own restaurant that sense of quality and confidence continued. The food was stunning. A piece of salmon from her kitchen prepared over a decade ago still stands for me as a marker of what can be done with fresh seafood.

Many chefs would have been content at founding their own restaurant and running an active catering business. But dee decided to spread the word farther by turning to writing. And with the same flair and attention to detail, she is excelling in a difficult world. In this, her third book, she brings us some of the recipes she cherishes most dearly. These are the dishes she feeds her family and friends, and a sparkling collection it is.

So have a taste of dee's world at home. You'll enjoy the person as much as the food.

JOHN GILCHRIST

John Gilchrist is Calgary's most recognizable food voice as CBC Radio One's long-serving restaurant reviewer on the "Calgary Eye Opener."

Introduction

Ten years ago, when I began to put my food on the page instead of the plate, I realized that my job was to bridge the growing divide between home cooking and restaurant food.

The gap has grown. It will never close. Even the advent of the Slow Food movement cannot bring the two worlds together. Few home cooks can replicate the extra hands, the time or the training that combine to produce the increasingly intricate foods that appear as edible art in our restaurants. Nor should we attempt to. Restaurants have food television to keep up with, and well-travelled palates to wow. It makes for a potently addictive brew of flash, flavours and entertainment. That's a lot for a home cook to compete with.

As a food professional, I have observed that many of the men and women who cook for a living have a dual sensibility about food. There is a big difference between what they cook at work, to impress or turn heads, and what they choose to feed themselves and their families.

What I hear is a groundswell of interest in "real." It's in the voices of kids who are beginning to think that the kitchen is a cool place to hang out, the keen interest from folks learning to feed themselves in midlife, and the passion with which cooks and consumers talk about regional cuisine and locally sourced ingredients.

It seems that in spite of the increasing commercialization of food, diners really want the intimacy of making and sharing food at the kitchen table. What a relief! I had feared for years that "real" cooking, food from family kitchens, was at risk. But I have changed my mind. Home cooking is here to stay.

I, too, have worked as a restaurant chef. But my cooking life began at home, and it is to my home kitchen that I have returned in this book. Along with me, I bring my family's influence and some tales about my friends in their kitchens. Here is my home cooking. As my Grandma Sarah always said, it's nothin' fancy, but you are welcome to share it with me.

As you peruse this book, allow your curiosity free rein. It is a useful trait for a cook, a window you can open a crack, out of mild interest, or fling

SLOW FOOD

A culinary revolution is growing. In 1989, in Paris, a gathering of delegates from 15 nations signed the manifesto that created the Slow Food movement. "Slow" has taken root, and now has 65,000 members in more than 40 countries. It is the antithesis of fast food, the global weed that serves up mass-produced, soulless food, but Slow Food is not just the act of cooking over a low flame. At its roots, Slow Food is a joyful philosophy that actively supports hands-on artisanal producers, heirloom regional plant species and the pleasures of food.

Slow Food is personal. It attempts to reconnect our families to what we blithely discounted in the wide when you want to know every detail. When you just need to get dinner on the table, set your curiosity aside, but return to it later. Curiosity contributes to the making of a cook through new dishes and old ideas. On these pages you will find cooking methods that have been passed on from our grandmothers and great-grandmothers, methods that have not changed much through time and require only open-minded practice to master. But even mistakes have value. Some of my young students have gone home and reported, "Mom, dee says there are no mistakes in cooking, just experiments." Is life really that simple?

Relax. It is. Cooking can calm your nerves and restore a sense of rightness to a world disrupted by management meetings and big-city traffic. Cooking can help those of us who are not calm by nature; the fiery-spirited may find it helps to remember what was written in 1923 by Marcel Boulestin, long before gridlock and double-booked schedules: "A good cook is not necessarily a good woman with an even temper. Some allowance should be made for artistic temperament." So here is a salute to the fiery and the fierce, the temperament that brings good home cooking proudly to the table and says, "Here is what I made for you. Share it with me."

race to progress — our food supply, and our food producers. Our children do not know a weed from a carrot top, or what a hoe is for, or what pigs or goats eat. They don't know (and neither apparently do our governments) the difference between a herbivore and a carnivore, or what is fitting food for either. They think food originates in the over-processed packages that line our grocery shelves.

I want my unborn grandchildren to experience more than out-of-season fruit in a sterile supermarket. I want them to eat peaches so incredibly sweet and perfect they bring tears to their eyes. I want them to know where their nourishment comes from. Fast food has a lot to answer for: our kids have absorbed some not-so-cool lessons about food. "More, better, faster" has come to be, along with the profit motive, the predominant characteristic of a society focused on immediacy.

Knives and Other Useful Tools

A cook's toolbox is a strange and wondrous thing. In it can be found the usual, muddled together with the unexpected. Serious tools for serious cooks include a mallet for pounding meat (what else?), a mortar and pestle for grinding herbs and spices, zester, channel knife, melon-baller, piping bags with various tips, whisks in different shapes for beating food into submission, biscuit cutters (useful for scaling fish as well as the gentler art of cutting dough) and at least one rolling pin.

Any cook worth her salt jar has run a raid below stairs and brought the following up into the kitchen: a blowtorch, needle-nose pliers, a fine rasp, a selection of gaskets and slabs of cedar or alder. These are all the fine and delicate tools you might expect of a cook of haute cuisine. No kidding. Use the blowtorch to create crackling-hard sugar jackets of amber on your crème brûlée. Use the rasp to whisk fine threads of zest from the skin of a lemon, or pare rock-hard Parmesan into submissive heaps of grated cheese. Pull salmon pin bones with the needle-nose pliers. The gaskets might fit the blender or the espresso pot. The unsprayed wood? Soak it for awhile, then grill or roast your salmon on it.

Tools of the trade begin with knives. Top-quality knives are very thin, especially along the cutting surface; thinness is equated with sharpness. There are 3 basic chores performed by knives — chopping, slicing or cutting, and butchering. A *chef's knife, a paring knife and a boning knife*, in that order, perform these tasks best.

Chef's knives are best in a length of 8–12 inches (20–30 cm); shorter blades are not as efficient at chopping. Choose a knife that fits your hand size and feels balanced.

Paring knives are 3–4 inches (8–10 cm) long and come in different blade shapes: *bird's beak, miniature boning, fluting, clip point (granny), sheep's foot and spearpoint.*

Boning knives can be rigid or flexible, with a curved or straight edge that may be high-tipped, and are usually 5 inches (12 cm) long.

Knife manufacturers produce knives at varying levels of quality, with prices that reflect the difference. You get what you pay for. Here are the basic blends of metals to look for.

Carbon steel is an iron-carbon alloy with a long history. The blackened blade in your grandmother's kitchen is likely carbon steel. The iron content is stained, corroded and darkened by high-acid foods, salt, humidity and time. These knives are easily sharpened.

Stainless steel contains chromium, which strengthens and prevents oxidation or corrosion. These knives are relatively brittle, harder to sharpen and don't hold an edge as long as the alternatives. They are recommended for coastal dwellers, where high humidity and salt-laden air will pit or corrode any carbon steel blade.

High-carbon stainless steel is an offspring of stainless steel, with added molybdenum and vanadium. It is easier to sharpen and holds an edge longer than stainless. It resists rust, pitting and abrasion and is a more flexible metal that can recover from bending.

Careful care and storage keeps blades in good shape and protects you from injury. Wash knives by hand immediately after use — not in a dishwasher, which dulls blades. Store knives in a block or on a wall magnet (do not leave them loose in the "horrible drawer"). Coat high-carbon blades with food-grade mineral oil to prevent rust and oil wooden handles occasionally; wipe off residue before use. Do not place knives in the sink, where water can damage them and hide their sharp edges.

Dull knives are dangerous because they require force. Sharp knives need no force to do their job. Use a diamond core or ceramic steel, harder than the metal in your knife, and use it daily, or whenever you pick up your knife. Sharpen knives on a whetstone, take them to a specialist to be ground or buy a draw-through sharpener.

Safe cutting is another way to keep your precious hands and fingers safe. Use knives for cutting, slicing, chopping or butchering (not for opening jars or as hammers or levers). When cutting round items such as tomatoes or oranges, cut a thin slice from one side to establish a flat surface that will keep the food from wobbling.

Pantry
(A Bit on the Side)

Condiment Collecting

They call me the Condiment Queen. My oldest son, Darl, says that if a stranger looked in our fridge, she'd think I was a member of the Condiment of the Month Club. But even though my cupboard and fridge are crammed with condiments I have bought to experiment with, I still like to make my own. Homemade condiments add depth of flavour to simple dishes and a sense of festivity to plain tables. Most of these enhancements are quick to make and pay great dividends. A well-stocked pantry makes it much easier to pull together a meal from what might look, to outsiders, like a jumbled collection of jars.

Cooking from the pantry is still a smart move, just as it was when our grandmothers fed our grandfathers. The modern pantry has changed, and so have its contents: the New Age pantry encompasses a cupboard, the fridge and the freezer. Make the most of them. The pantry still can save us time, money and last-minute trips to the store. On days when we have no extra time for trips anywhere, when just getting home from work and putting dinner on the table is job enough, the pantry is our lifeline.

Managing Your Pantry

Use your freezer wisely, no matter what size it is. Buy the best, in bulk and in season if you can, then repackage your booty into usable, snug, appropriate freezer containers. If you cannot cope with a case of peppers or tomatoes in season, share with a friend. It is quicker to thaw stock and beans than to cook them, so make big batches every few months and freeze each in small tubs, perfect for potfuls of risotto, quick cassoulet or soup. In the summer or fall have a cooking bee with your buddy: make pesto, roast tomatoes for sauce and peppers for peeling, then reach for them all winter long. Make extra when you cook — it is no more work to double many dishes and have enough for the freezer. Label everything with name and date. You won't remember in 2 months just what is what, so save yourself from surprises.

Reorganize your shelves. Group foods by type or by geographic origin in the fridge or cupboard to reduce foraging time. Toss the deadwood, including old spices and stale herbs.

There is no point in settling for poor-quality food when good food is so simple to make, and so satisfying too. The pantry is just as useful now as it was in our grandmothers' time.

The Balancing Act

Balancing the flavour of a dish with a handful of condiments can be a bit like a precarious pedal on the circus high-wire. It takes perseverance, bravery and a certain amount of faith to get it right. For a cook, this means one taste after another, adding condiments one at a time until you get the flavour you want. Recognize the four components that make up taste in the western world: *sweet* (maple syrup, honey, fruit, Indonesian soy sauce); *sour* (wine, citrus juice, vinegar, pickles); *salty* (salt, anchovies, fish sauce or shrimp paste, cheese, bacon, ham); *bitter* (grapefruit, Campari, horseradish, coffee, chicory, fenugreek, black tea, tannic red wine). Asian cooks include *hot* (hot chili flakes, black pepper, Szechuan pepper, chile sauce or paste), and *umami* (in proteins and fermented food like soy sauce, balsamic vinegar, Parmigiano-Reggiano cheese), which means perfect balance, or wholeness.

Altering the flavour profile of a dish sometimes involves adding fat in the form of oil, butter, cream, nuts or cheese. If a sauce is too tannic, it can be softened by whisking in a knob of butter or a splash of oil. If a vinaigrette is too sharp but the other flavours balance, more oil (slowly added, tasting along the way) will solve the problem. A high-fat cheese or a dash of whipping cream will alter the balance of a sauce or gratin in the same way.

Salt is the first thing to reach for when food tastes flat. Add it in small increments. Salt can tone down an overly acidic dish or rein in a dish that is too sweet.

Sweet ingredients smooth out other flavours or counteract acids, salt or heat. Something sour (acid) will help to highlight a flavour or it can even out the edges of a too-sweet or too-hot dish. A dash of hot chili flakes or a few generous twists from the pepper mill can lighten a cloying or smooth-textured dish. Caramelize onions with a splash of balsamic for umami, which is usually provided by protein, such as chicken or beef, in meatless dishes.

Vanilla-Citrus Vinaigrette

VANILLA VINEGAR

Infusing vinegar is an easy and quick way to transfer flavours. My current favourite is vanilla vinegar. The intoxicating scent and taste of vanilla adds unexpected nuances to savoury dishes, especially asparagus, lobster and mixed greens. Choose a fairly mild, neutral vinegar you enjoy, such as Japanese rice vinegar or Champagne vinegar. Split 2 or 3 vanilla pods lengthwise, scrape out the seeds, then drop pods and seeds into the bottle of vinegar. Cover, label and let stand for a month before using.

Blended citrus juices make a very appealing salad dressing. Vanilla is unexpected in savouries and makes the palate sit up and take notice. Drizzled on roasted beets, tossed with grilled peppers and asparagus or spooned across a chicken thigh awaiting the grill or on shellfish straight from the pan, this vinaigrette is subtle, vaguely suggestive of something sweeter.

¾ cup (175 mL)	citrus juice
¼ cup (50 mL)	**Vanilla Vinegar (see left)**
1 Tbsp. (15 mL)	**smooth Dijon mustard**
2–4 Tbsp. (25–50 mL)	**honey, melted**
¼ cup (50 mL)	**olive oil**
1 Tbsp. (15 mL)	**minced chives**
1 tsp. (5 mL)	**minced fresh thyme**
~	**kosher salt and hot chili flakes to taste**

Strain the juice if necessary. Add the vinegar, mustard and honey, whisking in well. Slowly add the olive oil, whisking, shaking or stirring vigorously to blend and emulsify. Stir in the herbs, then season with salt and hot chili flakes. Refrigerate until needed, shaking or stirring well to reblend if it separates.

MAKES ABOUT 1 ¼ CUPS (300 mL)

VARIATIONS

Your pantry is a great source of inspiration for variations on vinaigrette. Change the oil or the vinegar, then add different spice blends, whisk in olive or caper paste (page 28), tiny bits of Pickled Lemons (page 24), a bit of Fresh Peach Chutney (page 22), or your favourite mustard. The results are as individual as you and your palate.

Gewürztraminer Vin

Although I am firmly in the "Riesling Rules!" camp of wine drinkers, I also love the generous nature of Gewürztraminer. It is great to drink and amazingly good to cook with. I use this dressing on chicken salad, pan-steamed salmon, tender greens, crunchy apple salads and in salads with contrasting textures.

1 bottle	**Gewürztraminer**
¼–½ cup (50–125 mL)	**melted honey**
2 Tbsp. (25 mL)	**Dijon mustard**
~	**kosher salt and hot chili flakes to taste**
½ cup (125 mL)	**sunflower oil**
2 Tbsp. (25 mL)	**minced fresh thyme**
~	**zest of 1 lime**
¼ cup (50 mL)	**lime juice (or less)**

In a nonreactive pot, simmer the wine over medium-high heat until it is reduced to about ½ cup (125 mL). Transfer the wine to a bowl and mix it with the honey, mustard, salt and chili flakes. Whisk in the oil slowly, mixing continually to form an emulsification. Stir in the fresh thyme. Taste, then add the lime zest and enough juice to give it the acidity level you like.

MAKES ABOUT 1 ¼ CUPS (300 mL)

Fresh Peach Chutney

Perfect for summer and fall, this peach chutney is a spirited look at fresh fruit. Make it now and enjoy it beside your favourite curry.

4	shallots, minced
½ cup (125 mL)	minced red onion
¼ cup (50 mL)	olive oil
2 cups (500 mL)	peeled and coarsely chopped fresh peaches
1 cup (250 mL)	white wine vinegar
2	cinnamon sticks
½ tsp. (2 mL)	ground cardamom
1 cup (250 mL)	brown sugar
½ cup (125 mL)	minced red bell pepper
4 Tbsp. (50 mL)	minced fresh cilantro or mint

Sauté the shallots and red onions in the olive oil over medium heat until tender and transparent, about 5 minutes. Add the remaining ingredients and simmer 45 minutes, stirring often to prevent sticking or burning. Remove the cinnamon stick. Cool and store in the fridge for up to a week or process in canning jars in a hot water bath and store in the cupboard for a year.

MAKES ABOUT 2 CUPS (500 mL)

dee's Spicy Pickled Asparagus

With thanks to Elna Edgar for the great idea. Hide a jar in the back of your most cluttered shelf in the fridge, then bring it out as a Caesar or martini garnish, as a nibble straight out of the jar before dinner, or as part of a composed summer salad.

¼ cup (50 mL)	**finely slivered fresh ginger**
¼ cup (50 mL)	**finely sliced garlic**
2 Tbsp. (25 mL)	**pickling spice**
1 Tbsp. (15 mL)	**kosher or pickling salt**
5 cups (1.25 L)	**white vinegar**
3 cups (750 mL)	**tarragon vinegar**
1 ½ cups (375 mL)	**water**
5 lb. (2.2 kg)	**fresh green asparagus**
3	**dried hot chilis**

Wash and sterilize 3 one-quart (1-L) jars in a boiling water bath. Sterilize the outer rings of 2-part lids, and immerse the flat lids in boiling water.

Combine the ginger, garlic, pickling spice, salt, vinegars and water in a heavy pot. Bring to a boil, then simmer for 5–10 minutes.

Trim the asparagus to fit the jars. Pack each hot jar with one ladle of hot brine and spices, then add the asparagus spears and dried hot chilis, using a chopstick to aid in the vertical alignment and packing. Ladle boiling brine and spices over the asparagus, pushing the ginger and garlic down along the inside walls of the jars.

Wipe the mouth of each jar clean, screw on the lids finger-tight, and process in a boiling water bath for 35 minutes. Remove the jars to a double-folded thickness of towel away from any draft. When the jars are cool, stash them in a cool closet or cupboard for a month to mellow.

MAKES 3 1-QUART (1-L) **JARS**

Susan's Winter Fruit Chutney

This spicy and intensely flavoured dish, from my friend Susan Hopkins of Red Tree Kitchen in Calgary, is lovely with Brie, great with Wild Roast Boar Kaleden Style (page 135), super with Spanish-Style Braised Duck Legs (page 216) and wonderful with Salt-Cured Foie Gras (page 43)! Aim for a sweet-acid balance. Susan suggests chopping the dried fruit into slivers because they expand so much when simmered. This keeps for several months in the fridge.

1 ½ cups (375 mL)	dry white wine
⅓ cup (75 mL)	white sugar
1	cinnamon stick
1 cup (250 mL)	lemon juice
1	bay leaf
1 ½ tsp. (7 mL)	whole coriander seed
1 ½ tsp. (7 mL)	ground black pepper
3 whole	star anise pods
½ cup (125 mL)	dried cranberries
¾ cup (175 mL)	dried figs, slivered
¾ cup (175 mL)	dried pears, slivered
¼ cup (50 mL)	golden raisins
¾ cup (175 mL)	dried pineapple
¾ cup (175 mL)	dried apricot, slivered
¼ cup (50 mL)	Thompson raisins
¼ cup (50 mL)	currants
1	orange, peeled and diced
1	Granny Smith apple, peeled and finely diced
~	kosher salt to taste
~	extra lemon juice as needed

Combine all the ingredients except the orange, apple, salt and lemon juice in a heavy-bottomed pot. Simmer on low heat until the fruit is fat and tender, adding water (about 1 cup/250 mL) to prevent sticking. Stir in the orange and apple and turn off the heat. Add salt and lemon juice to taste.

MAKES ABOUT 1 QUART (1 L)

PICKLED LEMONS

Pickled lemons are a classic Mediterranean condiment that is great with prawns, couscous, tagines, lamb braises, vinaigrettes and salad dressings. Quarter washed lemons ¾ of the way down the fruit, leaving the quarters attached at the stem end. Freeze overnight. Defrost, then stuff each with 1 tsp. (5 mL) kosher salt. Pack into 2 jars, sprinkling each layer with kosher salt, cracked coriander seeds, cinnamon sticks and bay leaves. Fill each jar with a blend of ¼ cup (50 mL) melted honey, 1 cup (250 mL) lemon juice and warm water to cover. Process the jars in a boiling water bath and age for a month before using. Refrigerate after opening.

Pineapple *and* Mango Compote

A tropical trio of flavours warms spirits worn down by a cold Canadian winter. Use this with Salt-Cured Foie Gras (page 43), Pavlova (page 246), or Buckwheat Crêpes (page 248).

1	**mango, peeled and diced**
1	**pineapple, peeled and diced**
4	**oranges, peeled and segmented**

(see Cut to the Quick, page 193)

Combine all fruit and mix gently. Keeps for 2 days in the fridge.

MAKES ABOUT 4 CUPS (1 L)

Balsamic Mustard

North America's most popular condiment is mustard. Serve this sweet and hot mustard with any sausage (pages 164–173), Choucroute Rapide (page 166) and Cherrywood-Smoked Venison Loin (page 148).

½ cup (125 mL)	**black mustard seed**
2 Tbsp. (25 mL)	**freshly ground yellow mustard seed**
½ cup (125 mL)	**balsamic vinegar**
¼ cup (50 mL)	**Japanese rice vinegar**
1–2 Tbsp. (15–25 mL)	**sugar, or to taste**
~	**kosher salt to taste**
1	**shallot, minced (optional)**
1 tsp. (5 mL)	**minced rosemary or thyme (optional)**

Pulverize ¾ of the black mustard seeds in a food mill. Add to the ground mustard, along with the remaining seeds and enough water to make a thick paste. Mix well and let stand, uncovered, for several hours. Add all the remaining ingredients, mix well and store in the fridge to mellow. Keeps for months in the fridge.

MAKES ABOUT 1 CUP (250 mL)

MUSTARD DIP

Choose your favourite mustard and your favourite oil. Whisk the two together, add a handful of minced herbs, a bit of honey, and you have a glaze, a dip, a spread and a beginning for a new salad dressing.

Malt Mustard

For Scotch-lovers, a strong and wicked mustard. But, like good Scotch, this mustard takes time. Don't even think about it for at least a month... then serve it with Wild Roast Boar Kaleden Style (page 135), any sausage (pages 164–173), or grilled beef, lamb or pork.

½ cup (125 mL)	**black mustard seeds**
½ cup (125 mL)	**yellow mustard seeds**
½ cup (125 mL)	**single malt Scotch**
¼–½ cup (50–125 mL)	**malt vinegar**
½ cup (125 mL)	**melted honey**
1 Tbsp. (15 mL)	**freshly ground nutmeg**
~	**kosher salt to taste**

Divide the mustard seeds into 2 even groups. Grind up half of each, then add enough water to moisten. Let stand several hours. Add the remaining ingredients, including the reserved mustard seeds. Mix well and store in the fridge to mellow for at least 4 weeks.

MAKES ABOUT 2 CUPS (500 mL)

More on Mustard

From vinaigrettes to rubs, bastes and sauces, ballpark hotdogs and street vendors' sausages, mustard has become the most popular condiment on the continent. Locally made mustards always cause a small tornado of discussion at the table. Who made them? Where do we get them? Why are they so much better than the mass-produced ballpark and French mustards that dominate the supermarket shelves?

Canada is one of the world's top five mustard-growers. We grow mustard seed on the Canadian prairie, where the cool climate and short growing season are ideal for this cousin of canola. All summer, the yellow heads of mustard wave in the wind beside our highways and byways. Come fall, ¾ of the harvest is shipped out of the country. We buy it back — as imported, expensive Dijon mustard or as pungent mustard oil that is processed in India or Bangladesh. Our country is still primarily an exporter of raw materials, from copper to wheat, beef, mustard seeds and hockey players.

Local mustards are produced in small pockets of the country by chefs, cooks and gardeners. They make their way onto shelves at farmers' market stalls and into specialty food emporia. You have to know where to look, and that can be like looking for a pitchfork in a field of mustard seed — but buying local mustard is worth the effort.

All-Purpose Lamb Rub

This traditional blend brings out the full flavours of lamb.

2 Tbsp. (25 mL)	**olive oil**
8 cloves	**garlic, minced or slivered**
1	**tangerine or orange, juice and zest**
2 Tbsp. (25 mL)	**minced fresh mint**
1 Tbsp. (15 mL)	**minced fresh rosemary**
1 Tbsp. (15 mL)	**minced fresh thyme**
1 Tbsp. (15 mL)	**Malt Mustard (see page 26) or Balsamic Mustard (see page 25)**
~	**freshly cracked black pepper to taste**

Combine all the ingredients. Rub onto lamb leg, rack or chops before grilling or roasting.

MAKES ENOUGH FOR 1 LEG
or 2 racks or 8 double-cut chops

Arugula Pesto

This pungent paste is wonderful in sandwiches, with pasta or grilled meats and fish, stuffed under the skin of chicken, with Succulent Oven Squash (page 105), Warm Flageolet and Borlotti Salad (page 99) and on grain or bean dishes.

2 bunches	**fresh arugula**
1 bunch	**parsley, preferably flat-leaf**
6–8 cloves	**garlic cloves**
½ cup (125 mL)	**finely grated best-quality Parmesan cheese**
¼ cup (50 mL)	**toasted pine nuts or walnuts**
½ cup (125 mL)	**lemon juice**
½ cup (125 mL)	**olive oil**
~	**kosher salt and freshly ground black pepper to taste**

Strip the leaves from the arugula and parsley, discarding the stalks. Using a food processor, blender or mortar and pestle, grind the garlic, cheese and nuts to a paste as coarse or fine as you like. Add the herbs, lemon juice and oil, and blend into a smooth paste. Season with salt and pepper. Store in the fridge for up to 10 days or freeze.

MAKES ABOUT 2 CUPS (500 mL)

BUTTER BLENDS

Soften unsalted butter and blend with minced garlic, lemon zest, chopped tarragon, chives, parsley, rosemary, thyme, cracked peppercorns. Or add smoked Spanish paprika and garlic with minced oregano and orange zest. Pack into ramekins or shape into small logs, wrap and freeze.

Use on grilled fish or meat, steamed or grilled vegetables, cooked rice or bulgur, roasted potatoes.

Ras El Hanout

I have been making variations of this blend for as long as I have loved curries (a long time!). This North African blend is as personal as any Indian masala. It brings together the sultry smells of the market; all you add is imagination. Hang tapestries, recline on a cushion, and pretend to be there. Use this market-inspired blend on squash destined for the oven, on turkey or duck, with robust fish like salmon, or on beef and bison.

1 tsp. (5 mL)	**powdered ginger**
1 tsp. (5 mL)	**red pepper flakes**
½ tsp. (2 mL)	**ground cardamom**
2 tsp. (10 mL)	**ground coriander**
1 Tbsp. (15 mL)	**ground cumin**
1 tsp. (5 mL)	**anise seed, ground**
1 tsp. (5 mL)	**ground star anise**
½ tsp. (2 mL)	**ground cloves**
1 tsp. (5 mL)	**turmeric**
½ tsp. (2 mL)	**lavender**
1 tsp. (5 mL)	**ground nutmeg**
1 tsp. (5 mL)	**ground cinnamon**
1 tsp. (5 mL)	**ground allspice**
2 tsp. (10 mL)	**cayenne**
1 Tbsp. (15 mL)	**ground black pepper**
½ tsp. (2 mL)	**mace**

Mix together and store in a cool dry place.

MAKES ABOUT ⅓ CUP (75 mL)

OLIVE PASTE

Olive tapenade (olivada) is another paste that deserves space in your pantry. Place good black or green olives on your cutting board, flatten each with your thumb or the heel of your hand, then pick out and discard the pit. Chop or purée the olives, then combine with cracked fennel seed, dried oregano or basil, finely grated orange or lemon zest and hot chili flakes to taste. Add a drizzle of olive oil. Vary it by starting with chopped capers and sun-dried tomatoes, or by adding threads of Pickled Lemons (page 24) to either mix. It tastes wonderful on lamb burgers, pasta, sandwiches, rice, beef, salmon, under the skin of chicken, with brandade. This keeps for several weeks in the fridge.

India's High Cs

Curry powder is a gimmick. In a nation of over a billion people, the notion of one spice blend to suit all needs is ludicrous. Cooks from across the sub-continent of India rely on the same spices, but develop personal preferences. Curry powder, a ubiquitous North American approach to unfamiliar blends of spices, is not a common sight in India, where every home cook blends spices individually for each dish. Use these spices to mix up your own blends.

Cumin may be used whole as a seed — dry-roasted, fried in oil, broiled — or ground raw, fried in oil or dry-roasted.

Coriander, the seed of the coriander plant, is equally versatile. Fry it whole, grind it, add it to blends, then add the fresh chopped leaf of the same plant, called cilantro, for a jolt of green.

Cardamom is a suave flavour unfamiliar to most North American palates. Cardamom can scent anything from chai to basmati rice pilaf. Buy the pods, green or black, and crack them in a mortar to remove the husk, then use the small black seeds within for a distinctive and smooth scent. Be cautious — this camphor-like spice is incredibly potent and can overpower anything in its path!

Cloves are associated with dessert in North America, but in India, this pungent spice makes an appearance in most masalas, in Moghul dishes, in pilafs, as a perfume for oil-fried vegetables and in richly flavoured onion-tomato based dishes. Use it sparingly.

Cinnamon is also considered a "sweet" spice in the West. In India, whole sticks are used in garam masala, and in southern dishes like dal, vegetables and rice pilaf.

Just Noshing

A Nibble Is as Good as a Nosh

There are times when a snack is enough. There are other times when a nibble is prerequisite to other things — dinner, a movie, a date or a detour. In a family that includes busy teenagers or growing toddlers, it is wise to collect bits and pieces that may not fit into a formal menu but are ideal as a light lunch or after-basketball snack. Many of these bites can be held in the hands with a napkin to protect school clothes, but there are a few that need tools, chairs and attention.

In our home, my diabetic spouse and hypoglycemic youngest son sometimes need a little practical help and encouragement when their fuel cells are completely depleted. That is when I go to the freezer and find the pecans or the muffins, or quickly heat up the stove and make some saganaki. I have learned there is no point in saying "Go eat something" to someone who needs to eat; it is far more effective to simply put food into their hands and quietly give them the chance to smell it. They'll eat, and so will you, even if it's just a companionable nibble or nosh.

Of course, those same pecans make admirable salad and pizza garnish in more formal circumstances, but it is good to know that sustenance is just moments away. Another home run for the well-stocked pantry!

That pantry will stand you in good stead when the starving teenager emerges, hungry, an hour after dinner, and sticks his head and half his torso into the fridge. He's bound to be back for a late-night prowl, so it's a sure bet that the last two slices of pizza — or the last four salad rolls — won't survive to see the morning. Better that than an empty box of crackers or tub of ice cream. Or a grumpy teenager.

Kitchen Kids

The world that kids grow up in today is not the same world inhabited by kids 40 years ago. Homes are busier, many headed by a single parent or 2 working parents struggling to meet the needs and time frames of all the family members. Dinnertime and the contents of the fridge and pantry have all changed too. Many homes rely on processed and packaged meals, or opt for quick fixes like takeout or pick-up.

As a result, many kids don't cook, don't know where their food originates, rarely see the ground that grows their greens. We may think the Italians are far ahead of us because the Slow Food movement began there in 1989, but they are struggling with the same issues — their kids' lack of knowledge about food, their distance from the garden and the prevalence of fast food in children's diets.

The answer, not surprisingly, is a slow process. Plant a garden. Cook together. Visit a farmer. Here's how you can approach the subject in your own kitchen.

- **Be curious.** Try unfamiliar foods. Kids won't eat adventurously if parents don't. Explore faraway foods if you can. Closer to home, visit ethnic markets and the library.

- **Strengthen your own skills** so you can help your young ones learn. Take cooking classes or send your child, then share what was learned. Read cookbooks, and discuss them as you might already discuss your favourite novel.

- **Integrate your children** into meal planning and preparation, including shopping and gardening, from an early age. Little ones can smash and peel garlic, wash greens, grate cheese, core apples, peel carrots and spuds, slice vegetables, stir liquids and whisk with vigour. Older kids graduate to scrambled eggs, Caesar salad, French toast, quesadillas, stir fries, muffins.

- **Buy raw foods** rather than packages, a lot of cans or processed junk foods. If it's in the house, it will get eaten, so simply minimize temptations.

- **Consider planting a garden**; if you don't have space, there may be plots for rent. Alternatively, take your kids to pick-your-own gardens or grow herbs in pots.

- **Establish ground rules** early in the game. Teach them to locate everything and put it away when they are done. Live by cleaning as you go. Divide clean-up chores.

- **Buy knives that fit small hands.** A serrated 4-inch (10-cm) round-ended blade is perfect for the enthusiastic sawing motions of youngsters. Move on to bigger knives when your child is bigger and you are both more at ease with knives. Keep knives sharp. Dull knives are wickedly dangerous because they require more force to do the job and do more damage as a result. (See Knives and Other Useful Tools, page 14.)

- **Remember that cooking with kids takes longer**, feels more chaotic and inevitably produces unpredictable results. Build in extra time and patience. Don't try it on a busy night when you are tired and the kids are hungry. Choose a weekend and block off the whole afternoon. Then step back and let them do their part.

- **Potential land mines** are expecting kids to be as quick or efficient as we are, negating their choices, and generally expecting them to behave like grown-ups.

The most important message is to enjoy the process. Have fun and don't sweat the small stuff. Tension in the kitchen creates an arena for a power struggle where the issue sometimes has little to do with what's on the plate. Kids who associate food and the kitchen with stress and discomfort aren't likely to grow into adults who love spending time puttering in a kitchen. Children who do grow up in the kitchen become competent cooks who can sustain themselves and the others in their lives. The lesson extends beyond the kitchen to encompass curiosity and open-mindedness in life. And that is a very good thing.

Tiger Prawns in Crispy Jackets
with Thai Dip

These delicious prawns are always in hot demand. You can never have enough money or prawns, so plan accordingly. These are always devoured as soon as they emerge from the pan, so don't stand on ceremony. Now is better than later. A cool, clean, lean German Riesling, with its lower alcohol, would leave more room for more prawns! Beer, on the other hand, is filling — how many prawns did you buy?

1 tsp. (5 mL)	**baking powder**
½ cup (125 mL)	**flour**
1–2 Tbsp. (15–25 mL)	**chopped parsley**
1–2 Tbsp. (15–25 mL)	**chopped tarragon**
~	**salt to taste**
⅔ cup (150 mL)	**cold carbonated water**
1 lb. (500 g)	**tiger prawns, peeled and deveined**
~	**vegetable oil for the pan**
1 recipe	**Thai Dip**

In a small bowl, combine the baking powder, flour, parsley, tarragon and water. Mix thoroughly.
Coat the prawns in the mixture and fry them quickly until golden in hot oil. Serve hot with Thai Dip.

SERVES 2—4

Thai Dip

Use as a dip or as a seasoning base in stir-fries. Alternatively, simmer the mixture over high heat to reduce the volume by half, then use it as a glaze on fish, lamb and beef.

4 Tbsp. (50 mL)	**light brown sugar**
4 Tbsp. (50 mL)	**rice wine vinegar**
4 Tbsp. (50 mL)	**water**
2 Tbsp. (25 mL)	**Thai fish sauce**
2	**seeded and diced red chiles**
1 Tbsp. (15 mL)	**grated fresh ginger**

Mix all the ingredients together.

MAKES ABOUT ½ CUP (125 mL)

Turkey-Stuffed Salad Rolls
with Double Dips

These are fat-free, tenderly delicious, and use up great quantities of cooked turkey. They are good for lunch and are quickly and easily made by kids of any age. Dried rice paper can be found in Asian markets; buy several packages of differing diameter, and store them on the "Asian ingredients" shelf in your pantry. Leave out the noodles if you prefer. If you have leftover BBQ duck or pork, use either in place of the turkey. Rice beer is the perfect accompaniment for these treats!

1 lb. (500 g)	slivered cooked turkey, white and dark meat
1 bunch	cilantro, leaves only
4 cups (1 L)	cooked bean thread noodles, thoroughly drained and chopped into manageable lengths
2 Tbsp. (25 mL)	minced garlic
2 Tbsp. (25 mL)	finely grated fresh ginger
1 bunch	green onions, sliced
1 bunch	Thai basil, shredded
1 package	rice paper sheets
1 recipe	Vinegar-Chili Dip
1 recipe	Hoisin Dip

Combine the turkey, cilantro, noodles, garlic, ginger, green onions and basil in a bowl. Mix well. Set out a bowl of hot water. One sheet at a time, dip the rice sheets in the warm water. Leave the sheet in the water for 2–3 minutes; when it feels soft and pliable, remove it and lay it out flat on a clean, dry kitchen towel. Gently lay a second towel over the sheet to pat it dry so it will adhere to itself. Place a large spoonful of the filling on the lower third of the sheet in a line that leaves ½ inch (1 cm) of the edge uncovered at each end. Tuck in the edges and roll up the sheet to enclose the filling. Repeat until all the filling is used up. Serve cold with the dips.

MAKES ABOUT 20 ROLLS

continued...

THAI BASIL

Thai basil, widely available in Chinese markets, sometimes called licorice or anise basil, is a purple-tipped, showy cousin of Italian basil. It is spicier than Italian basil and has an anise-like overtone. It gives food a vibrant frisson of flavour and aroma that suits its Southeast Asian origins. Thai basil encourages spontaneity. In real life, I am the organized, results-oriented woman who attends to every detail and makes every deadline. In my dream life, I am the slightly irresponsible, flamboyantly gorgeous, wild socialite with the scent of Thai basil in her hair.

VARIATION: *Spring Rolls*

If crunchy munches are more your thing than soft and supple salad rolls, use spring roll wrappers to make spring rolls instead.

Make a paste of flour and water. Lay out a wrapper and brush the edges with the paste. Centre the filling on the diagonal in a straight line, leaving the edges clear. Roll on the diagonal from one corner, tucking in the ends after the first turn. Pan fry in hot oil and serve hot.

Vinegar-Chili Dip

This traditional dip is good for salad rolls or crispy spring rolls.

1 cup (250 mL)	**rice wine vinegar**
½ cup (125 mL)	**water**
2–3 Tbsp. (25–45 mL)	**white sugar**
¼ tsp. (1 mL)	**hot chili flakes or paste**
~	**kosher salt to taste**
1 tsp. (5 mL)	**finely grated carrot for garnish**
1 tsp. (5 mL)	**chopped peanut for garnish**

Combine and adjust to taste.

MAKES ABOUT 1 ½ CUPS (375 mL)

Hoisin Dip

Use this dip as a sauce for stir-fries if you have any left over.

½ cup (125 mL)	**hoisin sauce**
2–3 Tbsp. (25–45 mL)	**lemon juice**
1 Tbsp. (15 mL)	**minced cilantro**
1 Tbsp. (15 mL)	**minced garlic**
1 Tbsp. (15 mL)	**grated fresh ginger**
½ tsp. (2 mL)	**hot chili paste**
¼–½ cup (50–125 mL)	**water**

Combine and adjust to taste.

MAKES ABOUT 1 CUP (250 mL)

Tzatziki

Confession time. I never did like yoghurt, even though it is good for me, until I learned to drain it, making a rich yoghurt "cheese" (called labneh by Lebanese cooks). Use yoghurt that does not contain gelatin, otherwise the whey won't separate. Draining the yoghurt and squeezing the grated cucumber help to create a dip that is rich and creamy in texture. Of course, adding good olive oil doesn't hurt either. Serve this with Greek Feast Souvlaki (page 138), go cross-cultural with Thai Lamb (page 153) or use it as a dip with pita or vegetables.

1 24-oz. tub (1 750-mL tub)	unflavoured, gelatin-free yoghurt
1	Long English cucumber
2–4 cloves	garlic, minced or finely grated
½ cup (125 mL)	olive oil
~	kosher salt and freshly ground black pepper to taste
2 Tbsp. (25 mL)	minced parsley

Line a fine mesh strainer with a damp kitchen towel and dump the yoghurt into the sieve. Let it drain for at least half an hour. Discard the whey. Grate the cucumber and squeeze it dry. Mix the yoghurt with the cucumber, garlic and olive oil. Season with salt and pepper. Stir in the parsley.

MAKES ABOUT 2 CUPS (500 mL)

Saganaki

I love Greek restaurants, but they never serve enough saganaki! To get as much as you REALLY want, make it at home. Find a good Mediterranean market, and buy the Greek cheese called kefolitiri. Eat this standing up around the stove, wrapping each bite in a bit of pita bread.

2 slices (½ x 4 x 6 inch) (1 x 10 x 15 cm)	**kefolitiri**
4 Tbsp. (50 mL)	**flour**
1	**egg**
~	**olive oil for sautéing**
1	**lemon, juice only**

Slice the cheese in half if it won't fit your pan. Mix the flour and egg together, thinning as needed with water to make a batter about as thick as pancake batter. Dip the cheese in the batter, completely coating all sides. Heat the oil in a sauté pan. Gently slide the cheese into the hot oil. Sauté on medium heat, turning it once. When the centre of the slice feels soft and gives under your finger, transfer the cooked cheese to a plate. Pour the olive oil from the pan on top of the cheese and immediately squeeze the lemon juice over it. Serve hot with pita.

SERVES 2—4

Savoury Filo Strudel

Make party filo in tidy little packages, but at home, make them big enough to warrant a knife and fork. Replace the onion marmalade with a fruit chutney if you wish. Heighten the flavours by choosing smoked bacon and air-dried sausage. And don't stint on filling — make each bite fat! Pour Tempranillo or Pinot Noir red and perhaps a Riesling or fruity Pinot Gris for a white — your pick.

Onion marmalade

3	onions, minced
2 Tbsp. (25 mL)	minced double-smoked bacon (optional)
1 link	air-cured sausage (optional)
4 cloves	garlic, minced
2 Tbsp. (25 mL)	butter
2 Tbsp. (25 mL)	brown sugar
2 Tbsp. (25 mL)	balsamic vinegar or sherry vinegar
½ tsp. (2 mL)	dried thyme or fresh rosemary
~	kosher salt and freshly cracked black pepper to taste

Combine all the ingredients in a sauté pan and simmer over slow heat until the onions are tender and dark, about 30–45 minutes. Transfer the mixture to a bowl and let it cool.

Filo strudel

2 bunches	spinach, washed and stemmed
2 links	spicy Italian sausage
½ tsp. (2 mL)	dried oregano
½ tsp. (2 mL)	dried basil
2 Tbsp. (25 mL)	minced fresh cilantro
1	tart apple, grated
1 cup (250 mL)	crumbled feta cheese
~	kosher salt and freshly cracked black pepper to taste
1 lb. (500 g)	filo
1 cup (250 mL)	melted butter

continued...

Wilt the spinach in a hot non-stick pan. This takes 15–30 seconds, no more. Remove from the heat, squeeze out the water and mince finely. Add the spinach to the onion marmalade. Poach the sausages in simmering water. Slice lengthwise into quarters, then mince finely. Transfer to the spinach mixture. Let the mixture cool. Add the herbs, apple and feta, then season with salt and pepper.

Unwrap and unroll the filo. Lay the stack of sheets flat on a counter. Remove one sheet and lay it across a cutting surface. Cover the remaining filo stack with plastic wrap, making sure all the edges and corners are covered. Brush the sheet lightly with melted butter, then add a second and third sheet, buttering each.

Slice the buttered filo lengthwise into 4 strips. Place about ⅓ cup (75 mL) of the filling on the top of each strip, leaving a ½-inch (1-cm) border of uncovered dough around the filling. Fold the filo and its filling over into a tidy package, pinching in the sides with your fingers as you roll and fold. Continue folding to enclose the filling and create a tidy oblong package. Lay the package on a parchment-lined baking sheet and pinch the ends so they look a little like a Christmas cracker. Continue until the filling is used up. Lightly butter the exterior of all the strudel.

Preheat the oven to 375°F (190°C). Bake the crackers until golden brown, about 30–40 minutes. Serve hot.

MAKES 20 STRUDELS
(serve 2—3 strudels per person)

Caramelized Pecans

There is nothing shy about these sugar-coated nuts. They are the best midday snack, the best pizza topping, the best salad garnish, the best accompaniment to a glass of red wine. Don't be tempted to sample them straight out of the pan — that melted sugar is hot enough to seriously burn your mouth. Let them cool and crisp before sampling. These are great with a glass of bubbly — Italian Prosecco perhaps.

2 cups (500 mL)	**pecan halves**
2 Tbsp. (25 mL)	**unsalted butter**
2 Tbsp. (25 mL)	**sugar**
½ tsp. (2 mL)	**ground star anise**
½ tsp. (2 mL)	**cayenne**
~	**kosher salt to taste**

Put the nuts into a colander or strainer and pour boiling water over them to minimize the tannins in the skins. Drain well, then place the nuts and all other ingredients in a sauté pan. Cook over medium-high heat for about 7 minutes, stirring well, until the nuts are dark and glossy. Spread them out in a single layer on a baking sheet. Any leftovers can be frozen; bring back to room temperature before serving, although they are surprisingly good straight out of the freezer!

MAKES ABOUT 2 CUPS (500 mL)

Warm Canadian Chèvre Fondue

Fondue is ideal for entertaining. Most cheese dips are served cold, but this one is warm, perfect for chilly nights and a houseful of friends. Use a wee candle under your old fondue pot to keep this at dipping consistency. If the dip thickens, add a bit of milk or cream to thin it. Don't try to freeze the finished dip, but you can make it several days in advance and reheat it on the stove or in the microwave. Serve this with Susan's Winter Fruit Chutney (page 24) or Fresh Peach Chutney (page 22) as an accompaniment. Chèvre loves to keep company with a crisp Sauvignon Blanc or a soft, sultry Pinot Noir.

1 Tbsp. (15 mL)	butter
1	shallot, minced
1 tsp. (5 mL)	sherry vinegar
½ tsp. (2 mL)	sugar
½ cup (125 mL)	cream cheese
½ cup (125 mL)	milk
1 Tbsp. (15 mL)	cornstarch
½ lb. (250 g)	Canadian chèvre
3 Tbsp. (45 mL)	minced fresh chives
1 Tbsp. (15 mL)	minced fresh parsley
¼ tsp. (1 mL)	hot chili flakes
~	good crusty bread or baguettes for dipping

In a small pot, melt the butter. Add the minced shallot and cook over medium heat until tender, about 5 minutes. Add the sherry vinegar and sugar. Mix well. Add the cream cheese. Stir the milk and cornstarch to combine, and add the mixture to the pot. Bring to a boil, stirring constantly. Break the chèvre into pieces and add it to the mixture, stirring until smooth. Add the chives, parsley and hot chili flakes. Serve warm with cubes of crusty bread for dipping.

SERVES 4–6

Salt-Cured Foie Gras

How is it, you ask, that a foie gras dish made it into a book on home cooking? Two reasons. One, foie gras is considered a food group in its own right by dedicated Francophiles and food lovers. Two, no heat applied means this is a totally painless way to splurge on a rich, rich dish, with no splatters, splutters or splashes. Add a selection of dips and fruit chutneys, including Pineapple and Mango Compote (page 25) and Susan's Winter Fruit Chutney (page 24), your favourite crisp crackers or homemade crostini, and a crowd of friends. Serve the incomparable sweet wine of the Languedoc in France, St.-Jean de Minervois Muscat.

1	**duck or goose foie gras**
4 ¼ cups (1 L)	**milk**
4–6 cups (1–1.5 L)	**kosher salt**

Soak the foie gras in the milk for 6–8 hours. Use your hands to gently pull the lobes apart and remove the veins from the lobes. Wrap the foie gras in cheesecloth and tie securely like a sausage. Place in a bowl sprinkled with a deep layer of kosher salt. Cover completely with salt and chill at least 16–24 hours. Remove the foie gras, brush off the salt, unwrap the cheesecloth and slice the foie gras thinly.

SERVES 10–12 greedy little pigs or a crowd of polite and restrained adults

Eggs Benny *with* Better than Béarnaise Sauce

This brunch classic is easier than it appears — it just requires good time management skills. It will wean you forever from hotel-style buffet Benny's. I can just see those silver lids being lifted at every plate.

1 recipe	**Better than Béarnaise Sauce**
8	**eggs**
1 bunch	**asparagus**
8	**baguette slices**
2–3 Tbsp. (25–45 mL)	**grainy or smooth mustard**
8 slices	**lean ham, back bacon or cold-smoked salmon**

Make the béarnaise sauce first. Transfer it into a warmed thermos jar or balance the bowl over warm — not hot — water, to keep it warm.

Fill a shallow, wide pot ⅔ full of water. Add a splash of vinegar and a tablespoon (15 mL) of salt. Bring to a boil, then reduce the heat to a simmer. Crack each egg, one at a time, into a small bowl, then slide the egg into the simmering water. Poach gently, uncovered, for about 4–6 minutes. The eggs should float when they are done.

When the eggs go into the water, steam the asparagus in a shallow pan of boiling water, for 2–3 minutes, just until bright green. Remove and keep warm. Toast the baguette slices under the broiler, spread each slice with mustard and top with ham, bacon or salmon. Briefly slide the baguettes and toppings under the broiler.

To assemble, place 2 hot slices of garnished baguette on each plate, asparagus beside. Gently put a poached egg on each slice, top the eggs and asparagus with sauce and serve promptly.

SERVES 4

POACHING EGGS

When poaching eggs, be sure the water is at a gentle simmer, not a rolling boil. Crack each egg into a bowl and slide it gently into the water, where they slowly and gently set. Adding a little salt, mild vinegar or lemon juice to the water aids in the coagulation of the albumen and helps achieve a smooth shape. Fresh eggs will give the best results because the whites are thick, rather than runny, and spread the least.

Better than Béarnaise Sauce

Enhanced with the sweet scent of vanilla, this classic emulsion is an ideal Sunday brunch treat. Use it with poached eggs, salmon and other fish, asparagus, lobster and grilled beef tenderloin. Don't flinch at the butter — we're talking better than Béarnaise here.

½ cup (125 mL)	tarragon vinegar
1	shallot, minced
2 Tbsp. (25 mL)	fresh tarragon leaves and stalks (or 1 tsp./5mL dried)
1 tsp. (5 mL)	whole peppercorns
2	egg yolks
1 cup (250 mL)	melted unsalted butter
1–2 Tbsp. (15–25 mL)	Vanilla Vinegar (see page 20)
2 Tbsp. (25 mL)	minced fresh tarragon or parsley

Infuse the vinegar with the shallot, tarragon and peppercorns in a small shallow pan. Simmer, reducing the volume to 1–2 Tbsp. (15–25 mL). Strain, discarding the solids.

Whisk the yolks in a stainless bowl and add the vinegar reduction. Whisk vigorously off the heat, then whisk vigorously over a hot water bath until the yolks lighten in colour and thicken noticeably. Remove from the heat, still whisking. Add the melted butter in a slow steady stream, whisking it in to form an emulsion. Add the vanilla vinegar to taste, then stir in the minced tarragon or parsley.

Bleu D'Auvergne *and*
Black Mission Fig Soufflé

Soufflés are not so complicated. They just take a few steps — a two-step, not a tango. Savoury soufflés are made by folding some of the whisked whites into a thick white sauce enriched with yolks. Grated cheeses, meat or vegetable purées and herbs are added for flavour, then the remaining egg whites are folded in. You get a taller soufflé if you use more egg whites than yolks. Think ahead, because a soufflé waits for no one. Have your family and friends seated and waiting, glass of wine in hand (try a sweeter Vouvray from the Loire).

2–3 Tbsp. (25–45 mL)	butter for ramekins
6	Black Mission figs, finely diced
⅓ cup (75 mL)	brandy
3 Tbsp. (45 mL)	unsalted butter
4 Tbsp. (50 mL)	all-purpose flour
1 ½ cups (375 mL)	milk
6	eggs, separated
1 cup (250 mL)	crumbled bleu D'Auvergne or other good blue cheese
1 Tbsp. (15 mL)	minced fresh thyme
~	freshly cracked black pepper to taste
¾ tsp. (4 mL)	cream of tartar

Preheat the oven: 400°F (200°C) produces a creamy centre and crusty outside; 325°F (160°C) bakes into a uniformly solid dish. Butter the insides of 8–14 ramekins (use a 6–8 oz./175–250 mL capacity.)

Mix the figs and brandy together. Let stand.

In a heavy sauté pan, melt the butter. Add the flour and cook until sandy-textured. Heat the milk in a separate pot, then add the hot milk to the flour mixture in small increments, stirring well to prevent lumping. Bring to a boil, then turn off the heat and add ½ cup (125 mL) of the hot sauce to the egg yolks, stirring briskly. Add the cheese, thyme and pepper and mix well. Drain the figs and fold them in.

In a clean glass bowl, whisk the egg whites until frothy, then add the cream of tartar. Beat to firm peaks. Lighten the texture of the egg yolk and cheese mixture by folding ¼ of the egg whites into the mixture, then fold in the remaining egg whites. Do not overmix.

Gently spoon the mixture into the ramekins, filling each about ¾ full. Transfer to a baking sheet and bake on the centre rack of the oven for about 20 minutes, until puffed but not completely set. Serve immediately.

SERVES 8–14, depending on ramekin size

Beating around the Bush about Eggs

In the 1980s, Europe and the USA experienced outbreaks of food poisoning that were traced to raw or mildly cooked eggs. The salmonella bacteria infected some laying hens, and others were infected in the shell, before hatching. Until such time as salmonella is eliminated, it is generally accepted in the USA and Europe that it is best to cook eggs until they are solid throughout. Canada's health and agriculture regulations are widely regarded as the most stringent in the world, and eggs raised in Canada are generally considered safe to be eaten raw, with the following provisos.

- Don't feed food containing raw eggs to persons with compromised immune systems, young children or pregnant women.

- Examine eggshells for cracks, and discard cracked eggs.

- Use eggs before the "best before" date.

- Don't keep leftovers containing raw eggs.

- Don't store eggs (or food containing raw eggs) at room temperature.

Manchego *and* Golden Potato Pizza

A beer-scented crust seems like a natural on a dark and stormy night. Make the sponge the day — or the hour — beforehand. Serve this as an hors d'oeuvre or as dinner with Maudite beer.

....

Sponge

1 Tbsp. (15 mL)	**yeast**
1 Tbsp. (15 mL)	**sugar**
½ cup (125 mL)	**all-purpose flour**
½ cup (125 mL)	**whole wheat flour**
1 cup (250 mL)	**Maudite or other full-flavoured ale**

Make the sponge in advance by mixing together the yeast, sugar, flours and beer. It should be fairly loose and fluid. If it appears dry, add more beer. Cover and refrigerate for anywhere between 1–12 hours.

....

Dough

2 cups (500 mL)	**all-purpose flour**
2 cups (500 mL)	**whole wheat flour**
1 Tbsp. (15 mL)	**yeast**
1 Tbsp. (15 mL)	**sugar**
3–4 cups (750 mL–1 L)	**Maudite or other full-flavoured ale**
1 Tbsp. (15 mL)	**kosher salt**
2 Tbsp. (25 mL)	**olive oil**

To make the dough, transfer the sponge to a mixing bowl. Add the flours, yeast, sugar, beer and salt. Mix well. Add more beer or flour as needed to achieve a soft, supple dough that kneads well. Turn the dough onto the counter and knead well for 5–10 minutes, or until the dough is smooth and elastic.

Pour the oil into the mixing bowl, swirl it around to coat the sides and bottom, and place the dough in the bowl. Roll the dough in the oil so its entire surface is generously covered in oil. Cover the bowl with plastic wrap and let the dough rise until doubled in bulk, 30–60 minutes, depending on the temperature of the room.

When the dough is doubled, knock it down by punching it once in the bowl. Turn the dough onto the counter and divide into 3 equal pieces. Shape each piece into a disc about 10 inches (25 cm) in diameter and transfer to a parchment-lined baking sheet. Let the dough rise again until double in bulk, 20–40 minutes.

Toppings

3 cups (750 mL)	cooked Yukon Gold spuds, thinly sliced
1 cup (250 mL)	sliced Kalamata olives
1 cup (250 mL)	sliced green Italian olives
2	red bell peppers, sliced
1	onion, sliced
6 cloves	garlic, sliced
1 Tbsp. (15 mL)	minced rosemary
1 Tbsp. (15 mL)	minced thyme or parsley
2 ½ cups (625 mL)	grated Manchego cheese
2 ½ cups (625 mL)	grated Medium Gouda cheese
3 Tbsp. (45 mL)	olive oil
~	kosher salt and freshly ground black pepper to taste

Prepare the toppings while the dough rises for the final time. Set the oven to 375°F (190°C).

Distribute the toppings on the pizza rounds, finishing with a drizzle of olive oil and a sprinkle of salt and pepper. Bake the pizza on the middle rack for about 20–25 minutes, or until crusty and golden. Serve hot.

MAKES 3 10-INCH (25-CM) PIZZAS

Savoyard Potato Pizza

It may sound a bit odd to use whipping cream or crème fraîche and potatoes so unexpectedly, but the results are truly wonderful. Serve this on "Movie Night" or on a weekend when you can settle in and not leave your house. Get the toppings ready while the dough rises. Open a rosé from the Languedoc in the south of France.

....

Dough:

2 Tbsp. (25 mL)	**yeast**
2 Tbsp. (25 mL)	**sugar**
½ cup (125 mL)	**warm-to-hot water**
4 cups (1 L)	**all-purpose flour**
1 Tbsp. (15 mL)	**kosher salt**
1 tsp. (5 mL)	**dried thyme or herbes de Provence**
1 cup (250 mL)	**warm-to-hot water**
2 Tbsp. (25 mL)	**olive oil**

In a countertop mixer, combine the yeast, sugar and the ½ cup (125 mL) water. Let stand for about 5 minutes, until it is puffy. Add the flour, salt, herbs and the 1 cup (250 mL) water. Mix well. Turn the dough onto the counter and knead well for 5–10 minutes, or until the dough is smooth and elastic.

Pour the oil into the mixing bowl, swirl it around to coat the sides and bottom, and place the dough in the bowl. Roll the dough in the oil so its entire surface is covered in oil. Cover the bowl with plastic wrap and let the dough rise until doubled in bulk, 30–60 minutes, depending on the temperature of the room.

When the dough has doubled in bulk, punch it down, divide in 4 pieces and shape into thin flat rounds. Let them rise again while you prepare the toppings.

MAKES 4 10-INCH (25-cm) **ROUNDS**

....

Toppings:

½ **cup** (125 mL)	**sautéed onion slices**
½ **cup** (125 mL)	**diced ham**
½ **cup** (125 mL)	**crisply cooked bacon, sliced or chopped**
½ **cup** (125 mL)	**pitted and chopped niçoise or Kalamata olives**
1 **cup** (250 mL)	**sliced cooked Yukon Gold potatoes (see Selecting Spuds, page 81)**
2 **tsp.** (10 mL)	**dried herbes de Provence**
1 **cup** (250 mL)	**whipping cream or crème fraîche**
2 **cups** (500 mL)	**grated Gruyère, Jarlsberg or Fontina cheese**
~	**extra virgin olive oil**
~	**kosher salt and freshly cracked black pepper**
~	**cornmeal for the tray**

Set the oven to 375°F (190°C). If you have a pizza stone, put it on the bottom rack of the oven to heat. Line several trays with parchment and lightly dust each with cornmeal. Evenly distribute the toppings on each round in the order listed. The important thing is to add the cream or crème fraîche and cheese at the end. Drizzle each pizza with oil, then sprinkle with salt and pepper. Bake the pizza for about 20—25 minutes, or until crusty and golden. Serve hot.

Sourdough Bread

Sourdough starter adds a wonderful tang to breads, and it's easy to maintain in your fridge. A baker friend of mine calls his starter "Judy"; I call mine "Herman," and bring him out to feed him several times a day or so in advance of making bread. If you bake weekly, your starter will be active and ready to use. If you are a sporadic baker, the starter may need feeding several times before it is active enough to leaven a loaf of bread. Feed it high-fat milk and flour to help tame the sharp "sour" nature of an ignored starter.

Starter:

2 cups (500 mL)	**sourdough starter**
2 cups (500 mL)	**water or milk**
2 cups (500 mL)	**all-purpose flour**

Mix the starter, water or milk and flour together in a clean jar or glass/ceramic bowl. Leave the bowl or jar on the counter for a day, uncovered. Several times over the next 24 hours, add ½ cup (125 mL) all-purpose flour and ½ cup (125 mL) milk or water when liquid begins to seep to the surface of the starter.

Transfer half the starter to a clean jar and refrigerate as your new "Herman." Put the remaining starter in a mixing bowl.

Bread:

3 ½ cups (875 mL)	**all-purpose flour**
½ cup (125 mL)	**whole wheat flour**
2 Tbsp. (25 mL)	**kosher salt**
4 Tbsp. (50 mL)	**olive oil**
~	**warm water or milk to form a dough**
2 heads	**roasted garlic, chopped**
1 cup (250 mL)	**chopped olives**

4 Tbsp. (50 mL)	**minced parsley and/or chives**
2 Tbsp. (25 mL)	**minced fresh rosemary**
~	**freshly cracked black pepper**

Combine the starter, both flours, salt, half the oil and water or milk. Mix to form a dough. Add all or some of the flavourings once the dough is mixed together. Turn out and knead until soft, smooth and supple, with well-developed gluten. Swirl the remaining oil around inside the bowl to coat all surfaces, then roll the dough in the oil so its entire surface is lightly oiled. Cover the bowl with plastic wrap and let rise in the fridge until doubled in bulk. Be patient. This could take 2 days.

Punch down and shape into 2 rounds or oval logs. Place on the back side of an inverted baking sheet and cover. Let rise another day or two.

Preheat an oven for an hour to 400°F (200°C). When you turn on the oven, put an empty, shallow heat-proof metal pan on the top rack and line the bottom rack or the floor of the oven with unglazed ceramic tiles or a ceramic baking stone. Slash the top of each loaf with the tip of a sharp knife. Try for a shallow, near-horizontal slice in the shape of a reversed letter C, or use a parallel set of lines. Brush the top of the dough with tepid water. Spray the tiles with warm water and fill the heated pan on the upper rack to create steam. Be careful! Immediately slide the bread rounds onto the tile or stone. Bake until crusty and baked through, about 15–30 minutes, depending on the thickness of the loaves.

MAKES 2 LOAVES

Cheese Biscuits

These biscuits freeze very well after baking, so go ahead and make a big batch. This is my favourite accompaniment for a pot of soup on a cold afternoon, and it's a quick piece of work to get them into the oven while your soup simmers. Faster than bread, more satisfying than crackers, biscuits fit the bill.

1 ½ cups (375 mL)	**all-purpose flour**
½ cup (125 mL)	**whole wheat flour**
½ tsp. (2 mL)	**kosher salt**
1 Tbsp. (15 mL)	**baking powder**
½ cup (125 mL)	**feta or Cheddar cheese, crumbled**
1 bunch	**minced green onions**
½ tsp. (2 mL)	**hot chili flakes**
¼ cup (50 mL)	**unsalted butter**
¾ cup (175 mL)	**buttermilk, sour cream or yoghurt**

Preheat the oven to 375°F (190°C). Line a baking sheet with parchment paper.

On the counter, combine the flours, salt and baking powder. Stir in the cheese and green onions, with the hot chili flakes to taste. Add the butter and work it in with your fingers or a pastry cutter until the mixture is mealy in texture. Add the buttermilk, sour cream or yoghurt and blend by lightly tossing the dry ingredients up with stiffly extended fingers, using your hands like two large salad forks. The dough will begin to come together into blobs. Pack it all together into a ball, flatten it out with a minimum of handling, and form into a rectangle about 1 inch (2.5 cm) thick. Fold in half, pat out lightly with your palms and fold over 3 more times. This helps to create layers without developing unnecessary gluten. Pat or roll out with a floured rolling pin to a thickness of about 1 inch (2.5 cm).

Cut out with a lightly floured 2-inch (5-cm) round cutter, combining all the scraps and cuttings to form additional biscuits. Arrange on the baking sheet, fairly closely together. These biscuits rise up, not out, so ½ inch (1 cm) clearance is fine. Bake in a preheated oven for about 20–30 minutes, turning the pan end for end at the halfway point to ensure even baking. Serve warm or at room temperature.

YIELDS 10 2-INCH (5-cm) **BISCUITS**

Apple Muffins
with Pecan-Maple Streusel

There was a time when I made muffins by the dozen. I counted it a worthwhile investment; muffins are a wonderful breakfast, and they lend themselves willingly to endless tinkering. And did I mention quick?

Streusel:

¼ cup (50 mL)	**all-purpose flour**
½ cup (125 mL)	**toasted and chopped pecans**
¼ cup (50 mL)	**maple syrup**
2 Tbsp. (25 mL)	**vegetable oil or melted butter**

To make the streusel, stir all the ingredients in a small bowl.

Muffins:

2 cups (500 mL)	**all-purpose flour**
½ cup (125 mL)	**whole wheat flour**
1 Tbsp. (15 mL)	**baking powder**
½ tsp. (2 mL)	**baking soda**
2 tsp. (10 mL)	**ground cinnamon**
½ cup (125 mL)	**raisins or dried cranberries**
½ cup (125 mL)	**toasted chopped pecans**
2	**eggs**
½ cup (125 mL)	**sugar, granulated or brown**
⅓ cup (75 mL)	**vegetable oil**
1	**tart apple, finely diced, peel on**
2 ½ cups (625 mL)	**buttermilk**

Preheat the oven to 375°F (190°C). Brush the muffin cups with oil or line with paper liners.

Stir together both flours, the baking powder, baking soda, cinnamon, raisins or cranberries and pecans. In a separate bowl, stir together the eggs, sugar and oil. Add the apple and buttermilk to the wet ingredients, then add the wet ingredients to the dry, mixing with a wooden spoon or spatula only until blended.

continued...

Spoon the batter into muffin pans, divide the streusel topping evenly over the muffins and bake 15–20 minutes, until set. Remove to a rack and let cool before removing from the oven. Serve warm.

MAKES 12 LARGE MUFFINS

Skillet Cornbread

Pull out your favourite black cast iron pan for this bread. It goes together quickly, bakes in a hurry, and then is gracious about not hanging around. (It never gets the chance!)

1 ½ cups (375 mL)	**cornmeal**
2 ½ cups (625 mL)	**all-purpose flour**
¾ cup (175 mL)	**sugar**
~	**kosher salt to taste**
3 Tbsp. (45 mL)	**baking powder**
1 tsp. (5 mL)	**ground allspice**
2	**eggs**
2 cups (500 mL)	**milk or buttermilk**
½ cup (125 mL)	**vegetable oil**

Set the oven to 400°F (200°C). Lightly butter and flour a 9-inch (1.5-L) round cake pan or black cast iron pan.

Combine the cornmeal, flour, sugar, salt, baking powder and allspice in a bowl. Combine the eggs, milk or buttermilk and oil in a separate small bowl, mixing well, then add to the dry ingredients. Mix just to blend, then gently pour into the prepared pan. Smooth the top and bake about 35 minutes, or until set and golden. Serve warm with butter.

SERVES 6–8

Steaming and Poaching

Steaming and poaching are more than just low-fat ways to cook eggs. Food cooked by steam or in liquid is tender in texture and subtle in flavour. Learning to appreciate the gentle art of infusions and indirect heat can be a bit of a leap for cooks raised on the robust flavours and crunchy crusts of grilling and sautéing. But sometimes getting straight to the point is too direct: slow and gentle is more effective. The gust of scent as you open the dish or unwrap the packet is a wonderful collateral benefit.

This is poaching and steaming for the uninitiated.

Poaching and steaming are perfect for delicate foods such as tender fish or seafood, boneless chicken breasts, fruit and vegetables or dumplings. Either can be done in the oven or on the stovetop, in a variety of styles.

When steaming, raw food sits above the simmering water, either in a steamer basket or arranged in a single layer on a plate, covered with a lid or parchment paper.

Food is immersed in liquid when poaching. Poaching liquid can be water, vegetable juice, stock, flavoured wine, or a bouillon infused with lemon, wine and herbs, as is commonly used to classically poach fish. The temperature of the liquid should not exceed a simmer — 185°F (85°C). The point is to keep the temperature down and watch the cooking time. A wide, shallow pan is best for poaching. Add a pinch of salt or a dash of vinegar or lemon juice to poaching water to help coagulate protein foods, avoiding the long strands that trail from eggs cooked in plain water.

Poaching is often used to add more flavour to bland or mild meats, fruit and vegetables. Adding vegetables, herbs, spices or citrus to the poaching liquid gives subtle nuances of taste to the food. Protein foods, such as chicken breasts, scallops or dumplings, are best removed from the liquid at the completion of cooking. Cool and store fruits in their poaching liquid to allow them to absorb even more flavour.

Saturday
Soup Supper

Filling the Pot

Soup means a collection of foods cooked in liquid. That's a pretty unromantic assessment of what has come to be known worldwide as the ultimate healing and nurturing food. Soup is imbued with the mythic power to heal broken hearts and cracked bones, to thaw skiers' frostbitten noses and to mend, like Time, all wounds.

The soup pot invites a style of cooking as varied as this week's fridge contents. Resist the temptation though, to empty the entire vegetable drawer into the soup pot. This is a death knell to the best soup; add too many ingredients and the pot becomes undefined and its character unstated. The other side of the coin is the ease with which soup accepts last-minute changes and substitutions. Slide onions in for leeks, use carrots for roasted red peppers, yams instead of Yukon Golds.

To my mind, the best soups arise from cold-weather cooking, when the slow simmer fills a home with comforting aromas. When it's too cold to venture outdoors, you have prime conditions for creating the finest soup. Springtime soup is an entirely different matter — lighter, more intensely flavoured, and quicker off the mark.

And don't fret that soup has to be an all-day proposition. Many soups can be cooked inside an hour, perfect for those days when the dog, the boss, the kids, the weather, are not as you would like them to be. Baby, it's cold outside. Snuggle up to a hot stove and put the soup on.

Chicken Stock *and* Variations

Stock is the gold standard, the twenty-four-carat basis for soups, sauces, gratins, cassoulets, stewed and braised dishes. It can be a poaching liquid and a deglazer of pans, and is a finishing agent in the form of *glace de viand*. Stock gives weight and depth to your cooking. The most versatile of all the stocks, chicken stock is neutral in character, and can stand in for fish stock in fish-based dishes and soups with the addition of a bit of anchovy or shrimp paste. It can just as easily sub for meat-based soups and dishes, especially if the bones are roasted first. Store raw chicken bones and cooked carcasses in the freezer, then use them as the base for stock-making, a far tidier process than starting with fresh.

2–3	chicken carcasses, fresh or frozen
1	onion, quartered
1 bulb	garlic, split horizontally
2	carrots, halved
2 stalks	celery
1	leek, split and washed
4–5	mushrooms, optional
1–2	tomatoes or trimmings, optional
1 bunch	parsley stalks
~	handful herb stalks (see A Baker's Dozen Steps to Perfect Stock, page 62)
1 tsp. (5 mL)	whole black peppercorns

Put the bones into a tall heavy pot. Cover with cold water and bring to a boil. Skim any impurities and fat from the surface. Add the remaining ingredients. Simmer for 2 ½–4 hours, replenishing the water if the level drops below the top of the bones. Strain, chill, de-fat and freeze the finished stock.

MAKES ABOUT 2 QUARTS (2 L)

VARIATIONS: **Veal Stock:** Substitute veal bones, sawed into 2-inch (5-cm) pieces by your butcher, for the chicken bones and carcasses. Brown the bones. (See A Baker's Dozen Steps to Perfect Stock, page 62.) Proceed for chicken stock but simmer veal stock for 8 hours.

continued...

Glace de viand (meat glaze) is used as a flavour agent, not as a liquid component. To make it, reduce 2 qt. (2 L) of veal stock to ½ cup (125 mL). Spoon into ice cube trays and freeze. When the cubes are solid, transfer into a freezer bag.

Fish Stock: Unless you are using crustacean shells, which freeze well, use fresh bones. Fish is generally too perishable to freeze bones for stock — the result often tastes a little less than fresh. Choose neutrally flavoured fish, like halibut, snapper, sole or other white fish for stock instead of strongly flavoured fish like salmon, which limits the uses of the stock. Put the bones in a pot, rinse thoroughly with cold water, drain and cover with fresh cold water. Continue as for chicken stock, omitting the carrots and simmering for just 45 minutes.

Vegetable Stock: Browning or roasting vegetables first makes for much more focussed flavours and a more appetizing colour. Vegetable stocks can be infused with other ingredients, like wild mushrooms or lemon grass, if it will enhance the flavour of the final dish. Use the same vegetables and flavourings as for chicken stock. Brown the vegetables first in a little olive oil and simmer for just 45 minutes before straining.

A Baker's Dozen Steps to Perfect Stock

1. **Roast bones** in a shallow pan in a hot oven for stock with deeper colour and flavour. Split and brown an onion in an ungreased pan for additional colour and flavour.

2. **Start with cold water** to make a clear stock.

3. **Skim repeatedly** to remove scum and fat from the top of the simmering stock.

4. **Simmer instead of boil** to avoid emulsifying any remaining fat into the stock.

5. **Avoid adding members of the cabbage family** (cabbage, brussels sprouts, cauliflower) or the stock will be sulphurous.

6. **Add fresh or frozen herbs and/or stalks** — parsley, sage, rosemary, thyme, oregano, basil, marjoram, bay.

7. **Add spices sparingly** — peppercorns are potent.

8. **Simmer for 2 ½–8 hours**, depending on the type of stock, uncovered.

9. **Do not add salt!** It will be concentrated if you simmer to thicken by reduction.

10. Make sure the **water level just covers the bones** so that the final liquid is strong and concentrated instead of diluted.

11. **Chill the stock**, then peel off any congealed fat before decanting the liquid into smaller tubs.

12. Keep your finished stock **in the fridge for up to 5 days**; after that, re-boil it before use.

13. **Store extra stock in the freezer** in labelled tubs of a useful size, depending on the size of your household. (For a family of four, 2-cup/500-mL and 3-cup/750-mL sizes are most practical.)

Asparagus Soup

When asparagus is abundant, make this soup and freeze some for a taste of spring later in the year. The asparagus tips, quickly blanched and added to the finished soup, give it an attractive fresh bright green colour. Try delicate Sauvignon Blanc from France or Italy with this.

3	**leeks**
2 ½ lbs. (1 kg)	**fresh asparagus**
1–2 Tbsp. (15–25 mL)	**butter or oil**
1 lb. (500 g)	**Yukon Gold potatoes**
4 cups (1 L)	**chicken stock**
1 cup (250 mL)	**whipping cream**
1 cup (250 mL)	**milk**
~	**kosher salt and freshly ground black pepper to taste**
½	**lemon, juice only**

Slice the leeks lengthwise, trim off the root and any tough or damaged outer green leaves, and slice crosswise into fine shreds. Transfer the sliced leeks into a colander and wash very thoroughly under running water. Place the cleaned leeks in a large heavy pot.

Trim off and set aside the asparagus tips. Trim and discard the tough bottom ends. Chop the remaining stalks into ½-inch (1-cm) lengths and add to the pot. Add the butter or oil. Cook the leeks and asparagus for 5 minutes, or until tender.

Peel and dice the potatoes, then add them to the pot along with the stock. Mix well and cover. Cook for 30–45 minutes at a simmer until all the vegetables are soft. Use an immersion wand to purée the soup if you wish. Add the cream and milk. Mix well.

Heat ½ inch (1 cm) of water in a small pan. Add the asparagus tips when the water boils, and briefly cook until the tips are bright green. Drain and discard the water, then add the tips to the finished soup. Season to taste with salt, pepper and lemon juice.

MAKES 3 QUARTS (3 L)

The Straight Goods on Sautéing

Sautéing — and fat — is not the enemy. Sautéing is a respected member of the cooking community, often serving as the first step in a series. Doing it right can make crispy food that does not absorb excess oil or butter. Doing it incorrectly can cause greasy sauces, soups and braises.

- **Choose a good pan** — non-stick, cast iron, lined copper, or stainless with a bottom of more conductive metal (aluminum, copper, nickel). Avoid glass or thin stainless without a heavy bottom, and select a style that is wider than it is deep.

- **Choose tender foods** that would also be suitable for broiling or grilling — fish that is firm-textured enough to withstand turning, poultry breast, chops, steaks, medallions, sliced vegetables.

- **Cut food into pieces** of uniform size and thickness.

- **Preheat the pan**, then add and heat just enough oil to lubricate the cooking surface of the pan. A non-stick pan greatly reduces the fat needed. Heat the oil to sizzling. (Check with the splatter water test; flick a few drops of water across the surface of the water. If the oil is hot enough, it will immediately hiss and burble. Alternatively, place a cube of bread in the oil; the bread will immediately begin to colour to golden if the oil is hot enough.)

- **Cook small pieces** of tender food over high heat in a single layer in the pan. Stir or toss with a gentle flipping action. Turn larger pieces with tongs — once. Minimal turning, poking and fussing lets the food colour and form a crust.

- **Cook food uncovered** (steam interferes with the formation of a crust). Use a pan that just fits the food. If the pan is overfilled, food will boil, rather than brown, and it will not be crisp. If the pan is too large, any juices that accumulate will burn in the open spaces.

Butternut Squash Soup
with Orange and Basil

In winter, when vegetable selection is narrow and expensive, fall back on winter squash. It makes a brilliant soup that will brighten the palate and the table. Choose butternut squash for its sweetness and firm texture. Omit the stock in this dish and the squash makes a wonderful vegetable side dish, sparkling with citrus, ginger and basil. Pour a fruit-driven Sauvignon Blanc.

½	leek, white and pale green parts only
1 Tbsp. (15 mL)	olive oil
1 Tbsp. (15 mL)	minced fresh thyme
1 Tbsp. (15 mL)	grated fresh ginger
2 Tbsp. (25 mL)	dried cranberries (optional)
4	whole star anise pods
1	medium butternut squash, peeled and cut into ½-inch (1-cm) dice
4 cups (1 L)	chicken or vegetable stock
1	orange, juice and zest
1 Tbsp. (15 mL)	unsalted butter
1 Tbsp. (15 mL)	sherry vinegar, or to taste
~	kosher salt to taste
2 Tbsp. (25 mL)	finely minced fresh basil

Slice the leeks lengthwise, trim off the root and any tough or damaged outer green leaves, and slice crosswise into fine shreds. Transfer the sliced leeks into a colander and wash very thoroughly under running water. Drain well.

Heat the oil in a large heavy pot. Add the leeks, thyme, ginger, cranberries if using, and star anise. Cook over medium-high heat, adding small amounts of water as needed, until the leek is tender, about 3 minutes.

Add the squash and stock, stir well and cook over medium heat for 20–30 minutes, stirring often, until the squash is tender and beginning to fall apart. Purée if desired. Stir in the orange juice and zest, butter, vinegar, salt and basil and pick out the star anise. Mix gently. Serve hot.

SERVES 8

CHOOSING AND PEELING BUTTERNUT SQUASH

Although they are relatively thin-skinned when compared to their thicker-skinned cousins like Hubbard squash, it still takes care to peel butternut squash. Start by choosing one with the smallest possible bulb and the thickest neck. Cut off the bulbous end and trim the end of the neck. Stand the neck on the cutting board and slice off the skin in successive downward vertical cuts. Peel the bulb the same way, then split it in half, seed it and cut it into usable sizes.

Kale *and* White Bean Soup

This robust soup shows up in most European cuisines, from Portugal north to Scandinavia, nearly always partnered with smoked pork — sausages or ham of some sort — and dried beans. I prefer Great Northern beans, but any variety will work equally well. Kale doesn't wilt like other greens, so don't be tempted to add extra to the pot. Substitute spinach, arugula, beet tops or chard for the kale. Like most soup, this is better if it can mature for a day in the fridge before being served. Check out some of the great Canadian Pinot Gris or Gamay.

1	leek
1 Tbsp. (15 mL)	olive oil
1	large onion, diced
4–6 cloves	garlic, minced
4	carrots, diced
1	bay leaf
4 slices	bacon, diced (or ½ cup/125 mL diced ham or 2 spicy sausages, sliced)
½ tsp. (2 mL)	dried thyme
1 Tbsp. (15 mL)	sweet paprika
1 head	kale, coarsely chopped and central rib discarded
1 lb. (500 g)	Yukon Gold potatoes, diced
2–3 cups (500–750 mL)	cooked white beans (see Cooking Beans, page 79)
4–6 cups (1–1.5 L)	beef or chicken stock
~	kosher salt and freshly cracked black pepper to taste
~	drizzle of white wine vinegar
4 Tbsp. (50 mL)	minced fresh parsley

Slice the leeks lengthwise, trim off the root and any tough or damaged outer green leaves, and slice crosswise into fine shreds. Transfer the sliced leeks into a colander and wash very thoroughly under running water. Place the cleaned leeks in a large heavy pot with the oil over medium-high heat, and add the onion, garlic, carrots and bay leaf. Cook until the vegetables are tender, allowing them to brown a little. Add the meat and cook thoroughly. Discard any extra fat. Stir in the thyme, paprika, kale, potatoes, beans and stock. Bring to a boil, then cover and reduce the heat. Simmer until all the ingredients are tender, about 35–40 minutes. Season with salt, pepper and vinegar to taste. Stir in the parsley just before serving.

SERVES 6 GENEROUSLY

Hot *and* Sour Soup

Like any good chicken soup, this is good for whatever ails you. Do not be discouraged by the long list of ingredients; the cooking time is really brief. California Riesling or a sweeter rice beer would be great with this!

Meat and marinade:

2 Tbsp. (25 mL)	**sherry vinegar**
1 Tbsp. (15 mL)	**dark soy sauce**
2 Tbsp. (25 mL)	**cornstarch**
1 tsp. (5 mL)	**ground star anise**
1 tsp. (5 mL)	**ground black pepper**
¾ lb. (375 g)	**lean pork or boneless, skinless chicken thighs, finely slivered**

Combine marinade ingredients in a bowl, add the meat and let stand while you prepare the rest of the ingredients.

The rest:

12	**black Chinese mushrooms**
½ lb. (250 g)	**dried rice noodles**
1 Tbsp. (15 mL)	**vegetable oil**
1	**onion, finely sliced**
6 cloves	**garlic, minced**
1 Tbsp. (15 mL)	**grated fresh ginger**
4	**carrots, finely julienned**
3 stalks	**celery, thinly sliced on an angle**
½ head	**sui choi, finely sliced**
6–8 cups (1.5–2 L)	**chicken stock**
1 cup (250 mL)	**cubed firm tofu**
1 Tbsp. (15 mL)	**honey**
½ cup (125 mL)	**rice vinegar**
1 tsp. (5 mL)	**hot chili paste**
3 Tbsp. (45 mL)	**fish sauce**
1 Tbsp. (15 mL)	**dark soy sauce**
2 Tbsp. (25 mL)	**minced cilantro**
3	**green onions, minced**

continued...

Rehydrate the mushrooms by simmering them, covered, in hot water for 5 minutes. Remove and discard the stems; strain and save the water. Julienne the mushrooms. Rehydrate the noodles by covering them with boiling water and leaving them to stand while you chop and slice.

Heat the oil over medium-high heat, add the onion and sauté for 5 minutes. Add the garlic, ginger, carrots, celery and mushrooms. Sauté until tender, about 5 minutes. Add the mushroom-soaking water and the sui choi, stock, pork and its marinade and the drained rice noodles. Simmer for 3–5 minutes, stirring several times. Add the tofu, honey, vinegar, chili paste, fish sauce and soy sauce. Simmer until the tofu is heated through. Taste and adjust the balance. Add the cilantro and green onions. Serve promptly.

SERVES A CROWD, 8–10

Shellfish Bisque *with* Fino

Bisque has a luxurious image, but it is a dish made from scraps and leftover shells, lily-gilded with cream and booze. No half-measures here, except for when you ladle out the rich result. If you have some lobster, shrimp or crab, sauté it, cut into small pieces, season it with salt, cayenne and lemon juice, and use small spoonfuls as garnish for this impossibly delicious soup. This will become your benchmark for what bisque *should* taste like when you dine out at fine French restaurants. Serve your very best buttery Chardonnay.

1	**leek**
2–4 Tbsp. (25–50 mL)	**unsalted butter**
2	**onions, minced**
1 head	**garlic, minced**
3 stalks	**celery, minced**
3–4	**carrots, minced**
1–2	**bay leaves**
1 tsp. (5 mL)	**dried thyme**
8 cups (2 L)	**shrimp, crab or lobster shells, raw or cooked**
2 Tbsp. (25 mL)	**sweet Hungarian paprika**
½ cup (125 mL)	**tomato paste**

~	**freshly cracked black pepper to taste**
½ cup (125 mL)	**brandy**
½ bottle	**dry white wine**
4–6 cups (1–1.5 L)	**white fish stock (see Fish Stock, page 62)**
2 cups (500 mL)	**whipping cream**
~	**kosher salt and cayenne to taste**
~	**lemon juice to taste**
½ cup (125 mL)	**fino sherry**
4–6 Tbsp. (50–90 mL)	**cornstarch dissolved in cold water**
~	**whipping cream for garnish**
~	**fresh parsley or chives for garnish**

Slice the leeks lengthwise, trim off the root and any tough or damaged outer green leaves, and slice crosswise into fine shreds. Transfer the sliced leeks into a colander and wash very thoroughly under running water.

Melt the butter in a large heavy pot. When it foams, add the leek, onions, garlic, celery, carrots, bay leaves and thyme. Cook over high heat until the vegetables are tender, about 5 minutes. Add the shells and stir well. Continue cooking until the shells colour and become fragrant. Stir in the paprika and tomato paste, stir well, then add the pepper and brandy. Stir in the wine. Bring to a boil, then add the stock.

Simmer until the liquid is fragrant, about 20 minutes. Strain through a fine sieve or chinois, pushing with the back of a wooden spoon to extract all the liquid and discarding the pulp and shells. Return the liquid to the pot. Add the cream, then balance the flavours with salt, cayenne and lemon juice. Add the sherry. Return briefly to a boil, then stir in the cornstarch mixture to thicken. Cook for a minute, or until lightly thickened. Serve in small portions, garnished with a drizzle of cream and a sprinkle of minced parsley or chives.

SERVES A CROWD, 8–10

FREEZER GOLDMINES

The freezer holds a lot of secrets that look like gold to cooks. Unfortunately, some of that gold resembles dross to the non-cooks we love. One day, Jeff was organizing things in the freezer, and he suggested that maybe we get rid of the junk that filled it — to make room for other, more important stuff, of course. He was talking about my hoard of lobster and shrimp shells, my bags of chicken bones and kaffir lime leaves, and the other odds and sods that only look like detritus. Guard your gold like a dragon, and do not let your loving non-cook convince you to abandon what will become something delicious!

Tomato Saffron Sole Consommé

The famous short story writer Saki once wrote that a clear soup is more important in life than a clear conscience. Yes, it is delicious. No, it is not difficult — consommé just sounds hard. This one is quickly made from fish so finely textured that it takes minutes, not hours, to cook. It is vital to begin with cold ingredients, otherwise, the all-important "raft" that clarifies the soup will not form. The end result is a highly flavoured broth of intense clarity and purity, despite the absolute absence of fat. The flavours are the classics of southern France — fennel, tomato, saffron and orange, with slivers of fresh basil to complete the picture. Pour a slightly chilled French Chablis or other lighter white Burgundy.

1	leek, minced
8 cups (2 L)	fish stock, cold
3	sole fillets, chopped or puréed
2 lbs. (1 kg)	white fish bones (sole, halibut, snapper), chopped or broken into 2-inch (5 cm) lengths
1	onion, minced
1	carrot, minced
1 stalk	celery, minced
2 Tbsp. (25 mL)	minced parsley
1 sprig	fresh thyme
2	bay leaves
~	pinch of saffron
½ bulb	fresh fennel, diced finely
1–2	ripe tomatoes, seeded and diced finely
4	egg whites, lightly mixed with a fork
~	kosher salt and cayenne to taste
1–2 Tbsp. (15–25 mL)	lemon juice
2 Tbsp. (25 mL)	slivered fresh basil
1	orange, zest only, blanched and slivered

Slice the leek lengthwise, trim off the root and any tough or damaged outer green leaves, and slice crosswise into fine shreds. Transfer the sliced leek into a colander and wash very thoroughly under running water.

In a heavy pot off the heat, combine the leek, cold stock, sole, bones, onion, carrot, celery, parsley, thyme, bay leaves and saffron. Add most of the fennel and tomato, reserving a couple spoonfuls of each for garnish. Add the egg whites. Mix well. Bring to a gentle simmer, stirring until the ingredients coagulate into a "raft." At that point, stop stirring. Instead, use a tablespoon to loosen the edges of the raft so it doesn't stick to the sides of the pot.

Keep the heat slow and gentle so that no large bubbles form that might break up the raft. Simmer 45 minutes. Use a pair of wooden spoons or some other large tools to hold the raft in place while you carefully strain the soup through a sieve or fine mesh chinois lined with a clean, damp kitchen towel. Discard the raft.

Adjust the seasoning of the consommé with salt, cayenne and lemon juice. Garnish with the reserved tomato and fennel, along with the basil and orange zest.

SERVES 6

TO SEED OR NOT TO SEED

There is absolutely nothing wrong with tomato seeds or juice. But sometimes they add visual clutter and unwanted moisture to a dish. When you want neither, choose meaty Roma tomatoes, cut the tomato horizontally along the equator, squeeze each tomato half over a bowl, and discard the resulting juice-seed mixture. If you want the liquid but not the seeds, squeeze the halves over a sieve, discard the captured seeds and use the juice, cleverly caught in a bowl beneath the sieve.

Cream *of* **Winter Vegetable Soup**

Purées can be rich or lean, as the cook desires. This simple version makes a refined but substantial soup that is a meal unto itself or a prelude to other courses. Celeriac is a lumpy root that is largely ignored. It makes glorious soup, suave and sophisticated, with a flavour that is unforgettable — once you know what it is. Add texture with croutons of any shape, or use a simple but visually appealing garnish of minced fresh herbs or a drizzle of herb-infused oil. Italian Pinot Grigio or Pinot Bianco would be pleasant with this healthy bowl of soup.

3	**leeks**
2 Tbsp. (25 mL)	**unsalted butter**
2–3	**carrots or parsnips, sliced**
4 cloves	**garlic, minced**
2 sprigs	**fresh thyme, minced**
1 lb. (500 g)	**diced yams or celeriac**
4 cups (1 L)	**vegetable or chicken stock**
½ cup (125 mL)	**whipping cream**
~	**kosher salt and freshly cracked white pepper to taste**

Slice the leeks lengthwise, trim off the root and any tough or damaged outer green leaves, and slice crosswise into fine shreds. Transfer the sliced leeks into a colander and wash very thoroughly under running water.

In a heavy pot, melt the butter, then add the leeks, carrots or parsnips, garlic and thyme. Sauté until the leeks are tender, about 5–7 minutes. Add the yams or celeriac and stock, and bring to a boil. Cover, reduce the heat and simmer until the vegetables are tender. Purée, then stir in the cream. Adjust the flavour with salt and pepper. Thin with additional cream or stock if the soup is too thick. Serve hot.

SERVES 4–6

Stone Soup

This is the ultimate winter potful, a peasant soup full of unassuming cabbage, smoky pork and tender beans. The whole is greater than the sum of the parts, so make enough to share. It easily switches to a vegetarian style — just leave out the meat and use vegetable stock or water in place of the chicken or beef stock. Turn it into a vaguely mulligatawny-like soup by adding a good blend of curry powder when sautéing the vegetables. Serve with crusty Sourdough Bread (page 52) or Cheese Biscuits (page 54.) Alsatian wines marry well with this soup, or try a Pinot Gris or Auxerrois.

2–3 slices	bacon, diced
½ cup (125 mL)	slivered ham
1 Tbsp. (15 mL)	olive oil
1	onion or leek, diced
4–6 cloves	garlic, minced
1	bay leaf
2 stalks	celery, diced
2–3	carrots, diced
1 tsp. (5 mL)	dried basil
1 tsp. (5 mL)	dried oregano
½ tsp. (2 mL)	dried thyme
¼ head	Savoy or Napa cabbage, finely sliced
2–3	Yukon Gold potatoes, cubed
1 cup (250 mL)	cooked beans (I like Great Northern, but any variety will do)
¼ cup (50 mL)	raw lentils or barley
8 cups (2 L)	chicken or beef stock
¼ cup (50 mL)	raw rice or pasta shells
~	kosher salt and freshly cracked black pepper to taste

Sauté the bacon and ham until the bacon is almost crisp. Discard any extra fat. Add the oil, onion or leek, garlic, bay, celery, carrots, basil, oregano and thyme. Cook until tender, adding small amounts of water as needed to prevent browning. Add all the remaining ingredients, except for the salt and pepper. Cook, covered, over moderate heat until tender. Adjust the flavours with salt and pepper. Serve hot.

FEEDS A SMALL VILLAGE OF 12–14

Cheese *and* Onion Soup

Crusty Sourdough Bread (page 52) is a good match for this sophisticated use for cheese ends. Use a mixture of cheeses, but be sure to include a good melter, like fontina, and something assertive, either a blue, a sharp cheddar, manchego or Asiago. Depending on the cheese used, a wine with good acidity will work well to balance out the richness of the ingredients.

1	**leek**
1 Tbsp. (15 mL)	**butter**
1	**onion, sliced**
4–6 cloves	**garlic**
6–8	**medium potatoes, sliced**
~	**kosher salt and hot chili flakes to taste**
6 cups (1.5 L)	**chicken stock**
½ cup (125 mL)	**whipping cream**
2 cups (500 mL)	**cubed or grated cheese**
~	**minced chives or other fresh herb to garnish**

Slice the leek lengthwise, trim off the root and any tough or damaged outer green leaves, and slice crosswise into fine shreds. Transfer the sliced leek into a colander and wash very thoroughly under running water.

Heat the butter over medium heat in a heavy saucepan, add the leek, onion and garlic and sauté until tender. If necessary, add a little water to prevent browning. Add the potatoes, season with salt and hot chili flakes and stir in the stock. Cover and cook until tender.

Purée, adding additional stock to thin the consistency as needed. Purée finely for a smooth, refined soup or less for a chunkier, more robust finished texture. Don't over-process, or the potatoes will turn glutinous and sticky! Add the cream, taste, then add the cheese. Stir until the cheese melts, heating it gently if necessary, but remaining well below the boiling point. Garnish with herbs and serve.

SERVES 6

Turkey Chowder

Using stock instead of milk or cream makes a more flavourful, leaner soup that is less prone to curdling as it simmers. That leftover bottle of French rosé will serve you well here.

1	leek
2 slices	side bacon, slivered
1	onion, minced
2	carrots, diced
1 stalk	celery, diced
6 cloves	garlic, minced
½	red pepper, diced
1 cup (250 mL)	corn, canned, fresh or frozen
1	bay leaf
1 tsp. (5 mL)	dried thyme
½ cup (125 mL)	dry white wine
2 cups (500 mL)	diced Yukon Gold potatoes
4 cups (1 L)	chicken or vegetable stock
1–2 Tbsp. (15–25 mL)	cornstarch dissolved in cold water
¼ cup (50 mL)	whipping cream
~	kosher salt and hot chili flakes to taste
3	green onions, minced
1	lemon, zest only
1–2 lbs. (500 g–1 kg)	diced cooked turkey

Slice the leek lengthwise, trim and slice crosswise into fine shreds. Transfer into a colander and wash under running water.

Sweat the bacon in a heavy stockpot. Discard all but 1 Tbsp. (15 mL) fat. Add the leek, onion, carrots, celery, garlic, red pepper and corn and cook them without colouring, adding small amounts of water as needed.

When the vegetables are tender, stir in the bay leaf, thyme and wine. Bring to a boil, then add the potatoes and stock. Simmer, covered, until the potatoes are tender.

Return to the boil and stir in the dissolved cornstarch, allowing to thicken, adding more as needed. Add the cream, salt, hot chili flakes, green onions, lemon zest and turkey. Heat through and serve hot.

SERVES 6

Monday
Beans & Greens

Homely Veggies

My household includes two hungry teenagers, a hungry adult male and me. One teen inclines toward vegetarianism; the adult male is as carnivorous as they come, and thinks that "vegetable" is a four-letter word. As for pulses, that vast family of dried beans that includes chickpeas, lentils and split peas, he tends to think that they, like his asparagus, are best cooked until soft. He *is* right about the beans.

Pulses can't get any respect. Many people think that beans are a sign of hard times and hard luck, and are just plain hard-to-like. It is a slight to a noble food. The reality is that many North Americans only know insipid baked beans from a can, or undercooked, crunchy, bound-to-give-you-gas beans from a bad buffet or summer barbecue.

Cooks from other countries know better. In Spain, Catalan cooks "smother" fava beans and sausage, and Basque cooks in the Pyrenees simmer beans "*al-pil-pil*" in earthenware pots. Spanish beans with pork are called *cocido* and *porchas*; cooks in the south of France make *cassoulet* from the same ingredients. In Brazil, cooks make cassoulet's kissin' cousin, *feijoada*.

My best beloved, the carnivore, is an insulin-dependent diabetic. He more than many of us should be eating beans regularly. Pulses are better for diabetics than potatoes or white bread. According to the Canadian Diabetes Association, pulses are high on the favoured list for diabetics because they have a relatively low glycemic index (GI) value. That means they raise blood glucose levels more slowly than high glycemic foods like potatoes and white bread. Elevated blood glucose levels can contribute to damage to the eyes, kidneys, heart and blood vessels, so long-time diabetics face serious health challenges "later" if they don't mind their diet "now."

I had never thought of lentils as a treat before. But knowing about the value of low glycemic foods for my diabetic sweetie was enough impetus to send me scurrying into the kitchen to cook up batch after batch of beans.

Cooking Beans

A bean is a bean, no matter its name. So whether you opt for flageolets francais, Painted Pony, Jacob's Cattle, Rattlesnakes, Great Northern or plain old white navy beans, they all get treated the same way. Rinse them and pick out any pebbles. Cook them in a heavy-bottomed, big-bellied pot with lots and lots of water. Watch the water level; there is no rescuing burnt beans. Add a few fennel seeds as a digestive aid, but no salt, which inhibits cooking. Crunchy texture is not acceptable — beans must be soft to release their minerals and to be digestible, and undercooked beans cause gas. Don't stop cooking if they stay crunchy — simmer on! It just means the pulses are older, and need more time and liquid. Soaking and rinsing beans before cooking can strip out gassy carbon dioxide, but it also strips out the nutrients. It's easier — and tidier — to simply simmer pulses in abundant water. Once they are tender, add salt, a bit of vinegar and whatever you like for flavour. Freeze the extras for next time — it's faster to thaw frozen than to cook dried.

CONDIMENT BEANS

Many cooks make endless variations of Condiment Beans. Empty your fridge's burgeoning collection of condiments — salsa, chutney, herb paste, marmalade — into the pot with the cooked beans, but don't expect the same dish twice. Add a smoked pork hock and the results are magnificent. A slightly sneaky approach is to add a cup or two of cooked beans to slowly simmering braised duck legs, venison or lamb shanks.

Oregano and Lemon Potatoes

This is a good example of when it's best not to mess with a very good thing. In most Greek restaurants, this is the side dish that goes out beside the slow-braised lamb, the deep-fried calamari, the skewered meats. At home, it's easy to make in the oven or on the grill if it is already running. Just make extra — they disappear quickly! My Greek girlfriend Cat, who always greets guests with gusto, says these potatoes are like "Aggalitses" or little kisses, because they are so good to share.

1 lb. (500 g)	round potatoes (See Selecting Spuds, page 81)
6 cloves	garlic, minced
4–6 Tbsp. (50–90 mL)	olive oil
1 tsp. (5 mL)	dried rubbed oregano
1	lemon, juice only
1 cup (250 mL)	water (more as needed)
~	kosher salt and freshly ground black pepper to taste

Peel or scrub the potatoes. Slice them into quarters and toss with the remaining ingredients. Spread on a baking sheet with a lip and bake, uncovered, at 375°F (190°C), until tender, about 90 minutes. Stir often, turning the potatoes so that all the surfaces are coated. Add more water as needed — there should always be moisture in the pan.

SERVES 4

Olive Oil Mashed Potatoes

In the Languedoc, in south-central France, I ate mashed potatoes laced with olive oil. "This isn't very French!" I whispered to my friend Judy. No, but they sure are good. Use your very best olive oil, increasing the oil volume if you make this dairy-free. I invariably select Yukon Gold potatoes because I enjoy their flavour and rich golden colour, but russets work just fine too. If it isn't the middle of winter, when potatoes show their age with thick skins and bruises, simply wash the potatoes and cook them skin on for maximum nutrition and a slightly rustic look.

2 lbs. (1 kg)	**raw potatoes, preferably Yukon Golds or russets**
½ cup (125 mL)	**extra virgin olive oil (more as needed)**
½ cup (125 mL)	**milk (optional)**
~	**kosher salt and hot chili flakes to taste**
~	**minced chives (optional)**

Peel the potatoes, then immediately put them into a pot. Add cold water to a depth of 2 inches (5 cm) and a generous pinch of salt. Cover the pot and cook the potatoes over medium heat until they are tender.

Drain the potatoes. Use a hand masher to mash them in the pot while they are still hot. Add the oil and milk, if using, and season with salt and hot chili flakes. If you like, add a handful of minced chives.

SERVES 4

HERBED CRANBERRY POTATO CAKES

Make extra mash one night for dinner, and bind any still-warm leftovers with egg, spike it with herbs and chopped cranberries, form into fat patties 2 inches (5 cm) across and refrigerate. The next day, heat the oven to 450°F (230°C), drizzle the patties with oil and roast uncovered until golden and crusty. Serve hot.

Selecting Spuds

You'll get better results if you know what potatoes you are getting and why. Choosing the wrong potato can mess up the texture of a dish, so match the spud to the idea.

Round red potatoes with white flesh are called "waxy." Their firm and moist texture makes for wonderful potato salad, scalloped potatoes, soups, boiling and steaming — anywhere shape is needed. Favourite varieties include Red Bliss and Red Pontiac. **Round whites** have medium starch content, which helps these tan-skinned potatoes hold their shape when cooked. Look for Katahdin and White Rose. **Russets**, the most widely used potato in North America, are classified as "mealy." That means they are high in starch and light and fluffy when cooked, making

them ideal for French fries and baking in the jacket. Russets have brown "netted" skins and white flesh. Varieties include Burbank, Norland and Norgold. **Yellow-fleshed** potatoes include Yellow Finn, Bintje and Yukon Gold. These dense-textured potatoes are slightly lower in starch than russets, but are still superlative mashers, with a buttery flavour and colour. **Fingerlings**, also called banana potatoes, are low in starch, and are best for roasting and salads. **New** refers to immature potatoes that are harvested early. Look for a flimsy, easily removed skin like parchment. New spuds are high in starch, which limits how well they brown. They are best boiled and served simply.

Campfire Potatoes
and Vegetables

On the grill or over an open fire, these crisp vegetables will scent the air with rosemary and garlic. Make extra — half the spuds will disappear before dinner is served. Toss any leftover vegetables with Vanilla-Citrus Vinaigrette (page 20) for the next day's lunch.

1 lb. (500 g)	**small new potatoes**
2 heads	**garlic**
¼ cup (50 mL)	**olive oil**
2–3 sprigs	**fresh rosemary, minced**
~	**kosher salt and freshly cracked black pepper to taste**
12–16 stalks	**young asparagus**
2	**zucchini**
1	**onion**
1–2	**red, yellow or orange bell peppers**
12–14	**medium field mushrooms**
~	**kosher salt and freshly cracked black pepper to taste**

Scrub the potatoes and trim them into even sizes if necessary. Cut off the tips of the garlic bulbs to just expose the tops of the cloves. Brush the potatoes and garlic generously with oil. Place in a single layer in an old cake pan or baking sheet, the garlic cut side down. Sprinkle with the rosemary, salt and pepper. Place on the fire or grill and cook, turning now and then, until tender, 20–40 minutes depending on the size and type of potatoes.

Snap off the woody ends of the asparagus. Cut the zucchini into ½-inch (1-cm) slices on an angle. Peel the onion and slice it into 8 pieces lengthwise through the root. Slice the bell peppers into fat batons. Wash the mushrooms. Lightly rub the remaining olive oil over all the vegetables to coat their cut surfaces. Sprinkle with salt and pepper, then arrange in a single layer in a grilling basket or on a metal rack. Grill over direct heat, turning several times, until well-marked and tender, about 10 minutes. Serve hot or cold.

SERVES 4—6

---

10 REASONS FOR BUYING FOOD LOCALLY

....

10

Locally grown food is fresh. It was likely picked yesterday or today.

9

Local produce is good for you. It has not had time to lose nutrients during long freight trips.

8

Local food tends to be GMO-free. Many small farmers use GMO-free seeds, often heritage varieties that are impossible to find in commercial markets.

7

Local food preserves open space. Cities are rapidly encroaching on farm land.

6

Local food supports farm families. Put money in the pockets of the people who grow the grains. Fewer folks now live on farms than ever before. Who will feed us if we all move into town?

Succotash Gratin

Use up your proliferation of summer vegetables in this indulgent, sweet and succulent gratin. Make a large panful and take it to a potluck, or enjoy the leftovers tucked inside omelettes or alone for a fabulous breakfast. Replace the cream with an equal amount of milk or chicken stock (and several tablespoons of flour sprinkled among the potato layers) if this version is too rich.

2 lbs. (1 kg)	new potatoes, thinly sliced
2 cups (500 mL)	corn kernels (about 6 ears' worth)
2 cups (500 mL)	cooked white beans
3	red or yellow bell peppers, sliced
1	zucchini, thinly sliced
½ cup (125 mL)	sliced green olives
3 Tbsp. (45 mL)	minced fresh dill
~	kosher salt and freshly ground black pepper to taste
2 cups (500 mL)	whipping cream
2 cups (500 mL)	grated cheese (Swiss, Cheddar, manchego, Jarlsberg or a mixture)

Blanch the potatoes in boiling water for 5–7 minutes to parcook them. Drain the potatoes well. Layer the potatoes with the corn, beans, bell peppers, zucchini and olives in a shallow gratin dish with a 3-quart (3-L) capacity. Sprinkle the top with dill, salt and pepper. Pour the cream over top and add the cheese. Put the gratin on a baking sheet to catch drips and bake at 425°F (220°C) for 45 minutes or until bubbly and brown. Serve hot.

SERVES 8—10

5

Local food builds community. Look into the eyes of the people who grew your food. They won't call it a commodity; they'll call it dinner, and can tell you exactly how it was raised.

4

Local food keeps your taxes in check. Farm land is taxed at a lower rate than urban land.

3

Local food supports a clean environment. Small family farms are likely to grow cover crops to prevent erosion and replace soil nutrients. Cover crops also help combat global warming. Many small farms also support species of wildlife, insects and birds.

2

Local food preserves genetic diversity. Heritage produce that doesn't travel well but tastes real is likely to be grown by growers without a vested interest in long-distance shipping. So are fragile foods that ripen slowly and don't keep long.

1

Local food is about the future. Supporting farmers today means we may have farmers in the future.

Sui Choy *in* Coconut Milk

Any cabbage will work in this sweet and mellow Thai-style dish, but the gentle flavour of sui choy, napa or savoy cabbage are the best bets. Flowering yow choy is slightly stronger in flavour; for a milder finish, choose baby bok choy. Serve this dish with plain or Coconut Rice (page 124), finely-textured noodles or as an accompaniment to curries, grilled meats or fish. Add cubed tofu or cooked white beans for a meatless main dish. As with any stir-fry, have all the ingredients sliced and measured before you begin to cook.

1 Tbsp. (15 mL)	vegetable oil
½	small onion, finely sliced
4 cloves	garlic, minced
1 Tbsp. (15 mL)	grated fresh ginger
3	kaffir lime leaves
½ cup (125 mL)	julienned red bell pepper
½ cup (125 mL)	grated carrot
1 tsp. (5 mL)	finely minced jalapeño
½ head	sui choy or savoy cabbage, julienned
14-oz. tin (398-mL tin)	coconut milk
1 tsp. (5 mL)	shrimp paste
1 tsp. (5 mL)	fish sauce
1 tsp. (5 mL)	sugar or honey
1	lime, juice only
~	kosher salt to taste
3 Tbsp. (45 mL)	minced cilantro

Heat the oil in a large sauté pan, then add the onion, garlic, ginger, lime leaves, bell pepper, carrot and jalapeño. Cook over high heat, stirring, until the vegetables are tender and transparent, about 5 minutes. Add small amounts of water to prevent browning. Stir in the cabbage, coconut milk, shrimp paste, fish sauce, sugar or honey and lime juice. Mix well, cover and simmer for about 5 minutes, or until the cabbage is tender and wilted. Season with salt, stir in the cilantro and serve immediately.

SERVES 6 AS A SIDE DISH

Gai Lan *in* Black Bean *and* Marmalade Sauce

Choose more assertive greens to stand up to the big flavours in this dish. Mustard greens or flowering gai lan are slightly pungent choices that blend well with strong tastes. If your pantry does not contain marmalade, use plum preserves and extra vinegar or lemon juice. If red peppers are out of season, use half a dozen slivered mushrooms instead. Fermented black beans are available in Asian markets; if you cannot find them, leave them out and call this dish "Gai Lan in Hoisin and Marmalade Sauce"! This is good with barbecued pork or duck dishes, as well as with richer fish, such as salmon and tuna.

1 Tbsp. (15 mL)	**vegetable oil**
6 cloves	**garlic, sliced**
1 Tbsp. (15 mL)	**grated fresh ginger**
1	**small onion, finely sliced**
1	**red bell pepper, cut in 1-inch (2.5-cm) dice**
2 Tbsp. (25 mL)	**hoisin sauce**
2 Tbsp. (25 mL)	**orange marmalade**
¼ cup (50 mL)	**rice vinegar or lemon juice**
2 Tbsp. (25 mL)	**light soy sauce**
1 bunch	**gai lan, chopped into 1-inch (2.5-cm) lengths**
1 Tbsp. (15 mL)	**fermented dried black beans, rinsed**
2 Tbsp. (25 mL)	**cornstarch dissolved in cold water**

Heat the oil in a large sauté pan, then add the garlic, ginger, onion and bell pepper. Cook the vegetables over high heat, stirring, until they are tender and transparent, adding small amounts of water as needed to prevent browning. Add the hoisin, marmalade and vinegar or lemon juice. Mix well, then stir in 1–2 cups (250–500 mL) of water to thin the paste. Mix in the gai lan, cover and steam the vegetables for about 5 minutes, or until tender. Add the black beans and dissolved cornstarch and boil briefly until the mixture thickens. Serve hot.

SERVES 6 AS A SIDE DISH

Orange Ginger Baby Bok Choy

I love these cute little vegetables. You can vary this dish by adding curry paste, coconut milk and green beans cut into 2-inch (5-cm) lengths.

1 Tbsp. (15 mL)	**vegetable oil**
6	**baby bok choy, split lengthwise**
4 cloves	**garlic, sliced**
2 Tbsp. (25 mL)	**thinly sliced fresh ginger**
½ cup (125 mL)	**orange juice**
1 cup (250 mL)	**chicken stock**
4	**whole star anise pods**
2 Tbsp. (25 mL)	**cornstarch dissolved in cold water**
1	**orange, zest only**
2 Tbsp. (25 mL)	**minced cilantro**
~	**kosher salt and hot chili paste to taste**

Heat the oil in a shallow pan. Add the bok choy, cut side down, and cook over medium-high heat to brown the surfaces. Add the garlic and ginger. Sauté briefly. Add the juice, stock and star anise. Cover and cook on the stovetop over medium heat until the bok choy is tender, about 10 minutes. Add the dissolved cornstarch and boil the sauce briefly. Stir in the orange zest and cilantro and season with salt and chili paste.

SERVES 6

"One Hot Mama" Brussels Sprouts

For a Thanksgiving dinner, assemble this in advance. Add a bit of cream if you want to gild the lily, and slide the finished dish into the oven to heat through after you take the turkey out.

1 ½ lbs. (750 g)	Brussels sprouts
1 Tbsp. (15 mL)	vegetable oil
1	onion, finely diced
4–6 cloves	garlic, minced
½ cup (125 mL)	diced ham
½ tsp. (2 mL)	hot chili paste, or 1 jalapeño, seeded and finely diced
4 Tbsp. (50 mL)	minced fresh basil
~	kosher salt and freshly cracked black pepper to taste

Set the oven to 375°F (190°C). Trim off the ends of the Brussels sprouts and thinly slice them. Heat 2 inches (5 cm) of salted water in a sauté pan. Add the Brussels sprouts when the water is boiling. Cook over high heat until bright green and tender. Drain, discarding the water. Set the Brussels sprouts aside.

Reheat the pan, add the oil, then the onion, garlic and ham. Cook until the onions are tender, about 5 minutes, adding small amounts of water as needed to prevent browning. Stir the mixture into the Brussels sprouts along with the hot chili paste or jalapeño, basil, salt and pepper. Serve hot.

SERVES 6–10 AS A SIDE DISH

Caesar Salad

I admit to being a purist when it comes to this particular salad. I like romaine; I like homemade croutons; I especially like the best Parmesan, freshly grated. If you are more adventurous, substitute radicchio, change the cheese to feta, add slivered good green olives, use wonton crisps for croutons. But me? Hail Caesar!

....

Dressing:

1 Tbsp. (15 mL)	**smooth Dijon mustard**
4 cloves	**garlic, minced**
1 3-oz. tin (1 85-mL tin)	**anchovies, mashed or puréed**
1 Tbsp. (15 mL)	**lemon juice**
1	**egg yolk**
1 cup (250 mL)	**olive oil**
2 Tbsp. (25 mL)	**Worcestershire sauce**
2 Tbsp. (25 mL)	**red wine vinegar**
½ tsp. (2 mL)	**hot chili paste**

Combine the mustard, garlic, anchovies, lemon juice and egg yolk. Whisk well, until light and fluffy. Slowly drizzle in ½ cup (125 mL) of the oil to form an emulsion. Stir in the remaining ingredients, thinning if needed with a little water or lemon juice, then add the remaining ½ cup (125 mL) oil.

....

Croutons:

4 slices	**white or brown bread**
4 Tbsp. (50 mL)	**olive oil**
½ tsp. (2 mL)	*each* **dried oregano, basil, thyme, black pepper**

Slice the croutons into ½-inch (1-cm) cubes. Arrange in a single layer on a baking sheet. Drizzle the oil over the cubes. Sprinkle the herbs and pepper over the cubes. Bake at 300° F (150° C) until golden brown. Cool, then store in an uncovered jar at room temperature.

....

Assembly:

1 head	**romaine lettuce**
½ cup (125 mL)	**grated Parmesan cheese**

Wash the lettuce, dry it in a salad spinner and tear into bite-size pieces. (Do not cut the lettuce with a knife; it will rust much more quickly.) Toss the lettuce in a bowl with the Parmesan, croutons and 1 cup (250 mL) of the dressing, or to taste. (Refrigerate any leftover dressing for up to 4 days.) Serve promptly on chilled plates.

SERVES 6—8

Wilted Spinach *with* Shallots, Garlic *and* Pancetta

Eat your greens! In the depths of winter, look past the overpriced imported lettuces to the sturdy, rustic selection of kales, spinach, beet tops and chard. If you prefer chard, beet greens or kale to spinach, separate the rib, slice it finely, then sauté it with the shallot and garlic.

2	**shallots, finely diced**
3 cloves	**garlic, minced**
2–4 Tbsp. (25–50 mL)	**olive oil**
4 slices	**pancetta, diced**
3 bunches	**spinach, washed and stemmed but not dried**
~	**kosher salt and freshly cracked black pepper to taste**
~	**lemon zest to taste**

Wilt the shallots and garlic in half the olive oil. Do not allow to colour. Add the pancetta and sauté until crispy. Discard extra fat if you like. Add the spinach, wilting it over high heat until it collapses but is still bright green. Add the remaining olive oil if you like, and season with salt, pepper and lemon zest. Serve hot.

SERVES 4

*Teaching kids — and adults —
about emulsions is easily done
while making salad dressing.
An emulsion is a mixture of
2 liquids that would normally
not combine. Some emulsions,
like vinaigrettes, are temporary,
and return to their component
forms in layers shortly after
being blended. Others, like
mayonnaise, are permanent,
and form a new substance that
is different from either original
part. A permanent emulsion is
more stable if you use fresh eggs
and add an acid (lemon juice or
vinegar) to the egg yolks before
adding the oil. Fresh eggs have
higher amounts of lecithin,
and acid helps maintain the
pH level of yolks at a level that
minimizes curdling. How you
add the oil is crucial, too; in
a temporary mixture, you can
get away with just dumping
the ingredients into a jar and
shaking it madly. But for a
permanent emulsion, such
as Caesar dressing or Better
Than Béarnaise Sauce (see
page 45), the oil or butter is
added in a slow drizzle, while
whisking constantly. If the
mixture separates or curdles
because the oil was added too
rapidly, it can be whisked into
another egg yolk in a clean bowl,
slowly, as if it were oil.*

Curried Silky Spinach

Any English friend will love this gently flavoured and subtly textured dish. Think in mere seconds while you wilt the spinach, then gently reduce the cream to the thickish consistency that will coat a spoon. It is a lovely side accompaniment to any curry. This makes a fine soup — just add chicken stock and whiz it in a food processor or blender.

2 Tbsp. (25 mL)	**vegetable oil**
½	**onion, finely minced**
2 cloves	**garlic, sliced**
1 Tbsp. (15 mL)	**Ras El Hanout (see page 28) or curry powder**
1 tsp. (5 mL)	**mustard seed**
1 lb. (500 g)	**fresh spinach, washed and stemmed**
½ cup (125 mL)	**whipping cream**
~	**kosher salt and freshly ground black pepper to taste**

Heat the oil in a large, shallow sauté pan. Add the onion, garlic, curry powder and mustard seed; cook the vegetables until transparent, about 5 minutes. Add the spinach in large handfuls, stirring well. Cook just long enough to wilt the greens, less than a minute, turning with tongs. Drain off any accumulated liquid. Add the cream and bring it to a quick boil to reduce and thicken. Season with salt and pepper. Serve hot.

SERVES 3 – 4

AN OIL IS NOT AN OIL IS NOT AN OIL

We need fat in our diets. That is a fact, even if fat has become the biggest culinary culprit of our time. Fat is not to blame; inertia is. Add exercise to your diet, and your body will be healthier and happier. When you do use oil or fat, choose one that you like the taste of, not necessarily a mild, mass-produced and neutrally flavoured type. On salad, use avocado, olive, grapeseed or nut oil; in cooking, use olive, sunflower or safflower oil.

Grilled New Carrots
in Sherry Vinaigrette

New vegetables are a great excuse to get outside and turn on the grill. These are great at room temperature, so cook them before you grill your burgers or chops. Leftovers can find their way into risotto, pilaf, omelette or soufflé.

1 lb. (500 g)	**new carrots**
1–2 Tbsp. (15–25 mL)	**olive oil**
2 Tbsp. (25 mL)	**Dijon mustard**
1 Tbsp. (15 mL)	**minced fresh thyme or tarragon**
1 Tbsp. (15 mL)	**melted honey**
¼ cup (50 mL)	**sherry vinegar or Vanilla Vinegar (see page 20)**
~	**kosher salt and pepper to taste**
¼ cup (50 mL)	**olive oil**

Lightly oil the carrots with the 2 Tbsp. (25 mL) oil. Preheat the grill to medium-high. Grill the carrots until tender, 5–10 minutes.

Meanwhile, make the vinaigrette by whisking together the mustard, thyme or tarragon, honey, vinegar, salt and pepper. Slowly add the remaining ¼ cup (50 mL) oil, whisking to emulsify. Remove the carrots from the grill. Drizzle with the dressing and serve hot or warm.

SERVES 4–6

SIT! NOW EAT YOUR CARROTS... GOOD DOG!

Eat your carrots raw, and feed one to your mutt as well. Veterinarians agree that carrots are great treats for dogs, better in fact than many of the processed cookies and dog treats that are sold at the grocery. It's a treat that will work well to counteract obesity, too. Use slices of vegetables as motivation and reward for your dog. (And if the carrot is good enough, your kids might want it too.) My animals' vet, Brian McBride, says that most vegetables and fruit are safe for dogs; avoid garlic and onions, and remember that dogs are prone to gas from too much broccoli and other crucifers.

Grilled Leeks *and* Onions

Sometimes the simplest things are the best. Use this mélange of smoky flavours and tender textures as a base for grilled meats and fish, toss it on a disc of dough for a robust flatbread, add cream and serve it on pasta or in risotto with grilled sausage, or scoop spoonfuls onto grilled crusty bread for a messy lunch.

4	**leeks**
1	**red onion**
1 head	**garlic**
~	**olive oil for the grill**
~	**sherry vinegar or balsamic vinegar to taste**
1 tsp. (5 mL)	**minced fresh thyme**
~	**kosher salt and pepper to taste**

Trim the outer green leaves of the leeks, leaving enough root attached to hold leek halves intact. Slice the leeks in half lengthwise, wash well to eliminate hidden grit, and simmer in salted water for 5 minutes. Drain well, then lightly oil.

Peel and slice the onion lengthwise into 8 or 10 segments, depending on the size of the onion. Lightly oil. Cut off the top of the garlic, exposing the cloves, and brush with oil. Preheat the grill to medium-high. Grill the leeks, onion and garlic until tender and well-marked by the grill bars. Remove to a bowl. Peel the garlic and toss the cloves with the leeks, onion, vinegar, thyme, salt and pepper. Serve warm.

SERVES 4

Roasted Roots

More proof that simple is good. Raid your condiment cupboard for your favourite oil and vinegar for a bit of extra flavour. Serve warm or cold, alone or on sturdy greens.

3	**carrots, thinly sliced lengthwise**
2	**parsnips, thinly sliced lengthwise**
1	**onion, thinly sliced**
1 head	**garlic, peeled and separated into cloves**
1–2 Tbsp. (15–25 mL)	**olive oil**
~	**kosher salt and freshly ground black pepper to taste**
1–2 Tbsp. (15–25 mL)	**minced parsley**
~	**a splash of herb-infused vinegar** **or the juice and zest of 1 lemon (optional)**
~	**drizzle of infused oil (optional)**

Preheat the oven to 425°F (220°C). Combine the carrots, parsnips, onion and garlic with the oil. Spread the vegetables in a thin layer on a parchment-lined baking sheet. Sprinkle with salt and pepper. Bake uncovered for 20–45 minutes, until tender-crisp and well-coloured, tossing from time to time. Remove to a bowl and mix in the parsley and the optional vinegar or lemon and infused oil. Serve hot or at room temperature.

SERVES 4

VARIATION: *Roasted Beets*

Beets are the exception to this basic method of roasting root vegetables. Roast beets whole, in their jackets, until they give to a gentle squeeze. Peel them while they are still warm, and dress them in a small amount of your favourite vinaigrette.

Citrus-Dressed Asparagus *and* Smoked Salmon *on* Wild Rice *and* Spinach

Asparagus officinalis, an edible member of the lily family, has been popular for over 2,000 years. It is nowhere nearly as showy as its cousins but is among the most elegant of the kitchen's vegetable stars. When they are in season, use fresh berries on the plate in place of the oranges. These classic spring flavours combine texture and flavour with stylish simplicity. Think Mother's Day brunch, think late-night suppers, think of all those times when you don't feel like doing too much, but really want something light and yummy (preferably cooked by somebody else!).

½ cup (125 mL)	wild rice
~	kosher salt to taste
1½ cups (375 mL)	Vanilla-Citrus Vinaigrette (see page 20)
1 bunch	fresh asparagus
2	bagels
½ cup (125 mL)	Canadian chèvre, preferably St. Maure or St. Loup
2 Tbsp. (25 mL)	minced fresh chives
1 bunch	fresh spinach, washed and stemmed
4	oranges, peeled and segmented (see Cut to the Quick, page 193)
8 slices	lox or cold-smoked salmon

Combine the wild rice with at least 4 times as much water in a small pot. Add a pinch of salt. Cover with a snug-fitting lid and place over high heat. When the rice comes to a boil, reduce the heat and simmer, covered, until the grains begin to crack apart and are tender to the bite, about 45 minutes. Drain and place in a bowl. Stir in half the vinaigrette. Set aside.

Put 1 inch (2.5 cm) of water into a large sauté pan. Place on the stove and bring to a boil. Snap off the thick ends of the asparagus where they break easily, discarding the tough ends. Add the asparagus to the water and cook uncovered for about 3 minutes, until it is bright green. Drain and run cold water over the asparagus to chill it. Drain well and set aside on a plate.

Slice each bagel horizontally in half. Toast or broil each slice, then spread with the chèvre. Sprinkle the chives on the cheese.

To assemble the salad, toss the spinach and orange segments in the remaining vinaigrette, reserving 2 Tbsp. (25 mL) of dressing. Divide the spinach and orange segments among 4 plates, forming as tall a heap as possible on each plate. Place the wild rice beside the spinach. Toss the asparagus in the reserved vinaigrette, then arrange the stalks on the plates, leaning them against the wild rice and spinach. Add 1 bagel round, then drape 2 slices of lox or smoked salmon over each salad. Serve promptly.

SERVES 4

Asparagus *and* Roasted Pepper Salad

If you are grilling fresh asparagus for this dish, you might wish to dress it up by first wrapping the raw spears with thinly sliced pancetta or prosciutto.

1 lb. (500 g)	dee's Spicy Pickled Asparagus (see page 23)
	or fresh green asparagus
1	red bell pepper
1	yellow bell pepper
1 head	romaine lettuce
¼ lb. (125 g)	your favourite blue cheese, cubed or crumbled
¼ cup (50 mL)	Kalamata or other black olives
¼ cup (50 mL)	spicy green olives
¼ cup (50 mL)	toasted pine nuts or pecans
~	drizzle extra virgin olive oil or avocado oil
1	lemon, juice only
~	kosher salt and freshly ground black pepper to taste

If using fresh asparagus, steam or grill it. Set aside.

Grill the peppers directly on the flame of your gas range, on the grill or under the broiler until the skins are blackened on all sides. Put the peppers in a plastic bag for 5 minutes. Peel off the blackened skin, remove the seeds and membranes, and slice into strips.

Arrange whole or torn lettuce leaves on each plate. Divide the asparagus and cheese among the plates.

In a small bowl, combine the roasted pepper strips, olives and nuts. Add oil and lemon juice to taste, season with salt and pepper, and mix well. Spoon evenly over each plate. Serve immediately.

SERVES 4

Roasted Pepper Salsa

Use this in quesadillas, with grilled meats, in salads, in risotto or pilaf, on puréed soups, anywhere you need a splash of colour and flavour.

2	red bell peppers
1	ancho or morita chile
6–8	kumquats (or 1 whole orange)
1 head	roasted garlic
1 Tbsp. (15 mL)	minced fresh thyme, cilantro or chives
1 tsp. (5 mL)	minced fresh rosemary
2	green onions, minced
1 Tbsp. (15 mL)	grated fresh ginger
1 Tbsp. (15 mL)	shredded fresh basil
1 tsp. (5 mL)	Spanish paprika
¼ tsp. (1 mL)	smoked Spanish paprika (see note at right)
1 Tbsp. (15 mL)	olive oil
1 Tbsp. (15 mL)	sherry vinegar or white wine vinegar
~	kosher salt and freshly cracked black pepper to taste

Put the bell peppers under a broiler or directly onto the flame of the stove or grill until they blacken on all sides. Remove to a plastic bag for 5 minutes to steam, then peel off the blackened skin and remove the seeds and inner membranes. While the peppers steam, simmer the chile in a small pot with just enough water to cover. Purée or chop the softened chile into a fine pulp.

Finely slice the peppers. Finely slice the kumquats or segment the orange (see Cut to the Quick, page 193). Toss the sliced pepper and kumquats or orange with the remaining ingredients. Serve at room temperature.

MAKES ABOUT 2 CUPS (500 mL)

SMOKED SPANISH PAPRIKA

Some Spanish pepper varieties are dried, some smoked, prior to being ground into powder. The finest Spanish paprika, pimentón, is smoked over oak, and originates in La Vera in the southwestern area of Spain known as Extremadura. The peppers raised in La Vera trace their roots back to the sixteenth-century monasteries, and have been labelled a DO, or Denominacion de Origen as an indication of quality. La Chinata produces a fine example, sweet and pungently smoky at once, particularly wonderful in sausage-making, in paella and on meats. Use this cautiously; even though it is labelled "sweet," a little goes a long way to contributing depth of flavour and heat.

Braised Fennel *with* Bay Leaves

Fennel is one of those vegetables that can slip through the cracks because it is unfamiliar. Its licorice flavour becomes surprisingly mild and mellow with cooking.

2	**fennel bulbs, stalks discarded**
2 Tbsp. (25 mL)	**olive oil**
1 Tbsp. (15 mL)	**grated fresh ginger**
1	**orange, zest and juice**
½ cup (125 mL)	**fruity white wine**
1	**tart apple, finely sliced or grated**
3	**bay leaves**
1 cup (250 mL)	**chicken stock**
1	**orange or blood orange, segmented (see Cut to the Quick, page 193)**
1 Tbsp. (15 mL)	**minced tarragon**
~	**kosher salt and freshly cracked black pepper to taste**

Preheat the oven to 375°F (190°C). Slice the fennel into ½-inch (1-cm) slices. Heat an ovenproof frying pan over medium-high heat, add the oil, then brown the fennel slices in the oil. Add the ginger, orange juice and zest, wine, apple, bay leaves and stock. Bring to a boil, then cover snugly with parchment paper and a lid. Place in the oven and cook until tender, about 30 minutes. Remove the fennel and keep it warm. Boil the liquid until it is reduced by half, then return the fennel to the pan. Stir in the orange segments and tarragon. Season with salt and pepper. Serve hot.

SERVES 4

Warm Flageolet
and Borlotti Bean Salad

Borlotti beans, or Italian cranberry beans, make a good excuse for culinary puns. Serve this warm in late fall. In late spring, at the first potluck of the season, it is wonderful chilled, spiky with the bite of arugula and ginger.

2 cups (500 mL)	**cooked flageolets (see Cooking Beans, page 79)**
2 cups (500 mL)	**cooked borlotti beans**
2 Tbsp. (25 mL)	**pomegranate molasses (see note at right)**
½ cup (125 mL)	**Arugula Pesto (see page 27)**
¼ cup (50 mL)	**olive oil**
2 Tbsp. (25 mL)	**sherry vinegar**
4 Tbsp. (50 mL)	**minced parsley**
2 Tbsp. (25 mL)	**grated fresh ginger**
1	**orange, zest only**
⅓ cup (75 mL)	**dried cranberries, chopped**
¼ cup (50 mL)	**raw cranberries, chopped**
~	**kosher salt and freshly ground black pepper to taste**

Toss all the ingredients in a large bowl, seasoning to taste. Cover and chill for at least 3 hours to allow the flavours to meld and mingle. Reheat or serve cold.

SERVES A CROWD, 12–14

POMEGRANATE MOLASSES

Thick, garnet-glowing, and sweet-tart, pomegranate molasses is a very concentrated and intensely flavoured reduction of pomegranate juice. Add it by the spoonful to vinaigrettes, stir it into a lamb tagine, and use it to braise, baste and marinate fish, fowl and red meat. You will find pomegranate molasses at Middle Eastern groceries.

Red Beans
with Smoked Pork Hock

"Red beans and ricely yours" is how Louis "Satchmo" Armstrong signed his correspondence. Here is the straight goods, much as you would find it on Monday menus in New Orleans's old quarter. Leftovers become Tuesday's soup and Wednesday's quesadillas. Make sure the beans are tender enough to squish between your fingers. Serve with steamed rice.

8 cups (2 L)	**cooked kidney beans**
1 cup (250 mL)	**tomato juice**
2	**onions, diced**
3	**green onions, minced**
1	**green bell pepper, diced**
2 Tbsp. (25 mL)	**minced garlic**
1 lb. (500 g)	**baked ham, cut in 1-inch (2.5-cm) cubes**
1 lb. (500 g)	**smoked pork hock**
~	**freshly cracked black pepper, cayenne and hot chili flakes to taste**
2	**bay leaves**
½ tsp. (2 mL)	**dried thyme**
½ tsp. (2 mL)	**dried basil**
2 cups (500 mL)	**water**

Combine all the ingredients in a large heavy pot. Bring to a boil, then reduce the heat and cover. Simmer, stirring occasionally, until tender, 2–3 hours. Add water as needed. Taste and add salt as needed.

SERVES A CROWD, 12–16

Porchas

I ate this succulent bean dish in a small traditional *comidas* in northern Spain, where cooks make the most of their pork products. There, this is made with shreds of leftover *jamon*, air-cured pork leg. Use smoked pork hock, ham, prosciutto, capicolla or pancetta if you didn't dare smuggle a *jamon* home on your last trans-Atlantic flight. Add lashings of olive oil to the cooked dish for extra richness and mouth feel. Expect this to take at least 4 hours of simmering time. Any extras can find their way into lunch quesadillas or the next pot of soup.

2 cups (500 mL)	**dried Emergo or Great Northern beans**
2 Tbsp. (25 mL)	**olive oil**
4 cloves	**garlic**
2	**onions, minced**
1 tsp. (5 mL)	**anise seed, cracked**
2	**bay leaves**
1 cup (250 mL)	**shredded cooked smoked pork hock, ham, pancetta or prosciutto**
~	**kosher salt and freshly ground black pepper to taste**
~	**sherry vinegar to taste**
~	**olive oil to taste**

Cook the beans slowly in generous amounts of water, covered, until tender, adding water as needed (see Cooking Beans, page 79).

Heat the oil in a frying pan over medium-high heat. Add the garlic and onion and sauté over low heat. Add the anise seed and bay. Stir this mixture into the beans when they are half cooked, after about 3 hours. Add the pork and continue cooking for another 2 hours or until tender. Season with salt, pepper, vinegar and oil. Serve warm.

SERVES 10–12

Seasonal Mushrooms and *Green Beans in* Garlic

In northern Spain, we saw baskets, bushels and mountains of fresh mushrooms flooding the market stalls. Hand-lettered labels written in Catalonian identified each — *girgola, murgola, trompeta de la mort, xiitaque,* and the most beguiling, the golden *rovello,* streaked with green on its underside and gills. Add good olive oil or butter, shards of garlic and freshly blanched green beans for an irresistible side dish or light lunch plate. Simplicity!

2 cups (500 mL)	**fine green beans, trimmed**
2 Tbsp. (25 mL)	**unsalted butter or olive oil**
4 cloves	**garlic, sliced**
2 cups (500 mL)	**assorted fresh mushrooms, sliced or quartered**
~	**kosher salt and freshly ground black pepper to taste**
½ cup (125 mL)	**fino or amontillado sherry**
½ tsp. (2 mL)	**ground sumac (optional)**

Blanch the beans in boiling salted water until just crispy and still bright green. Drain, rinse in cold water and set aside.

Heat the butter or oil, add the garlic and mushrooms, and sauté until crispy. Add the beans and toss over high heat to reheat. Season with salt and pepper. Add the sherry and bring to a quick boil. Sprinkle with sumac, if using. Serve hot.

SERVES 4

Shanghai Shiitake

Shanghai noodles originate from north and east China, around Shanghai. They are fat, sturdy wheat noodles that soak up lots of sauce. Find them fresh in coolers in Asian markets. Use them in stir-fries, with sauces and in soups. They cook quickly, within 4–5 minutes. To add a little colour to what is decidedly a brown-toned dinner, offer Grilled New Carrots in Sherry Vinaigrette (page 91) or serve a chutney or salsa alongside some rice.

1 Tbsp. (15 mL)	vegetable oil
2	onions, cut into 1-inch (2.5-cm) dice
12 cloves	fresh garlic, sliced
2 Tbsp. (25 mL)	minced fresh ginger
½ lb. (250 g)	fresh shiitake mushrooms, sliced or whole
½ lb. (250 g)	barbecued pork, slivered
2 Tbsp. (25 mL)	light soy sauce
4 Tbsp. (50 mL)	hoisin paste
¼ cup (50 mL)	sherry
1 Tbsp. (15 mL)	hot chili paste
1 tsp. (5 mL)	honey
1	orange, juice and zest
¼ tsp. (1 mL)	ground anise seed
2 tsp. (10 mL)	roasted sesame oil
1-lb. package (500 g)	Shanghai noodles

In a non-stick sauté pan, heat the oil over medium-high heat. Add the onion, garlic and ginger. Cook until the vegetables are transparent and tender. Add the mushrooms and cook until tender. Add all the remaining ingredients, stir well, add a little water as needed, and cover. Simmer until tender, stirring well. Put the noodles into a sieve or colander, run hot water over them to loosen and soften them, gently separating the noodles with your hands. Add the noodles to the hot sauce. Simmer for 5 minutes and serve hot.

SERVES 4–6

Merlot-Infused Wild Mushrooms

This dish can be roasted a day in advance, then reheated on top of the stove if the oven is otherwise engaged. If you cannot find any fresh wild mushrooms, use field mushrooms fortified with rehydrated dried wild mushrooms of whatever type you like and can find. Serve this as a side dish, as a bed for poached eggs, as a base for omelettes, with roasted or grilled lamb or venison, in risotto or on flatbread.

2 lbs. (1 kg)	**fresh wild mushrooms**
1 head	**garlic, peeled and separated into cloves**
1	**onion, finely minced**
1 Tbsp. (15 mL)	**minced fresh thyme**
1 Tbsp. (15 mL)	**olive oil**
1 cup (250 mL)	**Merlot**
~	**kosher salt and freshly ground black pepper to taste**

Preheat the oven to 450°F (230°C). Slice the mushrooms and spread them on a baking sheet in a single layer. Sprinkle the garlic, onion, thyme, oil and wine over the mushrooms. Roast uncovered for 30–45 minutes, or until the mushrooms are tender. Drain off any liquid into a shallow pan, place over high heat and reduce it to a glaze-like consistency. Mix the glaze with the mushrooms. Serve warm.

MAKES 4 CUPS (1 L)

Succulent Oven Squash

Use any squash, but acorn offers convenient individual portions.

3	**acorn squash, halved and seeded**
3 Tbsp. (45 mL)	**herb-infused olive oil**
3 Tbsp. (45 mL)	**grated or diced ginger**
1–2 tsp. (5–10 mL)	**ground star anise**
3 Tbsp. (45 mL)	**minced fresh basil**
3 Tbsp. (45 mL)	**maple syrup**
~	**kosher salt and hot chili flakes to taste**

Preheat the oven to 375°F (190°C). Place the squash halves cut-side up on a parchment-lined baking sheet. Brush the oil over the cut surface, then fill the seed cavities with the ginger, star anise, basil and maple syrup. Bake until tender when pierced with a fork.

SERVES 6

Orange *and* Jicama Salad

This refreshing salad usually includes chayote, known as christophene in the West Indies and France. Jicama, a Central and South American tuber reminiscent of sweet mild radish, is more readily available locally.

½	**jicama, peeled and finely sliced into batons**
4	**oranges, peeled and segmented (see Cut to the Quick, page 193)**
½ cup (125 mL)	**snow peas, finely sliced**
¼ cup (50 mL)	**finely sliced red onion**
2 Tbsp. (25 mL)	**olive oil**
¼ cup (50 mL)	**orange juice**
~	**kosher salt and freshly ground black pepper to taste**
~	**minced chives and fresh thyme for garnish**

Toss all ingredients in a large bowl. Serve chilled.

SERVES 4

Squash Threads

It is impossible to walk through an autumn market without falling for the vibrant oranges and golds, the muted blues and greens of winter squash. Unfortunately, once they get home and have worn out their welcome as ornaments on the harvest table, many cooks are at a loss about what to do with them. Winter squashes are protected by a very tough skin that repels all but the most determined. Choose Hubbard, butternut or other winter varieties, and use a sharp knife to cut the squash into manageable sections. Some cooks use a potato peeler, others use a knife, but if you work on small pieces, a squash can be stripped of its hard skin without risking hands, fingers or other body parts.

2 lbs. (1 kg)	**squash**
2 Tbsp. (25 mL)	**unsalted butter**
1 Tbsp. (15 mL)	**grated fresh ginger**
1–2 tsp. (5–10 mL)	**Ras El Hanout (see page 28) or curry powder**
2 Tbsp. (25 mL)	**finely slivered fresh basil**
~	**kosher salt and hot chili flakes to taste**

Peel the squash and discard the seeds. Coarsely grate or julienne the squash with a food processor or mandoline. Heat the butter, add the squash, ginger, spice powder to taste, basil, salt and chili flakes. Sauté over high heat for 5 minutes, or just until tender but not soggy. Serve hot.

SERVES 4

Peas *and* Paneer

This blend of fresh homemade cheese and peas is a classic pairing. Cook the curry while the homemade cheese drains. For added richness, stir in coconut milk at the end of the cooking time. For crunch, top with toasted cashews, almonds, peanuts or coconut.

8 cups (2 L)	**milk**
½ cup (125 mL)	**lemon juice**
1 Tbsp. (15 mL)	**olive oil**
1	**onion, sliced**
4 cloves	**garlic, minced**
2 Tbsp. (25 mL)	**grated fresh ginger**
2 Tbsp. (25 mL)	**Ras El Hanout (see page 28) or curry powder**
2 cups (500 mL)	**water or stock**
3 cups (750 mL)	**peas**
2 cups (500 mL)	**diced cooked potatoes cut in ½-inch (1-cm) cubes**
1–2 Tbsp. (15–25 mL)	**honey**
1	**lemon, juice and zest**
½ tsp. (2 mL)	**hot chili paste**
~	**kosher salt to taste**
1 Tbsp. (15 mL)	**cornstarch, dissolved in water**
2 Tbsp. (25 mL)	**cilantro leaves**

To make the paneer, heat the milk to a full boil. While it is boiling, stir in the lemon juice. As soon as the milk starts to separate, turn off the heat. Line a fine-meshed strainer with a clean, dampened kitchen towel and slowly pour the hot milk through, discarding the liquid. Let the solids stand and continue to drain as you make dinner.

Heat the oil to sizzling in a medium sauté pan. Cook the onion, garlic and ginger until they are tender but not coloured. Stir in the curry powder, then add the water or stock and bring to a boil. Stir in the peas and potatoes and cook until they are hot. Balance the flavours with the honey, lemon, hot chili paste and salt. Bring to a boil and add the dissolved cornstarch; cook until the sauce is clear. Add the paneer, stirring very gently. Garnish with cilantro leaves and serve hot.

SERVES 4

Red *and* Yellow Curry

Thanks to Janet Webb of J. Webb Wine Merchant for sharing this garlic tip after a trip to Thailand. Remember as you slice your vegetables that finely cut pieces will cook more quickly than big chunks. Serve over rice or rice noodles.

1 Tbsp. (15 mL)	**vegetable oil**
1	**onion, diced**
1 Tbsp. (15 mL)	**grated fresh ginger**
3	**kaffir lime leaves**
1	**red bell pepper, cut in ½-inch (1-cm) dice**
2 tsp. (10 mL)	**yellow curry paste**
1–2 cups (250–500 mL)	**water or vegetable stock**
2 cups (500 mL)	**raw potatoes, cut in ½-inch (1-cm) dice**
1 19-oz. can (1 540-mL can)	**chickpeas, rinsed and drained**
6 cloves	**garlic**
~	**vegetable oil for pan-frying**
½ lb. (250 g)	**green beans, trimmed and cut into 1-inch (2.5-cm) lengths**
1 12-oz. can (1 340-mL can)	**coconut milk**
1 Tbsp. (15 mL)	**cornstarch, dissolved in cold water**
2 Tbsp. (25 mL)	**honey**
½	**lemon, juice only**
2 Tbsp. (25 mL)	**minced basil, cilantro or mint leaves**
~	**kosher salt to taste**

Heat the oil in a heavy large sauté pan. Add the onion, ginger and lime leaves, and cook over medium-high heat until the onion is tender, about 5 minutes. Add the bell pepper and cook for several minutes, until the pepper begins to soften. Stir in the curry paste, water or stock, potatoes and chickpeas. Cover, bring to a boil, and reduce to an active simmer.

While the curry simmers, finely slice the garlic into slivers. Heat ½ inch (1 cm) of vegetable oil in a small pot and quickly cook the garlic without letting it get too brown. Be careful — it cooks very quickly, and burnt garlic is bitter. Remove the garlic from the pan with a slotted spoon and cool it on a plate lined with paper towel.

When the potatoes are tender, add the green beans and replace the cover, adding more water if needed. Steam the beans to tender, then add the coconut milk and dissolved cornstarch. Bring the curry to a brief boil to cook the starch, then reduce the heat. Stir in the honey, lemon juice, herbs and salt. Serve immediately, garnished with additional herbs and the garlic chips.

SERVES 6 GENEROUSLY

Tuesday
Noodles & Grains

Making Decisions as Well as Dinner

Cooking real food takes time, more time than opening take-out packages or defrosting something in a cardboard box. I know this is not news. Of interest is what we choose to eat when we have no time.

The tried-and-true favourite of many adults and children in a hurry is some form of noodles. When I was growing up, it was macaroni and cheese with canned tomatoes and crispy crumbs on top. Now it's just as likely to be orrechiette with regionally produced goat cheese, sun-dried tomatoes and crispy crumbs on top.

Whether you are cooking for your kids or your inner child who craves a plateful of comforting pasta, noodles are healing, healthy, heart-warming and handy. Admittedly not everyone eats white flour and cheese, prime requirements of a plate of linguini with Asiago. But there are soba noodles redolent of buckwheat, soft rice noodles and crispy rice sticks that puff into fun in hot oil, and mung bean noodles, poetically called "glass noodles." None of these noodles need cheese. Asian noodle shops have been in existence for over a thousand years. Miso and noodles might be the perfect fast food after all.

Of all the grains around the world, rice is the most widely consumed. In over half the world, rice is life: almost one billion households depend on rice for their livelihood. This important grain has been recognized by the United Nations, which proclaimed 2004 as the international Year of Rice. (Not its first such recognition: in 2800 BC, rice was named one of China's Five Sacred Crops, along with soybeans, wheat, millet and barley; and the UN's Food and Agriculture Organization previously proclaimed the Year of Rice in 1966.) For something so simple, rice can look complicated to people who didn't grow up in a rice-eating culture. Long grain, short grain, sticky or fluffy, steamed or boiled, learning about rice can take a lifetime of eating and travelling.

Many of us take a Puritan approach to our eating habits, thinking it won't affect the flavour of what should nourish us. What works better is permission to enjoy our food. Truth is, the Dr. Seuss play-with-your-food rules are in effect. Won't people notice if we mix a dose of pleasure with our Parmesan? I hope so. It will help us live longer, more joyfully. Eat your noodles. They are a wonderful introduction to the wide world of food.

A 12-Step Program for Novice Cooks

1. **Trust your tastebuds.**
   They don't let you down in the best restaurants, and they won't let you down in the kitchen. Good cooks only cook — and serve, and eat — food that they like. If your tastebuds tell you something about a dish, consider it valuable intelligence gathered by a highly trained espionage agent. Act on it. (See The Balancing Act, page 19.)

2. **Read the recipe.**
   Understand what to do and how to do it. Figure out what the end result should be. If it's a complicated recipe to impress your guests, strip it down to essentials first. And practice before the big game. Do not go in cold.

3. **Assemble ingredients before you begin to chop or cook.**
   This is called *mise en place* by the pros, and it saves them mad dashes to the walk-in fridge when the heat's on and the dining room is full. At home, it will save you — or your spouse — a panicky gallop to the grocery store. Or it may convince you to try another dish or lead you down the path to inventive cooking. You don't have pecans, but you do have hazelnuts. The fishmonger cannot give you perch, but he has whole tilapia. Teach yourself when and what you can (and cannot) substitute. Assemble a good pantry. It's the best timesaver of all.

4. **Buy the best.**
   In food, as in everything else commercial, you get what you pay for. Cheap food can be a great seasonal bargain, but sometimes it is cheap for a reason. High-quality, sharp, well-maintained knives are magically time efficient. Wonderful pots made from heat-conductive materials mean your food will cook without sticking or burning, sometimes in less time, and certainly with less stress and fuss. Not only that, but good pots and knives make great inheritances for kids who have learned how to use them.

5. **Keep the cerebral juices flowing.**
   Problem solve. If you have questionable results, don't immediately blame yourself and your relationship with your stove. Be skeptical; there are many poorly written recipes and cookbooks on the bookshelves. Don't believe it all. Don't forget, either, that those

foodie evangelists on late-night television have armies of staff behind the scenes making perfect popovers or pastry. Even if your attempt at brisée pastry is not a perfect 10, it may still eat well, and that is the most important thing.

5. **Use all your senses.**
   Cooking and eating are sensual experiences. Involve your 5 senses during creation and consumption. Listen for the "ping" of properly sealed jars, touch your chop to gauge its doneness, watch the size of the bubbles in the cream while you reduce the sauce, smell the toasty heat of mustard seeds when they begin to pop in the hot pan. Taste everything.

6. **Taste. Taste. Taste.**
   All along the way, taste what you are making. Taste your ingredients at every stage that is safe. Assess food that is flat, needs salt, needs sweetening, needs acid, needs heat. (See The Balancing Act, page 19.) Learn what unseasoned turtle beans taste like, what an unfinished beurre blanc tastes like, what unsalted beef tastes like. Sample as many varieties of salt that you can find, and learn which you prefer. Then do the same for olive oils, plums at the farmer's market, and everything in between.

7. **Learn what you like.**
   Sometimes this means you inadvertently find out what you don't like. Ultimately, the only way to learn is to put something in your mouth and taste it. Be open-minded; just because it smells bad doesn't always mean it will taste yucky. You are entitled to an opinion once you have tasted it.

8. **Learn something new.**
   Your cooking has gone over to the dark side. You are stuck in a rut. Take a cooking class, read a food mag, go to the library. There is no new food anywhere in the world — it has all been cooked already, somewhere, by someone — but as the consignment stores say, it's new to you. Cook something you have never made before. Then cook it again, and change it. Cultivate curiosity.

10. **Never apologize.**
    This should be Rule #1! Everyone has to begin at the beginning. It means that the chicken breast may be a little hacked up the first time you use your boning knife to remove the meat from the bones. But you can disguise the fact by cutting the meat into bite-size pieces and serving it as a stir-fry this time. Next time, when the edges are tidier, pan-steam the boneless breast and build a Panang curry sauce.

11. **Buy a good timer.**
    Then use it. By the time you smell the nuts burning in the oven, it may be too late. Good cooking involves multi-tasking that would be the envy of any computer geek. It is easy to lose track of how long the genoise has been baking because you are preoccupied making the ganache. (And you really do not want to ruin the chocolate!)

12. **Have fun.**
    It helps to remember that cooking is a pleasant pastime. Find ways to make it fun. Hang out with confident cooks. There is nothing so confidence-building as seeing a good cook casually tossing things into the pot with no recipe in sight. It rubs off. Whatever you choose to cook, add laughter. It is the finest spice of all.

Sun-Dried Tomato
and **Arugula Pappardelle**

This warm salad laced with bits of sharp olive and crunchy bites of bacon provides ample opportunity to support local growers and producers. Find good bacon and sausage at the farmer's market; if your arugula has bolted, use spinach; try locally made cheese. This is best served on wide-cut noodles such as pappardelle; failing that, use a good fettuccine. Open an Italian Chianti or Primitivo with this.

1 lb. (500 g)	**pappardelle**
4 slices	**bacon, diced**
4 cloves	**garlic, slivered**
2 tsp. (10 mL)	**minced fresh rosemary**
2 Tbsp. (25 mL)	**olive oil**
3–4 links	**Italian sausage, finely sliced (see page 172)**
¼ cup (50 mL)	**slivered sun-dried tomatoes**
1 bunch	**arugula, washed and trimmed**
1 bunch	**green onions, minced**
½ cup (125 mL)	**sliced Kalamata olives**
½ cup (125 mL)	**sliced green Sicilian, French or Spanish olives**
~	**freshly cracked black pepper to taste**
~	**extra virgin olive oil for drizzling**
~	**finely grated Parmesan cheese for garnish**

Cook the pasta to al dente in a large potful of salted boiling water. While it cooks, make the sauce.

Cook the bacon in a large sauté pan until crisp. Pour out any excess fat, crumble the bacon and set it aside. Combine the garlic, rosemary and olive oil in the pan, and cook over medium heat until the garlic is tender, about 5 minutes. Add the sausage and sun-dried tomatoes. Sauté for several minutes, until the sausage is cooked through, then stir in the arugula. Toss the mixture until the greens wilt, then add the green onions and olives. Heat through, season with pepper, and stir in the bacon.

Toss the cooked pappardelle with the sauce, divide among warm pasta bowls, and top each serving with a generous drizzle of olive oil and a sprinkling of grated Parmesan cheese. Serve immediately.

SERVES 4

VARIATION:

Add thinly sliced beef tenderloin or flank steak to the pan for a heartier cold-weather pasta. Use a Canadian chèvre or blue cheese instead of Parmesan; for a crisp exterior, pop the whole thing into a shallow pan, drizzle it with olive oil and slide under the broiler to crisp.

Linguini *with* **Red Chard** *and* **Pecans**

This dish is a spin-off of a classic Catalan combination of greens with nuts and raisins, although the traditional pine nuts are replaced by toasted chopped pecans. You can stir in chèvre if you want a creamy finish, but the flavours are more clearly defined without the cheese. Beet greens are a good substitute for the chard. Pour a good Soave or a lighter Italian or Spanish red.

1 bunch	**red chard**
3 Tbsp. (45 mL)	**olive oil**
1	**onion, finely diced**
6 cloves	**garlic, minced**
½ cup (125 mL)	**finely diced ham or spicy capicolla**
½ cup (125 mL)	**Thompson seedless raisins**
½ cup (125 mL)	**chopped toasted pecans**
3 Tbsp. (45 mL)	**minced fresh parsley**
2 Tbsp. (25 mL)	**balsamic vinegar**
~	**kosher salt and freshly cracked black pepper to taste**
1 lb. (500 g)	**cooked linguini**
¼ lb. (125 g)	**Canadian chèvre (optional)**

Wash the chard, then fold each leaf in half lengthwise along the rib. Slice out the rib and finely sliver it. Coarsely chop the leaves. Heat the oil, then sauté the onion, garlic and meat over medium heat until the onion is tender and transparent. Add the slivered chard ribs and cook until they are tender, 5 minutes or so.

While the vegetables are cooking, soak the raisins in hot water. Cook the chopped chard leaves in boiling water, then drain well. Drain the raisins. Add the chard leaves, raisins, pecans, parsley and balsamic vinegar to the cooked mixture. Mix well and season with salt and pepper. Serve over hot linguini, adding a drizzle of olive oil if the sauce is too dry. Top with chèvre when you serve the pasta and sauce, if you like.

SERVES 4 – 6

Angel Hair Pasta *with* Brie, Basil *and* Pine Nuts

Quick and easy meals are the best bet for busy work nights. The ingredients for this rich pasta sauce can be prepared ahead of time. Just cook some noodles, toss together a sprightly salad and kick back to watch the Northern Lights and stars as they slowly wheel above you. That is the slow life. Italian Verdicchio will cut the richness in this simple but rich pasta.

4–8 cloves	**garlic, sliced**
2 Tbsp. (25 mL)	**olive oil**
1 handful	**fresh basil or parsley, chopped**
4	**ripe tomatoes, diced**
½ lb. (250 g)	**ripe Brie cheese, coarsely chopped**
~	**kosher salt and freshly cracked black pepper to taste**
1 lb. (500 g)	**angel hair or linguine**
½ cup (125 mL)	**toasted pine nuts**

Combine the garlic, olive oil, basil or parsley, tomatoes, Brie, salt and pepper in a bowl. Refrigerate until needed. Remove from the fridge about 30 minutes before dinner to take off the chill.

Bring a large pot of salted water to a boil. Add the pasta and cook until al dente. Drain well, then toss with the cheese mixture to coat thoroughly. Garnish with the pine nuts and serve immediately.

SERVES 4

Not Your Mom's
Macaroni *and* Cheese!

Yep, you have had this before, but maybe not in your mom's kitchen. This is simple enough for a capable child-cook to make as a surprise dinner for Mom. Serve your favourite lush Chardonnay with a bit of oak.

1 lb. (500g)	dried macaroni, penne, bowties or other short pasta
1	leek
4 Tbsp. (50 mL)	butter
1	onion, diced
1	red bell pepper, diced
4 cloves	garlic, sliced
2 stalks	celery, diced
6 Tbsp. (90 mL)	all-purpose flour
4 cups (1 L)	milk, heated
3	tomatoes, seeded and diced
2 cups (500 mL)	grated fontina
1 cup (250 mL)	grated old Cheddar or Asiago
1 cup (250 mL)	grated Parmesan
1 cup (250 mL)	frozen peas or green beans
½ cup (125 mL)	whipping cream (optional)
1 bunch	green onions, minced
1 Tbsp. (15 mL)	minced fresh basil
2 Tbsp. (25 mL)	minced fresh parsley
~	kosher salt and hot chili paste to taste

Cook the pasta in salted boiling water in a big pot for 10–15 minutes, until tender. Drain and keep warm. Preheat the oven to 375°F (190°C).

Slice the leek lengthwise, trim off the root and any tough or damaged outer green leaves, and slice crosswise into fine shreds. Transfer the sliced leek into a colander and wash very thoroughly under running water.

In a large pot, melt the butter. Add the leek, onion, bell pepper, garlic and celery. Cook over medium heat for 5–7 minutes or until tender. Add small amounts of water as needed to keep the vegetables from browning, then evaporate the water. Add the flour and cook over medium heat until sandy, about 3–5 minutes.

Add the milk slowly, mixing well with a wooden spoon in-between each addition. Bring to a boil, stirring well. Remove from the heat and stir in the tomatoes, cheeses, frozen vegetables, cream (if using), green onions, basil and parsley. Season with salt and chili paste.

Add the cooked pasta and mix well. Pour the pasta into a gratin dish.

Topping:

1 cup (250 mL)	**soft sourdough bread crumbs**
½ cup (125 mL)	**butter, melted**
½ cup (125 mL)	**grated Parmesan**

Combine the topping ingredients, mixing well. Sprinkle over the top of the pasta. Bake for 30 minutes, or until the crumbs are crusty and brown. Serve hot.

SERVES A CROWD or 4 teenagers

Gnocchi Parisienne

A forgotten classic, this dumpling is based on choux pastry, better known for its appearance as Long Johns, éclairs and gougères. Unabashedly rich, it is good with salad and sausages. No guilt. Serve with a crisp, dry white wine or a soft, oaky white wine.

1 cup (250 mL)	**cold water**
¼ cup (50 mL)	**unsalted butter**
1 cup (250 mL)	**all-purpose flour**
4	**eggs**
1 cup (250 mL)	**good-quality grated Parmesan**
¼ cup (50 mL)	**unsalted butter**
½ cup (125 mL)	**grated Parmesan or fontina, Jarlsberg or aged Cheddar**

Make a choux pastry first by bringing the water and ¼ cup (50 mL) butter to a rolling boil. Remove from the heat and add the flour. Mix well with a wooden spoon until the mixture becomes a smooth ball that pulls away from the edge of the pot. Allow to cool. Add the eggs one at a time, stirring well with a wooden spoon after each addition. Add the 1 cup (250 mL) grated Parmesan. Let cool while you bring a pot of water to a boil. Set the oven to 425°F (220°C).

Fit a plain tip in a piping bag, fill the bag with the mixture and pipe ½-inch (1-cm) lengths of dough into the boiling water (scrape a small knife across the opening to cut the dough to length if it doesn't stop flowing when you stop squeezing the bag). When the gnocchi float to the surface, about 3–5 minutes, scoop them out, drain well and toss in the remaining ¼ cup (50 mL) butter in a gratin dish. Sprinkle the top with the remaining ½ cup (125 mL) cheese and bake until bubbly, about 30 minutes. Serve hot.

SERVES 2–4

FILLING PIPING BAGS

There are cooks who go their entire lives without ever acquiring or using a piping bag. It is a specialized tool that is usually associated with pastry chefs and finicky work, not with the demands and needs of a busy family. Buy one anyhow, a relatively large one, about 12 inches (30 cm) in length, and buy a variety of tips: you will use them for choux pastry, whipped cream and sausage casings. To fill it, open the bag by folding the top third of the bag over to the outside. Drop a piping tip down the bag's gullet, then stuff the fabric of the bag surrounding the tip into the tip itself to plug it and keep filling from flooding out the bottom end as quickly as you fill it from the top. Next, pretend you are a puppeteer and slide your hand, thumb up, around the bag so it is positioned under the flap you folded over. Spoon filling into the bag, using your puppeteer's hand to scrape sticky stuff off the spatula directly into the bag. Do not fill the bag more than half full. Remove your hand from between the fold of bag, squeeze upwards to eliminate air bubbles, and close the top by folding the bag into vertical pleats. Use one hand to squeeze filling from the bag and the other hand to guide the tip of the bag.

Noodle Salad *with* Barbecued Duck, Snow Peas *and* Ponzu Dressing

When you plan a picnic, forget about mayo-based dressing and use a ginger-spiked vinaigrette to bind the flavours of this noodle salad. Mangoes are a juicy, fragrant addition, but Asian pears make a crispy alternative. Barbecued duck and pork are both available at Asian barbecue shops. Buy extra for the next time you make salad rolls. Rice beer is the best with this one.

1 lb. (500 g)	soba, egg or rice noodles
20–25	snow peas
1 lb. (500 g)	barbecued duck or pork, sliced
1	lemon, juice and zest
¼ cup (50 mL)	Japanese rice vinegar
1 Tbsp. (15 mL)	grated fresh ginger
1 Tbsp. (15 mL)	melted honey
2 Tbsp. (25 mL)	minced cilantro
1 Tbsp. (15 mL)	soy sauce
2 Tbsp. (25 mL)	vegetable oil
1	mango or Asian pear
2 Tbsp. (25 mL)	toasted cashews

Cook the noodles in salted boiling water. Drain and rinse with cold water. Heat a small pot or pan of water and briefly blanch the snow peas in boiling water. Combine the noodles, snow peas and duck or pork.

To make the ponzu dressing, whisk together the lemon juice and zest, vinegar, ginger, honey, cilantro, soy sauce and oil. Toss with the noodles, duck and peas. Chill. Just before serving, peel and slice the fruit. Add to the salad, toss gently, and garnish with the cashews.

SERVES 4

HEAVENLY NOODLES

A haven of noodles, my favourite noodle house is owned by Yosh Shima. Yosh makes soba noodles by hand, and serves them in a serene atmosphere amid stark surroundings. From him, I learned that soba noodles have an honourable spot in Japanese history, being the only acceptable food a monk on a quest could carry with him. But you don't have to join a monastery to enjoy soba noodles.

Persian Pilaf *with* Lemon

On a swing down Main Street in East Vancouver, I happened into a little Mediterranean grocery and came away with a package of "Zareshtz," the name scribbled by hand on the outside of the package. The shopkeeper sent me off with complete verbal instructions on how to use my little treasure, and I followed his instructions to the letter, with fabulous results. But then I ran out. I spent hours on the phone, on-line, and burrowing through books to find out just what it was I had run out of, but I finally had to invent a reasonable facsimile. Here it is, using rose hips.

1 Tbsp. (15 mL)	**olive oil**
½	**onion, minced**
2 cloves	**garlic, minced**
1 cup (250 mL)	**basmati rice**
~	**kosher salt to taste**
2 cups (500 mL)	**boiling water**
4 Tbsp. (50 mL)	**rose hips**
4 Tbsp. (50 mL)	**sugar**
1	**lemon, juice and zest**
¼ cup (50 mL)	**cold water**
~	**slivered toasted almonds for garnish**

Heat the oil in a heavy pot, add the onion and garlic and cook over medium heat until the onion is golden and fragrant. Add the rice, stir well and season with salt. Add the boiling water, stir, cover and reduce the heat to low. Set the timer for 16 minutes.

In a small pot, combine the rose hips, sugar, lemon and cold water. Bring to a boil and simmer until the fruit is tender.

When the rice is cooked, scoop ⅓ of it into a small bowl and stir in the rose hip mixture. Scoop the remaining rice into a bowl, top with the flavoured rice, and garnish with the toasted almonds. Serve hot.

SERVES 4

Real Dirty Rice *for Teddy*

When my good friend Ted first perused *Skinny Feasts*, which evolved from my vegetarian past, he said (like my dad), "Where's the meat?" At the time, I was a recovering vegetarian, and served much less meat than I do now. Here is my current approach, with meat, for Teddy.

4 Tbsp. (50 mL)	olive oil
2 lbs. (1 kg)	chicken livers, cleaned and diced
4 Tbsp. (50 mL)	brandy or cognac
6 cloves	garlic, minced
1	onion, minced
¼ cup (50 mL)	minced celery
¼ cup (50 mL)	minced red bell pepper
¼ cup (50 mL)	minced parsley
~	kosher salt, freshly cracked black pepper and cayenne to taste
3 cups (750 mL)	cooked basmati rice

In a heavy pan, gently heat the oil. Add the livers and sauté them quickly over high heat until the exterior is brown and the interiors remain pink, about 5 minutes, depending on the size of the livers. Tip the livers onto a clean plate and set aside. Add the brandy or cognac to the pan and scrape up the brown bits. Boil vigorously until the alcohol is reduced by half, then pour the remainder over the livers.

Reheat the pan, add a little more oil, then add the garlic, onion, celery and bell pepper. Cook for several minutes, until the onions are tender and translucent. Add the parsley, salt, pepper, cayenne and rice. Mix well. Top with the livers, mixing or not as your artist's eye dictates. Serve hot.

SERVES 4

AROMATIC RICES

The aromatic rices include basmati, Wehani, Texmati, wild pecan and Thai jasmine. They all have a pronounced perfume, nutty and subtle, when raw and cooked. Basmati rice that has been aged at least a year is preferred for its drier, finer texture and intense aroma.

Coconut Rice

Any curry fan is usually a fan of coconut rice. If you like, you can sprinkle toasted coconut over this fragrant rice after you transfer it into the serving bowl. Serve this with Thai Lamb (page 153), Red and Yellow Curry (page 108), Sui Choy in Coconut Milk (page 84) or Peas and Paneer (page 107).

2 cups (500 mL)	**basmati or jasmine rice**
1 ½ cups (375 mL)	**coconut milk**
2 ½ cups (625 mL)	**cold water**

Wash the rice under cold running water until the water runs clear. Bring the coconut milk and water to a boil. Add the rice, return to a boil, cover and reduce the heat. Set the timer for 16 minutes. No peeking!

SERVES 2–4

Cooking Rice

There are as many methods of cooking rice as there are cooks. Some cooks add salt; others don't. Some cooks, but not all, rinse their raw rice. If you rinse yours, drain it well in a sieve or colander before cooking. How much water is enough? This varies completely, depending on the type of rice. One rule of thumb when cooking long grain white rice is to put raw rice into a heavy-bottomed pot, then add cold water until it is a finger's width above the surface of the rice. Bring to a boil, cover with a snug lid, and reduce the heat to a simmer. Don't peek! If you do, the steam will dissipate and the cooking time is prolonged. White rice takes about 15 minutes to cook; brown rice takes about twice that.

Summer Couscous, Winter Bulgur

This is as close as I'll ever come to instant food. Couscous and bulgur need only boiling water, a lid and 10 minutes. Add flavour and big-time texture with dried fruit, fresh herbs and a drizzle of good oil and vinegar. Turn any leftovers into a lunchtime salad by adding chopped grilled vegetables, diced apples, nuts and slivers of cooked beef, chicken or lamb. This is great with fresh fish or lamb, Arugula Pesto (page 27), Fresh Peach Chutney (page 22), Pineapple and Mango Compote (page 25) or dee's Spicy Pickled Asparagus (page 23).

1 stick	cinnamon
1 cup (250 mL)	boiling water or stock
1 cup (250 mL)	couscous or bulgur
4 Tbsp. (50 mL)	dried cranberries, cherries, raisins, currants or minced apricots
3 Tbsp. (45 mL)	minced fresh tarragon
2	green onions, minced
2 Tbsp. (25 mL)	olive oil
1–2 Tbsp. (15–25 mL)	white wine vinegar or citrus juice
~	kosher salt and freshly cracked black pepper to taste

Add the cinnamon stick to the water or stock, cover and simmer for 10 minutes. Pour the liquid and cinnamon stick over the couscous and dried fruit in a heatproof bowl. Cover snugly and let stand for 10 minutes. Toss well with a fork, remove the cinnamon stick, and stir in the remaining ingredients. Serve warm or cold.

SERVES 4

COUSCOUS AND BULGUR

A staple since the twelfth century and one of the world's most uncomplicated foods, couscous refers to tiny pellets of semolina, but it also refers to the stew that accompanies the steamed semolina. Couscous is dried and will expand to many times its original volume, so the cook must allow the grains to thoroughly expand, or the diner's belly will be the unprepared expansion grounds. Steaming, not boiling, is the method to use. Boiling produces a porridge-like mess, while steaming results in fluffy, tender stuff that is great fun to eat with flatbread and sauce. The rehydrating liquid can be spiked with additional flavourings, like cinnamon, garlic or onion. To cook, simply pour boiling liquid over the granules, cover tightly, let stand for 10 minutes and fluff with a fork. It is easy to tell the difference between bulgur and couscous. Bulgur, which is parboiled crushed wheat, is reddish-brown, with straight-cut edges. It comes in several grades, or sizes. Couscous is golden brown and round, like a tiny belly button. Cook them the same way.

Mid-Week Meaty Mains

The Meat of the Matter

My family has grown accustomed to eating less meat than many others. When we do, it is rarely a roast. (Sorry, Mom!) When we do have some pork, beef, venison or lamb (my favourite), we lean heavily to braising what are generally called "less tender" meats, and grilling when we don't have time to babysit a braising pan in the oven.

Meat is an expensive commodity. Learn as much as you can about it; your choice of meat and method affect how well your money is spent. With meat as much as any other food, choose what you like. I avoid beef round — eye, inside and outside — because I don't like the grain or texture of those particular cuts.

Cuts that are grill-friendly also sauté well. Look for tenderloin, rib, ribeye, t-bone, New York strip loin, porterhouse, cross rib, blade, flank, sirloin tip. Cuts for braising or stewing include chuck (or shoulder), cross rib, blade, shoulder, short ribs, brisket, round, sirloin tip, and shank. Cuts that roast well are standing and prime rib, sirloin tip, rump, hip roast.

The rules also apply to smaller animals like lamb. Braise or stew the shoulder and the shanks. Roast the leg. Roast or grill the rack, chops and loin. Pork is so lean and tender now that it is possible to roast, grill or sauté virtually any part of the animal with happy results.

A few hours in an acid-based marinade will tenderize a tougher cut like flank or blade steak sufficiently for grilling or rapid, high-heat roasting. Maximum surface exposed equals maximum flavour and tenderizing effect.

However you cook it, meat should stand and rest after cooking if you intend to carve or slice it. This respite gives the protein strands a chance to relax, allowing the juices in the meat to redistribute evenly. The result is meat that is easier to slice, with more even colouring. Let large roasts stand for half an hour, and smaller pieces for 5–10 minutes.

Braising: Grey Skies Cooking

When the sky is overcast, the temptation is to curl up with a magnificent murder mystery and ignore the world. But the most devious plot is hard to follow if you get hungry. Sooner or later, you have to eat. Best to do the cooking part sooner — you'll be in the house all day solving the mystery anyhow. So plan on a soulful braise, or a rustic stew; the tantalizing scent will feed your senses while you read. And use the warm flavours of the Mediterranean basin. Their bright fragrance will make grey winter days seem less dismal.

But a wonderful braised meal is a little more complicated than simply tossing all the ingredients into a pot and leaving them to stew. Here's how to braise meat that will make fans of your mystery book club. Best of all, it is easy to make extra, and the flavours will be better after a day, so double up the recipe and invite the other bookworms over for dinner tomorrow.

BRAISING: THE PLOT THICKENS

Chapter One: Pick Your Victim and Set the Stage

Braising is a moist-heat method of cooking large pieces of meat. It is generally used for "less tender" (translation: "cheap and tough") cuts of meat that require slow simmering in liquid to tenderize while releasing their collagen into liquid form. The ideal cut of red meat for braising is the chuck, or shoulder, of lamb or beef. It also works with poultry legs because of their muscular structure.

Traditionally, a marinade with a high proportion of wine is used to tenderize and to boost a tough meat's flavour. The marinade can be used later as the cooking liquid, or it can be discarded. A cook in a hurry to get on with the plot can ignore marinades in favour of a perfunctory herb paste or a rub, or nothing at all, and go directly to the next chapter.

Chapter Two: Add Local Colour

Browning the surface of meat adds colour and complexity of flavour to the dish. If you used a marinade, remove the meat, pat it dry, and put the marinade onto the stove in a separate pot to boil. If you wish, dredge the meat in flour; the flour will absorb some of the fat and will serve as a thickening agent.

Floured or not, don't overcrowd the pan when you are browning meat, or the surface won't colour satisfactorily. Make sure the pan is hot, add enough oil to lubricate (and a little extra if the meat is floured), and add the meat in batches if it makes more than a single layer in the pan. Don't fuss; turn the meat once, after the surface is nicely coloured. If the meat is diced into cubes, turn it as often as you need to in order to colour each side.

Remove the meat to a clean plate. If there are nice crispy brown bits on the inside of the pan, add some liquid — water , stock or wine — and scrape the browned bits up. Pour the liquid on top of the meat and return the pan to the stove with a bit of oil in it. Add some large diced aromatic vegetables, herbs and spices, and cook for several minutes.

Chapter Three: Building the Case

Add a splash of wine, then the simmered and strained marinade if you are using it. Other possible liquids include vegetable juices, chopped tomatoes and stock. Bring the liquid to a boil. Add the meat. Spoon some of the sauce onto the meat. Cover, using an additional covering inside. First a piece of snug\fitting parchment if the braising liquid contains any acia ´vinegar, wine, citrus juice, tomatoes), then a piece of aluminum foil that is fitted inside the walls of the pot to sit directly on the top of the food, rather like an inverted tent, and then snugly folded over the rim of the pot. This jury-rigged internal lid helps to create the greatest amount of steam pressure to cook the meat.

Braise at 325°F (160°C) for at least 2 hours. The time will depend on the size of the piece of meat. A skewer inserted into the thickest part should come out freely when done. A whole shoulder of lamb takes 3—4 hours; chicken thighs and drums take 2—2 ½ hours. Don't rush it; the flavour and texture is best if arrived at slowly.

Chapter Four: Climax!

Remove the meat to a bowl and loosely cover. Strain the cooking juices, discarding the solids. Remove the fat. (If the dish is cooked a day in advance, the fat will congeal on top of the liquids when chilled; remove and discard the fat cap, slice the meat and reheat it slowly in its braising liquid, in the oven or on low heat.) Reduce the juices or thicken with a slurry of cornstarch dissolved in cold water (if you did not flour the meat before browning it).

THE RIGHT STUFF: CHOOSING A POT

Form follows function, the designers say. It is true in kitchens too. "Smouldering coals" is the rough translation of the French word "braise." Used on the hearth, a traditional braisière would slowly simmer for hours, hot coals below and around it and heaped into its concave lid. A reasonable modern facsimile will be made of material that diffuses and holds heat well, such as an enameled cast iron pot, heavy copper, stainless steel with a heavy bottom, anodized aluminum and earthenware or porcelain — if it can withstand direct heat on the stovetop. Look for 2 stout loop handles, and develop some muscles — most braising pans and Dutch ovens are heavy empty, heavier full.

Gauging Doneness

Use the tip of your finger to touch meat to assess doneness: rare meat of any type is still soft and flabby; well-done meat is springy and firm. If you cannot tell doneness by touch, poke a sharp fork or thin knife blade into the food to assess the colour of the juices. (You will lose only minimal juices.) Insert a carving fork into the thickest part of the meat (the thigh, on birds), count slowly to 10, remove the fork and touch it to the inside of your wrist. (Gingerly — it should be hot!) Then look at the colour of the juices from the meat: red juices indicate rare; clear juices indicate well-done.

If you don't want to rely on these clues, use the weight-time-temperature calculation (15–30 minutes per pound, depending on the oven's temperature) or use a thermometer, and make allowance for carry-over cooking: the internal temperature will rise from 5–15 degrees after the meat comes off the heat, depending on the size of the cut.

If you use a thermometer, here are the internal temperatures for any type of meat. For safety, birds must always be well-done, pork can be medium-rare, lamb and venison are best medium-rare, and beef can be what pleases you best.

- **rare: 125°F** (60°C)
- **medium-rare: 140°F** (75°C)
- **medium: 160°F** (70°C)
- **well-done: 175°F** (80°C)

CHOOSE YOUR WEAPON

Stewing
follows the same methods as braising, but is used for small cubes of meat, which are usually floured before being browned.

Fricassee
refers to the stewing process when applied to white meat, such as pork and veal and breast of chicken.

Blanquette
refers to the braising process for white meat, but omits browning the meat.

CUTTING BOARD SAFETY

Careful cooks avoid cross-contaminating their food. This means putting cooked meats and veggies onto a clean plate, never onto one soiled with raw meat juices. Never baste with marinades that have been in contact with raw meat unless you have boiled the marinade for a few minutes first. Consider using separate cutting boards for meat, vegetables, fish and fruit. Slice your vegetables first, before you slice raw meat on the same board.

Jeff's Lemon Ribs

Use this puckery baste on grilled side or back ribs. Some cooks prefer a "fall-off-the-bone" kind of texture that is achieved by simmering the ribs in hot water before basting and grilling them briefly at medium-high heat, but I absolutely hate the smell of pork as it simmers. Instead, I enjoy the toothier texture that accompanies slow-roasting the ribs in the oven or on a grill, basting them regularly. This dish calls for finger bowls and a soft fruity red like a Beaujolais. Beer would fit the bill as well.

2 slabs	**back or side ribs**
6 cloves	**garlic, minced**
1 tsp. (5 mL)	**orange-infused olive oil**
4 Tbsp. (50 mL)	**olive oil**
1	**lemon, zest and juice**
1	**orange, zest and juice**
½ tsp. (2 mL)	**dried thyme**
1 tsp. (5 mL)	**honey or molasses**
1 tsp. (5 mL)	**light soy sauce**
~	**lots of freshly cracked black pepper**
1 tsp. (5 mL)	**rice wine vinegar**
~	**kosher salt to taste**

Pull off and discard the membrane from the back of the ribs. Simmer the ribs, if desired, in a pot of water for 40 minutes, or simply lay them on a parchment-lined baking sheet.

Mix together the remaining ingredients. Smear half the baste onto the ribs. Cook over medium heat on a grill or in a 300°F (150°C) oven for 1 ½ hours, or until tender. (Time will be determined by whether or not the ribs have been blanched or not.) Ten or 15 minutes before the ribs are done, brush the remaining baste on the ribs.

SERVES 2—4

Pantry Pork Ribs

The alternative to sticky, sweet BBQ sauce from a bottle is to make a rub or baste from the contents of your pantry. Living with a diabetic means I have reinvented how I season ribs. A rich and "saucy" Zinfandel or Shiraz should team well with these.

2 slabs	**pork side ribs**
¼ cup (50 mL)	**sherry vinegar**
⅓ cup (75 mL)	**pomegranate molasses (see page 99)**
¼ cup (50 mL)	**olive oil**
3 Tbsp. (45 mL)	**Malt Mustard (see page 26)**
6 cloves	**garlic, minced**
1 Tbsp. (15 mL)	**Worcestershire sauce**
¼ cup (50 mL)	**sake**
½ tsp. (2 mL)	**hot chili paste**
¼ cup (50 mL)	**minced fresh herbs**
~	**kosher salt to taste**

Pull off and discard the membrane from the back of the ribs. Simmer the ribs, if desired, in a pot of water for 40 minutes, or simply lay them on a parchment-lined baking sheet.

Combine all remaining ingredients except the salt. Reserve ¼ of the mix for a baste. Smear the rest over the ribs, covering all the meat surface and the back of the bones.

Cook over medium heat on a grill or in a 300°F (150°C) oven for 1 ½ hours, or until tender. (Time will be determined by whether or not the ribs have been blanched or not.) Ten or 15 minutes before the ribs are done, brush the remaining baste on the ribs. Sprinkle with salt. Serve hot.

SERVES 4 teenaged males generously

Black Bean Baby Back Ribs

Ten years later, people still ask me how to do the ribs I served at my restaurant, Foodsmith. Offer lots of napkins; these are finger-lickers. This sauce is a knockout on salmon, with mussels, on lamb, with beef or venison, and on pork too. Serve this with Coconut Rice (page 124) and open a bottle of Riesling.

1 slab	baby back ribs
½ cup (125 mL)	hoisin sauce
2–3 Tbsp. (25–45 mL)	lemon juice
2 Tbsp. (25 mL)	fermented black beans, rinsed
1 Tbsp. (15 mL)	minced cilantro
1 Tbsp. (15 mL)	puréed garlic
1 Tbsp. (15 mL)	grated fresh ginger
½ tsp. (2 mL)	hot chili paste
¼–½ cup (50–125 mL)	water
~	cilantro leaves for garnish
~	toasted sesame seeds for garnish

Pull off and discard the membrane from the back of the ribs. Simmer the ribs in a pot of water for 40 minutes. Cool and slice between each bone to separate the ribs. Combine the hoisin, lemon juice, beans, cilantro, garlic, ginger, chili paste and water. Simmer for 5 minutes, add the ribs and simmer for an additional 5–10 minutes, allowing the sauce to thicken and glaze the ribs. Arrange on a plate and garnish with cilantro and sesame seeds.

SERVES 2

"Wild Child" Wild Roast Boar Kaleden Style

In 1999, on a driving holiday to Saltspring Island, I stopped in Kaleden at the south end of the Okanagan Valley to visit my long-time friend, Cindy. My girlfriend drove me out into what felt like the heart of the desert high in the hills on twisting narrow roads until we reached a farm I'd never have known existed. There, we bought a hefty loin roast from Fred and Mary Wendt, owners of Surprise Ranch, where they raised wild boar. Here's how we cooked the roast that night; don't be dismayed by what looks like a long process, because it goes together easily. Cindy's husband John, a "cellar rat" at a south Okanagan winery, opened several bottles of local Riesling to drink with this succulent roast.

Roast:

7.5-lb. (3.5-kg)	**wild boar or pork loin roast**
2 Tbsp. (25 mL)	**ground ginger**
1 Tbsp. (15 mL)	**sweet Hungarian paprika**
1 tsp. (5 mL)	**dried basil**
1 tsp. (5 mL)	**dried oregano**
1 tsp. (5 mL)	**dried marjoram**
½ tsp. (2 mL)	**powdered mustard**
⅛ tsp. (.5 mL)	**freshly grated nutmeg**
⅛ tsp. (.5 mL)	**ground allspice**
⅛ tsp. (.5 mL)	**hot chili flakes**
2 Tbsp. (25 mL)	**olive oil**
2 Tbsp. (25 mL)	**orange juice**
4 cloves	**garlic, puréed**
1 cup (250 mL)	**dry white wine**
½	**onion, finely minced**

Place the roast in a non-reactive container. Combine the remaining ingredients and smear over the meat. Cover and let stand in the fridge overnight if time allows; if not, proceed.

Preheat the oven to 325°F (160°C). Roast the pork, uncovered, for 2 ½ hours, or until medium-rare. Remove from the oven and from the pan. Let stand, loosely covered, while you make the pan gravy.

continued...

Gravy:

1 cup (250 mL)	white wine
1	onion, diced
1	carrot, diced
1 stalk	celery, diced
2 cloves	garlic, smashed
2 slices	fresh ginger, minced
1 sprig	fresh rosemary
2–3 sprigs	fresh thyme
4–5 stalks	parsley
10	peppercorns
2	bay leaves
2–3 cups (500–750 mL)	dark chicken stock
3–4 Tbsp. (45–50 mL)	cornstarch dissolved in cold water (optional)
~	kosher salt and freshly ground black pepper to taste
~	lemon juice to taste

To make the gravy, pour the drippings from the roast into a sauté pan, skimming off any extra fat. Place the roasting pan on the stove and deglaze the pan with the wine, scraping up any browned bits. Pour the deglazing liquid and the bits into the sauté pan. Add the onion, carrot, celery, garlic, ginger, rosemary, thyme, parsley, peppercorns and bay leaves. Add the stock and simmer for 30 minutes. Strain, discarding the solids. Return the liquid to the pan and reduce to thicken, or thicken with dissolved cornstarch. Season to taste with salt, pepper and lemon juice.

To serve, carve the meat and ladle the gravy over each portion.

SERVES 8–10

Pork *with* **Apple Beer** *and* **Cream**

The Normandy region of France is justly famous for its apples and dairy products, and this classic trilogy of flavours is tried and true. Serve this rich dish with a salad dressed in a slightly astringent vinaigrette and topped with apple slices, or with a simple potato or noodle side dish. Use chicken thighs, cooked to well-done, in place of the pork if you like. If you close your eyes, you could be in a tiny village in France. A lighter Gewürztraminer, Pinot Gris or Riesling would be stunning.

1 lb. (500 g)	**pork tenderloin**
2–3 Tbsp. (25–45 mL)	**butter**
1	**leek**
½	**apple, peeled and finely diced**
1 tsp. (5 mL)	**grated fresh ginger**
1 clove	**garlic, puréed**
½ cup (125 mL)	**apple beer (éphémère) or apple cider**
½ cup (125 mL)	**veal or brown chicken stock**
2 Tbsp. (25 mL)	**whipping cream**
½	**lemon or lime, juice and zest**
1 Tbsp. (15 mL)	**minced fresh thyme**
~	**kosher salt and freshly ground black pepper to taste**

Preheat the oven to 450°F (230°C). Clean the pork by removing the silverskin with the tip of a sharp knife. Heat the butter in an ovenproof sauté pan over medium-high heat and sauté the tenderloin for 1–2 minutes, rolling the meat to colour the entire surface. Remove the meat and pan to the oven and roast the meat until it is medium-rare and still pink at the centre (see Gauging Doneness, page 131), about 15 minutes, depending on the size of the tenderloin. Transfer the meat to a plate and cover loosely.

Slice the leek lengthwise, trim off the root and any tough or damaged outer green leaves, and slice crosswise into fine shreds. Transfer the sliced leeks into a colander and wash very thoroughly under running water.

continued...

Tip out and discard any excess fat from the pan. Wipe out the blackened or dark brown bits, then add the leek, apple, ginger and garlic. Cook over medium heat until the apple dice is golden. Add the beer or cider to deglaze the pan, scraping up the little brown bits. Boil until it is reduced by half, then add the stock and reduce it by half. Add the cream and boil until the sauce is the consistency you want. Add the juice and zest, thyme, salt and pepper.

Slice the meat thinly against the grain. Serve hot with the sauce.

SERVES 2–3

Greek Feast Souvlaki

This tender "meat on a stick" is found in tavernas across the Greek Islands. Entirely unpretentious and equally delicious, it is rubbed with the herbs that grow on the hills. Try a Greek wine — red or white, depending on the meat you use.

2 lbs. (1 kg)	**lamb shoulder, chicken breast or pork tenderloin**
~	**kosher salt and freshly ground black pepper to taste**
1 tsp. (5 mL)	**dried oregano**
3 cloves	**garlic, finely minced**
¼ cup (50 mL)	**olive oil**
1	**lemon**
1 cup (250 mL)	**Tzatziki (see page 37)**
6–8	**pita rounds, halved**
2–3	**tomatoes, diced**
½	**red onion, thinly sliced**
1 Tbsp. (15 mL)	**chopped fresh parsley**

Cut the meat into bite-size cubes. Season with salt and pepper, then toss with the oregano, garlic and oil. Marinate for 15 minutes or up to 2 hours.

Thread the meat onto skewers. Heat the grill or broiler to high and grill the meat, turning often. Grill about 10 minutes, or until juicy and tender. Sprinkle the meat with lemon juice when done.

Spread tzatziki inside each pita pocket. Arrange the meat on the sauce, pulling the skewer free, and add a bit of diced tomato and onion. Sprinkle with parsley. Serve with more tzatziki.

SERVES 6 – 8

Brined Smoked Pork

For everyday, use double-cut chops. To feed a crowd on New Year's Day, or to ensure leftovers for tomorrow's lunch, use a loin. Make the brine in advance and cool it, then store the pieces of pork loin in the brine, chilled, for 1 or 2 days, until you can get to it. This brine is good on venison, poultry and beef as well. The smoking technique works well for anything that can be cooked on a grill, from onions to duck or venison. Serve a fruity rosé from California or a lighter, fruitier style of red.

1 ½ cups (375 mL)	dry white wine
¼ cup (50 mL)	brown sugar
2 Tbsp. (25 mL)	kosher salt
2 tsp. (10 mL)	coriander seeds
2 tsp. (10 mL)	fennel seeds
2 tsp. (10 mL)	mustard seeds
1 Tbsp. (15 mL)	peppercorns
3	bay or kaffir lime leaves
1 Tbsp. (15 mL)	finely sliced fresh ginger
1	star anise pod
1	lemon or lime, zest only
½ tsp. (2 mL)	dried sage or tarragon
3 lbs. (1.5 kg)	pork loin, split lengthwise, or chops
1 Tbsp. (15 mL)	olive oil

continued...

To make the brine, combine the wine, sugar, salt, coriander, fennel, mustard, peppercorns, bay or lime leaves, ginger, star anise, lemon or lime zest, and sage or tarragon. Boil the mixture long enough to dissolve the sugar and salt, then simmer for 10 minutes. Let cool. Immerse the pork in the brine, cover and chill, turning now and then, for 1 or 2 days.

Soak several handfuls of fruitwood or hardwood chips in water for 20 minutes. Light the grill. Set one control on low, the other on medium-high. Pat the meat dry, then lightly brush it with olive oil.

Put handfuls of wet wood chips into a flat little tin, such as an old cake or bread pan, and put the tin on the cooler side of your grill, directly on the coals or heating element. When it begins to smoke, put the pork on the medium-hot side of the grill bars. Close the lid, and wait patiently until the pork is just cooked, 15–30 minutes for a loin, and 8–12 minutes for chops, depending on the thickness. Do not open the grill except to turn the meat once or twice, or you will lose the smoke collecting inside. If the wood is consumed, add another handful of wet chips. When the meat is done, its internal temperature should read 145°F (60°C).

SERVES 6–8

USING BRINE

In its simplest form, brining adds salt and acid to food as a preservative, as in pickled onions and chutneys. In its more complex form, brine ferments food, as in sauerkraut and dill pickles. Roll mops, or brined herring fillets, are a popular northern European treat; brined beef brisket is more commonly known as corned beef. Brining helps retains moisture in lean meat that might otherwise dry out on the grill. To make a simple brine, add salt, sugar, vinegar and whatever spices or flavourings the cook enjoys to boiling water. Two hours in brine is sufficient for chicken breast; large pieces of pork or venison can be brined for up to 2 days before cooking.

The World's Best Steak Sandwiches *with* Olive Aïoli

Flank steak's pronounced grain and leanness make it a prime candidate for misunderstanding and misuse. But a little attention can work wonders. Long marinating, quick cooking over high heat to no more than medium-rare, and careful carving — thin slices, against the grain — turn this meat into a modern classic. Have a big glass of Zinfandel and plug in a movie.

1 lb. (500 g)	**flank steak**
½ cup (125 mL)	**dark soy sauce**
2 Tbsp. (25 mL)	**sesame oil**
4 Tbsp. (50 mL)	**finely minced green onion**
6–8 cloves	**garlic, minced**
1 Tbsp. (15 mL)	**finely grated fresh ginger**
2 Tbsp. (25 mL)	**liquid honey**
1 Tbsp. (15 mL)	**toasted and ground sesame seeds**
1	**orange, zest and juice**
½ tsp. (2 mL)	**hot chili flakes**
1	**baguette, sliced**
1 recipe	**Olive Aïoli (see page 142)**

Place the steak in a non-reactive container. Mix the remaining ingredients well, then cover the beef with the marinade. Cover securely with plastic wrap and refrigerate overnight, or for up to 3 or 4 days. Remove the meat from the fridge 20 minutes before grilling to take the chill off. Discard the marinade.

Grill over high heat until medium-rare, about 10 minutes, although the exact time will vary with the size of the flank steak. Or roast at 450° F (230° C) for 20 minutes. Let rest a few minutes, then slice thinly against the grain. Serve the sliced meat on baguette slices, with aïoli spooned on top.

SERVES 4–6

Olive Aïoli

This is wonderful on meat and robust fish and even better on potatoes and pasta. Use it on sandwiches and salads, dip vegetables into it or drop spoonfuls onto hearty soups.

1	egg yolk
1 Tbsp. (15 mL)	Balsamic Mustard (see page 25)
½	lemon, juice only
½ cup (125 mL)	extra virgin olive oil
2–3	green onions or a handful of chives
1 tsp. (5 mL)	finely minced fresh rosemary
½ cup (125 mL)	finely minced Kalamata olives
½ cup (125 mL)	finely minced green olives
2 Tbsp. (25 mL)	capers
2 cloves	garlic, minced
~	hot chili flakes to taste
~	kosher salt to taste
1–2 tsp. (5–10 mL)	red wine vinegar

To make the aïoli, whisk together the egg yolk, mustard and lemon juice in a non-reactive bowl. Slowly drizzle in the oil, whisking thoroughly to form an emulsion. Add the remaining ingredients, balancing the flavours at the end with the chili flakes, salt and vinegar.

MAKES ABOUT 1 ½ CUPS (375 mL)

Flank Steak *or* Tenderloin *with* Mixed Greens *and* Tequila-Chile-Lime Dressing

This dinner satisfies Jeff's longing for red meat, hold the veg, and Darl's salad-loving tendencies. On days when you feel flush, splurge on tenderloin. Any other time, flank steak is a wonderful, flavourful, often-overlooked stand-in. Marinate flank for several days, if possible, to soften its texture, and be sure to roast or grill it only to medium-rare, then slice it thinly across the grain. Try this with other meats as well, but marinate fowl or pork for a few hours only. Offer a good Mexican beer and a fruit-forward red from the USA.

¼ cup (50 mL)	**lime juice**
1	**lime, zest only**
¼ cup (50 mL)	**tequila**
¾ cup (175 mL)	**olive oil**
2 Tbsp. (25 mL)	**orange liqueur**
½ cup (125 mL)	**minced cilantro**
2 Tbsp. (25 mL)	**minced parsley**
4 cloves	**garlic, minced**
1–2 tsp. (5–10 mL)	**Chimayo chili powder**
~	**kosher salt to taste**
2 Tbsp. (25 mL)	**grainy mustard**
2–4 Tbsp. (25–50 mL)	**liquid honey**
1	**flank steak (or 1 lb./500 g beef tenderloin)**
4 cups (1 L)	**mixed greens**

Combine the lime juice and zest, tequila, olive oil, liqueur, cilantro, parsley, garlic, chili powder, salt, mustard and honey. Set aside half to use as dressing. Immerse the meat in the remaining marinade and chill (flank for several days, tenderloin for no more than 8 hours).

Remove the meat from the marinade, discard the liquid and pat the meat dry. Grill or roast to medium-rare. Let stand 10 minutes, then drain any meat juices that accumulate into the reserved dressing and mix well. Slice the meat thinly. Toss the greens with the reserved dressing. Divide the greens and meat among 6 plates. Serve immediately.

SERVES 6

KOBE BEEF

If you can find Kobe beef at your butcher's, splurge and buy a flank steak. This pampered breed of cattle from Japan is intensely marbled, a direct result of high living, massages, and sips of beer. It means that flank steak eats like tenderloin, if you cook it properly. "Properly" in this case means quickly. Slice the raw meat very thinly and sear it in a hot cast iron pan to medium-rare, no more. Do not fuss or waste time, and serve it very simply, with good salt, freshly cracked pepper and good bread, mustard and salad greens.

Grilled Alberta Beef Tenderloin *with* Roasted Pepper Salsa

For an extravagant dinner, invest in a piece of tenderloin. For a more cost-effective daily meal, choose a piece of flank steak or a lamb rack or loin. Marinate the flank for several days, chilled, to get the best results. Add grilled vegetables and new potatoes for the full-meal deal. Set out a bowl of good olives as a suitably Spanish-influenced munch while dinner grills. Leftovers make killer sandwiches in crusty rolls. A Spanish Rioja with warm spicy notes would marry well with this dish.

1 Tbsp. (15 mL)	olive oil
½	orange, juice and zest
4 cloves	garlic, minced
1 Tbsp. (15 mL)	Spanish paprika
½ tsp. (2 mL)	smoked Spanish paprika
1 Tbsp. (15 mL)	grated fresh ginger
1 Tbsp. (15 mL)	minced fresh basil
~	freshly cracked black pepper to taste
1 lb. (500 g)	beef tenderloin
1 recipe	Roasted Pepper Salsa (see page 97)

Combine the oil, orange juice and zest, garlic, paprikas, ginger, basil and pepper. Coat the beef with the mixture, wrap well and chill until needed, at least 6 hours if possible. Remove from the fridge and let stand half an hour to remove the chill before cooking. Preheat the grill to medium-high and grill the tenderloin to medium-rare, or your preferred degree of doneness. Let stand 5–10 minutes before slicing. Serve with the salsa.

SERVES 2–4

Turkey-Stuffed Salad Rolls with Double Dips

page 35

Savoury Filo Strudel

page 39

Butternut Squash Soup with Orange and Basil

page 65

Citrus-Dressed Asparagus and Smoked Salmon on Wild Rice and Spinach

page 94

Shanghai Shiitake

page 103

Noodle Salad with Barbecued Duck, Snow Peas and Ponzu Dressing

page 121

**Persian Pilaf
with Lemon**

page 122

**Summer Couscous,
Winter Bulgur**

page 125

**Greek Feast
Souvlaki**

page 138

The World's Best
Steak Sandwiches
with Olive Aïoli

page 141

**Summer Salad with
New Potatoes and Beans
(and Lobster!)**

page 178

**Mussels in
Provençal Steam**

page 180

**Poached Sole
and Salmon in
Carrot Jus**

page 186

**Breast of Turkey
Stuffed with Cranberries
and Ginger**

page 204

**Far-Out Filo Napoleons
with Orange-Lime Mousse
and Fresh Berries**

page 238

**Dailyn's
Queen Cake**

page 252

Veal Medallions
with **Wild Mushrooms** *and* Oloroso Sherry Cream

Enjoy this dish on special occasions or when that beautiful bottle of Burgundy is calling your name. If you have a venison loin in the freezer, pull it out to cut into medallions in place of the veal. Uncork a luscious Pinot Noir or Pinot Gris for this special occasion dinner.

½ lb. (250 g)	veal, cut into medallions
2–3 Tbsp (25-45 mL)	butter
1	shallot, thinly sliced
2 cloves	garlic, thinly sliced
6	mushrooms, sliced
2 Tbsp. (25 mL)	dried wild mushrooms, rehydrated
1–2 Tbsp. (15-25 mL)	white wine or vermouth
½ cup (125 mL)	veal or brown chicken stock
¼ cup (50 mL)	whipping cream
2 Tbsp. (25 mL)	oloroso sherry
1 Tbsp. (15 mL)	minced fresh thyme
~	kosher salt and freshly ground black pepper to taste

Pound each medallion into a thin (¼-inch/.6-cm) slice. Heat the butter in a sauté pan and sauté the slices for 1–2 minutes each over high heat. Cook in batches to avoid overfilling the pan. Remove the meat to a plate as it is cooked, season with salt and pepper and cover loosely.

Add the shallot, garlic and mushrooms to the pan and quickly sauté. Add the wine or vermouth to deglaze and scrape up the little brown bits. Add the stock and cook until it is reduced by half. Add the cream and boil until it is reduced by half. Add the sherry, thyme, salt and pepper. Stir the meat into the sauce to coat it, then serve.

SERVES 2

Braised Veal *or* Venison Roll

Breast of veal and venison are both generally ignored in favour of more sexy cuts. That is hard to understand, because properly cooked, they are as tender as any high-rent piece of meat. Serve this with Olive Oil Mashed Potatoes (page 80) and your favourite salad. Try a hearty Côtes du Rhône with this flavourful dish.

2 Tbsp. (25 mL)	olive oil
2	onions, thickly sliced
1 head	garlic, separated into cloves and peeled
4	carrots, roughly chopped
2 stalks	celery, roughly chopped
2	bay leaves
3 sprigs	fresh rosemary
4 sprigs	fresh thyme
3–4 cups (750 mL–1 L)	bread, fresh cubes
1	onion, diced
2 cloves	garlic, diced
1 link	sausage, finely diced (optional)
2 Tbsp. (25 mL)	minced fresh parsley
1 tsp. (5 mL)	dried savoury
2–4 cups (500 mL–1 L)	rich brown stock
~	kosher salt and freshly ground black pepper to taste
3-lb. (1.5-kg)	veal or venison breast
½ bottle	robust red wine
4–5 cups (1–1.25 L)	rich brown stock
~	freshly cracked black pepper to taste

Heat the oil in a heavy sauté pan over medium-high heat. Add the sliced onions, whole garlic cloves, carrots, celery and bay leaves. Brown well, then add the rosemary and thyme. Transfer the browned herbs and vegetables to a brazier or heavy, ovenproof casserole.

For the stuffing, put the bread in a large bowl. Sauté the diced onion and garlic with the sausage, if using, until the vegetables are tender and the meat is cooked through. (If you don't use sausage, heat 1 Tbsp./15 mL oil in the pan before you sauté the onion and garlic.) Add the parsley, savoury, stock, salt and pepper. Mix well with the bread.

Preheat the oven to 375°F (190°C). Lay the meat out flat. Spread the stuffing over it in a thick layer, covering the meat from edge to edge. Roll up the meat and tie it with butcher twine. Return the sauté pan to the stove, add a little oil if needed, and add the tied roll of meat. Brown all the surfaces of the meat, then lay it on top of the vegetables in the brazier.

Discard any accumulated fat in the sauté pan. Add the wine and bring to a boil, then simmer for 5 minutes. Pour over the meat. Heat the stock to a boil and pour over the meat. Crack some pepper over the entire dish.

Place a piece of parchment over the surface of the food, then cover it snugly with a lid. Place on the centre rack of the oven and cook for 3 hours. Check the meat, and if it is tender and pulls apart easily, remove from the oven. Transfer the meat to a shallow gratin dish and loosely cover it, then return it to the oven to keep warm.

Strain the braising juices, pushing firmly on the solids with a wooden spoon to extract absolutely everything. Discard the solids and adjust the balance of the juices. Thicken with cornstarch dissolved in cold water if desired. Slice the meat thickly against the grain and serve with the sauce.

SERVES 6

Cherrywood-Smoked Venison Loin

This meat has a lovely texture, but only if you cook it to medium-rare. Cook it longer and it will be perilously like leather. Brining helps by adding moisture to the meat. (See Using Brine, page 140.) This is my rendition of a classic — serve it with mashed potatoes or noodles and a simple, cleanly flavoured orange and walnut salad in a sharply acidic citrus vinaigrette. Leftover smoked venison makes an outstanding sandwich, especially when it is thinly sliced, heaped on Sourdough Bread (page 52) and topped with Olive Aïoli (page 142) or Tzatziki (page 37). Drink a round, rich, berry-ripe Cabernet Franc with a hint of woodsmoke.

Brine:

¼ cup (50 mL)	Demerara sugar
¼ cup (50 mL)	kosher salt
3 cups (750 mL)	cold water
1 tsp. (5 mL)	juniper berries
4	bay leaves, crumbled
1	whole dried hot chile, crumbled
½ stick	cinnamon, crumbled
4	whole star anise pods
½ tsp. (2 mL)	whole allspice berries
4–6	whole cloves
½ tsp. (2 mL)	fennel seed
1 Tbsp. (15 mL)	peppercorns
2 tsp. (10 mL)	mustard seed
⅓ cup (75 mL)	gin

Combine the brine ingredients. Bring to a boil and simmer briefly, about 10 minutes. Cool.

smoked loin:

1 2-lb. (1-kg)   **venison loin**

2 Tbsp. (25 mL)   **olive oil**

1 tsp. (5 mL)   **dried oregano or basil**

~   **kosher salt and freshly cracked pepper**

Immerse the raw venison loin in the cooled brine. Let stand 12 hours in the fridge, turning from time to time.

Soak your preferred hardwood or fruitwood (cherrywood is lovely!) chunks in cold water for at least an hour or until thoroughly saturated.

Remove the meat from the brine and pat dry. Discard the brine. Rub the meat with the oil, and lightly dust with oregano or basil and a sparse sprinkle of salt and pepper.

Turn on the grill, setting the temperatures to high on one side of the grill and low on another.

Put handfuls of wet woodchips into a flat little tin, such as an old cake or bread pan, and put the tin on the cooler side of your grill, directly on the coals or heating element. When it begins to smoke, close the lid, and let a good head of smoke develop, about 10 minutes.

Place the venison on the hot side of the grill and cover the grill. Grill for 10 minutes for medium-rare, turning once. Remove the meat from the grill, let it rest 10 minutes, and carve thinly against the grain.

SERVES 4

Bison Curry *with* Coconut *and* Cilantro

You are likely to spend more time slicing and dicing than actually cooking when you make this lush curry. If no deer, antelope or bison roam your kitchen range, use beef. Put on a pot of Coconut Rice (page 124) before you begin, and serve some Fresh Peach Chutney (page 22) if you want to fill the plate. Match this with Riesling or Gewürztraminer.

Meat and marinade:

2 lbs. (1 kg)	bison tenderloin
1 Tbsp. (15 mL)	grated ginger root
4 cloves	garlic, minced
2 Tbsp. (25 mL)	vegetable oil
1 Tbsp. (15 mL)	Ras El Hanout (see page 28) or curry powder

Trim and thinly slice the meat into bite-size pieces. Combine the meat and marinade ingredients in a large bowl. Mix well and let the mixture stand while you prepare the vegetables for the sauce.

Sauce:

2 Tbsp. (25 mL)	vegetable oil
1	onion, diced
½	red bell pepper, diced
4 cloves	garlic, sliced
2 stalks	lemon grass, split and sliced
3	kaffir lime leaves
2 Tbsp. (25 mL)	Ras El Hanout (see page 28) or curry powder
1–2 Tbsp. (15–25 mL)	Panang curry paste (see Asian Ingredients, page 36)
¼ cup (50 mL)	white wine
2	Roma tomatoes, diced
2 Tbsp. (25 mL)	tomato paste
¾ cup (175 mL)	coconut milk
3	limes, juice only
2 Tbsp. (25 mL)	minced cilantro
~	kosher salt and freshly cracked black pepper to taste

Heat the oil in a large sauté pan. Add the meat and sauté over medium-high heat for several minutes, browning each side. Add the onion, bell pepper, garlic, lemon grass and kaffir lime leaves. Cook until the vegetables are tender, about 5 minutes, stirring often. Add the Ras El Hanout and curry paste, mix well and sauté for several minutes on medium heat. Add the wine and simmer briefly, then stir in the tomato paste and coconut milk. Simmer for 2–3 minutes, then add the lime juice to taste. Stir in the cilantro, salt and pepper. Add more coconut milk to thin the sauce if needed. Pick out and discard the lemon grass stalks. Serve hot.

SERVES 6

CITRUS FLAVOURS:
LEMON GRASS AND KAFFIR LIME LEAVES

Lemon grass adds a clean citrus note to curries and other dishes. Trim off the dry or woody tops and cut the rest in half lengthwise. Either mince the stalks into pieces fine enough to eat, or bruise the stalks with the flat of your knife and pick out the pieces before you serve. Dark green kaffir lime leaves have a haunting, perfume-like floral citrus scent. Buy lime leaves fresh or frozen in Asian markets; at home, double-wrap the package before storing it in your freezer or everything will smell of lime.

Beer-Braised Lamb Shanks

Every year, The Canadian Food and Wine Festival, set in the Rocky Mountains, is a highlight of my spring. Recently, the festival expanded to include great Canadian beer as well as wine, featuring Unibroue, a world-class artisan beer from Quebec. Find it, cook with it, drink it. Then go on the hunt for lamb shanks, or substitute beef short ribs, crossrib, blade or chuck.

1	leek
2 Tbsp. (25 mL)	olive oil
4	lamb shanks
1	onion, coarsely chopped
4	carrots, coarsely chopped
2 stalks	celery, sliced
1 head	garlic, cloves separated and peeled
1 tsp. (5 mL)	dried thyme
1 tsp. (5 mL)	dried oregano
1 tsp. (5 mL)	dried savoury
1 sprig	fresh rosemary
1 Tbsp. (15 mL)	freshly ground black pepper
1 lb. (500 g)	diced potatoes
2 cups (500 mL)	green lentils (optional)
4–6	Roma tomatoes, diced
1 12-oz bottle (1 350-mL)	Maudite or other dark ale
2 cups (500 mL)	veal or dark chicken stock
2 Tbsp. (25 mL)	cornstarch, dissolved in cold water
~	kosher salt and freshly ground black pepper to taste
~	minced parsley for garnish
~	finely grated lemon zest for garnish

Set the oven to 325° F (160°C). Slice the leek lengthwise, trim and slice crosswise into ½-inch (1-cm) pieces. Transfer the sliced leek into a colander and wash very thoroughly under running water. Drain well.

Heat the oil in a non-stick sauté pan and brown the meat on all sides over medium-high heat. Transfer to an ovenproof dish and brown the leek, onion, carrots, celery and garlic in the oil.

Add the thyme, oregano, savoury, rosemary and pepper. Layer the potatoes, lentils, if using, and tomatoes around the meat. Deglaze the pan with the ale and stock, bring to a boil and pour over the meat. Place a piece of parchment directly on top of the meat and vegetables, cover with the lid and place in the oven. Cook until the meat and lentils are tender, checking after 3 ½ hours. When done, remove the meat and cover with a piece of foil. Skim off any fat on the roasting juices, then bring the juices to a boil. Thicken with cornstarch, if desired. Adjust the seasoning with salt and pepper. Serve the shanks with the sauce, garnished with parsley and lemon zest.

SERVES 4 — 6 with lots of leftovers

Thai Lamb

This need not be hot, just roundly seasoned. Serve with Coconut Rice (page 124) and Thai Dip (page 34). Use leftovers in pita with Tzatziki (page 37). Try a big fruity brew or a soft and supple Gewürztraminer.

1 lb. (500 g)	**lamb loin**
2 Tbsp. (25 mL)	**minced cilantro**
~	**kosher salt and freshly ground black pepper to taste**
3 cloves	**garlic, finely minced**
¼ cup (50 mL)	**vegetable oil**
1	**lemon**
4 Tbsp. (50 mL)	**light brown sugar**
4 Tbsp. (50 mL)	**rice wine vinegar**
2 Tbsp. (25 mL)	**Thai fish sauce**
2	**red chiles, seeded and minced**
1 Tbsp. (15 mL)	**grated fresh ginger**

Cut the lamb into 1-inch (2.5-cm) cubes. Mix together all the remaining ingredients. Add the lamb and marinate for several hours. Thread the meat onto skewers. Preheat the grill or broiler to medium-high and cook the lamb to medium-rare. Serve Thai Dip in small bowls alongside the lamb.

SERVES 4

Phyllis's Innisfail Lamb Stew

It was Christmas Eve afternoon. I had a potluck to get to, and nothing specific on my mind to cook, other than I wanted to eat Alberta lamb. I puttered in the kitchen, and Phyllis perched on the stool beside the butcher block, drinking coffee, chatting and watching as I rummaged through cupboards, fridge and drawers, tossing in whatever caught my fancy. Like many spur-of-the-moment meals, it worked out better than many carefully choreographed events. Made with friends, served to friends, this is full of good wishes, Christmas cheer, and the rich flavour of lamb. Serve it with lots of crusty bread and a side order of Pineapple and Mango Compote (page 25), Susan's Winter Fruit Chutney (page 24) or Mustard Dip (page 25). Pour a rich, flavourful red Bordeaux, Spanish Rioja or Auzzie Shiraz with this.

2 lbs. (1 kg)	**lamb shoulder, cubed**
¼ cup (50 mL)	**all-purpose flour**
~	**kosher salt and freshly cracked black pepper to taste**
6 Tbsp. (90 mL)	**olive oil**
½ cup (125 mL)	**dry white wine**
3	**star anise pods**
4	**leeks**
6 cloves	**garlic, slivered**
4 Tbsp. (50 mL)	**Ras El Hanout (see page 28) or curry powder**
3 Tbsp. (45 mL)	**Pomegranate Molasses (see page 99)**
1 Tbsp. (15 mL)	**Worcestershire sauce**
8 cups (2 L)	**brown or chicken stock**
2 Tbsp. (25 mL)	**minced fresh thyme**
1 tsp. (5 mL)	**minced fresh rosemary**
1	**Gala apple, peeled and diced**
¼ cup (50 mL)	**dried cranberries**
¼ cup (50 mL)	**barley**
19-oz. tin (540-mL tin)	**chickpeas**
1	**orange, juice and zest**
2 cups (500 mL)	**peeled and cubed round potatoes (see Selecting Spuds, page 81)**
½ cup (125 mL)	**peeled and cubed yellow turnip**
2 cups (500 mL)	**carrot sticks**
½ cup (125 mL)	**slivered Brussels sprouts or napa cabbage**
4 Tbsp. (50 mL)	**minced fresh parsley**
~	**kosher salt and freshly cracked black pepper to taste**

Preheat the oven to 300°F (150° C). Toss the lamb cubes with the flour, salt and pepper in a plastic bag. Heat half the oil in a non-stick sauté pan, adding half the lamb when the oil is hot. Brown the meat, turning it to brown all sides and transferring it to an ovenproof braising pan as it is done. Repeat with the remaining oil and lamb. Add the wine to the sauté pan. Scrape the brown bits free over moderate heat, and tip the wine and bits into the stew pot. Add the star anise to the pot.

Slice the leeks lengthwise, trim off the root and any tough or damaged outer green leaves, and slice crosswise into ½-inch (1-cm) slices. Transfer the sliced leeks to a colander and wash very thoroughly under running water. Drain well.

Sauté the leeks and garlic in a little more oil, adding the Ras El Hanout or curry powder when the leeks are tender. Stir well, then transfer the mixture to the stew pot. Add the pomegranate molasses, Worcestershire sauce, stock, thyme, rosemary, apple, cranberries, barley, chickpeas, orange juice and zest, potatoes, turnips and carrots to the mixture in the stew pot. Bring it to a boil, cover, and transfer to the oven. Cook for 2—3 hours, or until the lamb is tender.

Remove the stew from the oven, stir well, and add the Brussels sprouts or cabbage. Stir again. Cover and let stand while you chop some parsley for garnish. Season with salt and pepper along with the chopped parsley. Serve hot.

SERVES A CROWD, 10—12

Classic Cinnamon-Scented Moussaka

The last time Darl and I made this, I (foolishly) thought we were cooking enough for several days. Was I ever surprised when nearly all of this humble dish disappeared at supper, devoured by 3 ravenous males! Substitute lean ground beef for the lamb or, for a meatless meal, leave out the meat and up the vegetable content with extra zucchini and peppers. This calls for a simple Rhône blend — substantial and spicy.

Meat sauce:

1 ½ lbs. (750 g)	globe eggplant (3 or 4 eggplants)
1 Tbsp. (15 mL)	kosher salt
½ cup (125 mL)	all-purpose flour, for dredging
2–3 Tbsp. (25–45 mL)	olive oil
2 ½ lbs. (1.3 kg)	lean ground lamb
1	large onion, cut into ½-inch (1-cm) dice
2 cloves	garlic, minced
2	roasted red bell peppers, cut into ½-inch (1-cm) dice
2	zucchini, cut into ½-inch (1-cm) cubes
2	bay leaves
1	cinnamon stick
4	whole allspice
½ tsp. (2 mL)	ground nutmeg
28-oz. can (796-mL can)	diced tomatoes
1 cup (250 mL)	dry white wine
4 Tbsp. (50 mL)	tomato paste
~	kosher salt and freshly cracked black pepper to taste
½ cup (125 mL)	feta cheese
2 Tbsp. (25 mL)	minced fresh parsley

Peel the eggplant and slice it into ½-inch (1-cm) slices. Place in a colander over a bowl or in the sink and sprinkle with the salt.

Lightly oil a 13 x 9-inch (3.5-L) cake pan or casserole dish. Preheat the oven to 400°F (200°C).

Lightly coat the eggplant slices with flour, shaking them in a plastic bag and discarding the excess. Line a baking sheet with parchment and place the eggplant on the baking sheet in a single layer. Drizzle the oil onto the eggplant and bake until brown, about 15 minutes, turning once. Remove the eggplant from the oven and decrease the oven temperature to 375°F (190°C).

Heat a heavy sauté pan. Add the lamb and cook, stirring frequently, until it is no longer pink. Discard any fat, then add the onion, garlic, roasted peppers, zucchini, bay leaves, cinnamon, allspice, nutmeg, tomatoes, wine and tomato paste. Simmer, covered, for 35 minutes, or until thickened. Remove the bay leaves. Season with salt and pepper.

Spoon half the tomato sauce into the baking dish. Lay the eggplant slices in one layer on top of the sauce. Sprinkle with the feta cheese and add the remaining meat sauce. Sprinkle the parsley over top. Set aside.

Béchamel sauce:

8 Tbsp. (125 mL)	**butter**
6 Tbsp. (90 mL)	**all-purpose flour**
4 cups (1 L)	**milk**
~	**kosher salt to taste**
½ tsp. (2 mL)	**ground nutmeg**
~	**hot chili paste to taste**
2	**eggs**
½ cup (125 mL)	**grated Parmesan cheese**
½ cup (125 mL)	**feta cheese**
~	**chopped flatleaf parsley for garnish**

For the béchamel, melt the butter in a heavy pot. Add the flour and cook the roux until it is sandy in texture. Heat the milk in a separate pot, then slowly add the milk in small increments, stirring well with a wooden spoon or whisk after each addition. Bring to a boil, then reduce the heat and simmer another 10 minutes, stirring often. Add the salt, nutmeg and chili paste to the sauce.

continued...

Use a fork to beat the eggs in a small bowl. Add some of the hot sauce (about 1 cup/250 mL) to the eggs, mixing well to temper them. Return the egg mixture to the sauce and mix well.

Pour the béchamel sauce over the meat sauce, smoothing the top. Sprinkle with a little more ground nutmeg and then the Parmesan and feta cheeses.

Bake for 30 minutes, or until hot. Remove from the oven and let stand for 10 minutes before slicing. Garnish each serving with parsley.

SERVES 8—10

Moroccan Lamb Tagine

The complex flavours in this wonderful tagine need very little embellishment. Preface it with a simple green salad, add Summer Couscous, Winter Bulgur (page 125), and sit down to enjoy a feast. Spanish red or white wines in the classic style are perfect choices.

2–3 lbs. (1–1.5 kg)	**lamb shoulder**
4 Tbsp. (50 mL)	**Ras El Hanout (see page 28) or curry powder**
1 head	**garlic, cloves separated and minced**
3 Tbsp. (45 mL)	**grated fresh ginger**
4 Tbsp. (50 mL)	**olive oil**
2	**onions, coarsely chopped**
1 stick	**cinnamon**
¼ tsp. (1 mL)	**saffron**
3 Tbsp. (45 mL)	**Pomegranate Molasses (see page 99)**
½ cup (125 mL)	**sliced Pickled Lemon (see page 24)**
½ cup (125 mL)	**sliced green Sicilian olives**
½ cup (125 mL)	**slivered dried apricots**
2 cups (500 mL)	**cooked chickpeas**
½ cup (125 mL)	**dry white wine**
1 cup (250 mL)	**veal or chicken stock**
~	**kosher salt and hot chili flakes to taste**
¼ cup (50 mL)	**minced fresh mint**

¼ **cup** (50 mL)	**minced cilantro**
¼ **cup** (50 mL)	**minced green onions**

Preheat the oven to 300°F (150°C). Cut the lamb into 1-inch (2.5-cm) cubes. Mix the meat with half the Ras El Hanout, half the garlic and half the ginger. Heat half the oil in a heavy sauté pan. Add the meat and brown it over medium-high heat on all sides, transferring it to a heavy braising pot as it is done.

Heat the remaining oil in the sauté pan. Add the onions and the remaining garlic and ginger. Brown the vegetables over medium-high heat, then transfer them to the pot with the meat. Add the remaining Ras El Hanout, along with cinnamon, saffron, pomegranate molasses, pickled lemon, olives, apricots, chickpeas, wine and stock. Bring the mixture to a boil. Cover with parchment paper and a snug lid. Transfer to the oven and cook for 3 hours, or until tender. Skim any fat from the pot. Season with salt and hot chili flakes. Serve on couscous or bulgur, sprinkling each serving with mint, cilantro and green onions.

SERVES 8–12

Thursday Night Modern Sausage

Reinventing Classics

In many cultures around the world, sausages were made from the garbage bin of the kitchen, from things no one wants to even know about, never mind eat. But that was then. Although they began as the thrifty butcher's way of using up trimmings, sausages have gone uptown.

Modern sausage is cool, trendy and good for you. It's also easy to make from prime lean meats flavoured with fresh herbs and spices. Making your own, like anything homemade, means the cook controls everything, from the selection of meats and spices to the amount of fat. It doesn't have to be just pork, although German and Alsatian sausage, based on pork, is justifiably famous. Contemporary sausage meats include turkey, chicken, lamb, beef, or game.

The Art of Sausage-Making

- Begin at the butcher's, unless you have a meat grinder attachment for your countertop mixer. Order some ground meat, medium or coarse, or a mixture, if you like a coarser-textured link.

- Back in your own kitchen, season the meat to taste. Some cooks find that sautéing, roasting or grilling any vegetable additions, such as onions, garlic, bell peppers, or shallots, makes a milder, more subtly seasoned sausage. Please yourself. But don't forget a generous amount of salt. Many cooks like to add a jar of berry compote when they make game sausages.

- Combine all the ingredients, mixing thoroughly. Add ice or ice water to help the mixture develop a slightly sticky texture. Test for seasoning by sautéing and tasting a bit of the blend before you commit yourself to stuffing or shaping patties. If you accidentally make the mixture too wet, add Japanese panko breadcrumbs to absorb the extra liquid. Make the links as hot (or not) as you like. (See The Balancing Act, page 19.)

- When the blend is balanced to your taste, shape patties of any size, just as you would hamburgers. If you have purchased casings, now is the time to rinse them. (See The Inside Story on Casings, at right.) Use a countertop mixer equipped with a "horn" designed to stuff sausage and attached to the meat grinder, or use a piping bag fitted with a plain tip. In either case, the entire length of the casing must be pushed onto the tip so it can be stuffed with the filling. It sounds more awkward than it is.

- Two people make the job easier if you are using a machine. One person can use the mixer's pusher to fill the hopper at the top, feeding the mixture down into the gullet of the mixer, while the other controls the filling as it enters the casing that is threaded onto the nose of the horn.

- Use your hands to pack and shape the sausage as it emerges, and don't overstuff. Leave a few inches empty at the beginning of the casing, and tie a snug knot after the meat has begun to extrude. (Otherwise, you get massive air bubbles, which can be pricked with a small knife or needle.) You need some slack between each link, about ½ inch (1 cm), to twist the links. You can do this as you go along, but it's easier to do later. Alternate twisting directions, 3 complete turns each time, to ensure the whole thing doesn't unravel like a Slinky losing its kinks.

- Wrap the sausages in freezer wrap or freezer bags, label them, and freeze any that won't be consumed within the next day or two.

- When you are done, don't wait for dinner. Strike up the grill or poach a few links right now to celebrate your efforts. And congratulations. You have just contributed to an enduring culinary tradition.

THE INSIDE STORY ON CASINGS

"Natural" pork casings (animal-derived, made from carefully washed intestines, if you must know…) are available for purchase at small butcher shops and packing houses.

To use them, put the bundle into a bowl of warm water in the sink, using a clothespin to clamp one end of a casing onto the edge of the bowl. When your sausage filling is ready, remove the clothespin and hold the casing open under running water. Let the water course through a manageable length of casing several feet long, then use sharp kitchen shears to sever the casing. Be sure to re-pin the new end to the bowl, and drain the piece you are ready to use. To store unused casings indefinitely, put them into a clean tub and add several large handfuls of kosher salt. Mix well, cover and refrigerate.

Canadian Cassoulet *with* Braised Duck Legs, Sausage *and* Great Northern White Beans

A potful of beans studded with smoky bacon is a powerful curative and restorative. After skiing in the cold, canoeing in the wet or golfing in the rain, returning home to the scent of simmering beans is bound to make you feel very cared for. Even better, your kitchen will smell of garlic, the perfect aromatherapy for long cold nights. Do not be dissuaded by the long list of ingredients — they add complexity of flavour, not difficulty. Drink a rosé from Corbières, in the south of France.

2	leeks
1 Tbsp. (15 mL)	olive oil
2	onions, thickly diced
2	carrots, coarsely chopped
2	celery stalks, coarsely chopped
8 cloves	garlic, sliced
4 slices	double-smoked bacon, diced
½ lb. (250 g)	ham, diced
2 links	sausage, sliced
2	bay leaves
2–3 sprigs	fresh rosemary
4–5 sprigs	fresh thyme
1 tsp. (5 mL)	dried oregano
1 tsp. (5 mL)	dried basil
1 or 2	star anise pods
½ stick	cinnamon, broken
1	lemon, zest only
1 Tbsp. (15 mL)	cracked peppercorns
1 cup (250 mL)	red wine
½ cup (125 mL)	Pomegranate Molasses (see page 99)
8 cups (2 L)	cooked Great Northern beans
½ recipe	Duck Legs in White Wine (see page 212)
8 cups (2 L)	chicken stock
1–2 Tbsp. (15–25 mL)	herb-infused wine vinegar
~	kosher salt and freshly ground black pepper to taste

Slice the leeks lengthwise, trim off the root and any tough or damaged outer green leaves, and slice crosswise into ½-inch (1-cm) pieces. Transfer the sliced leeks into a colander and wash very thoroughly under running water. Drain well.

Preheat the oven to 375°F (190°C). Heat the oil in a heavy ovenproof brazier, and cook the onions, leeks, carrots, celery, garlic and bacon, adding small amounts of water as needed to prevent browning. Once the vegetables are tender, allow the water to evaporate and the vegetables to brown for colour and flavour. Add all the remaining ingredients, except for the vinegar, salt and pepper.

Stir well and bring to a boil. Cover with a layer of parchment paper and a snug lid. Bake for 3 hours, adding more water or stock if the level of liquid drops below the surface.

Remove from the oven, skim any fat from the surface, taste, and add salt, pepper and a splash of vinegar as needed to balance the flavours. Serve in generous portions.

SERVES 8 hungry friends generously, with leftovers

Eating Locally

On a recent trip to the Languedoc in south-central France, I made it my mission to eat 3 things that define the food of the region. I tried nearly every cassoulet, duck confit and foie gras that presented itself. What I found, and where, was amazing: along the Canal du Midi, which threads its way for hundreds of kilometers from the Atlantic to the Mediterranean, I enjoyed a sophisticated foie gras. In Toulouse, I ate the best, simplest cassoulet filled with a wealth of sausages and topped with a leg of duck confit and crispy breadcrumbs in the traditional style. It was all good.

Choucroute Rapide

I was born in Alsace, not far from Strasbourg, which is "the" French sausage city. *Ma mère* made her own sauerkraut — tangy, spicy and delicious jars that we consumed in Reuben sandwiches for lunch, or with fat sausages for supper. If your mama doesn't make sauerkraut, buy some good stuff. Then make or buy some really good sausages, whatever you like — I am partial to white veal, bratwurst, and Hungarian, all in the same pot and all at the same time. Serve with a tasty mustard, pickles and steamed new potatoes in their jackets. Drink good beer or Alsatian Riesling with this.

2 Tbsp. (25 mL)	**olive oil or butter**
1	**onion, sliced**
3 cloves	**garlic, sliced**
1	**bay leaf**
½ tsp. (2 mL)	**whole coriander seeds**
¼ tsp. (1 mL)	**whole juniper berries**
6	**sausages, various types, sliced or whole**
½ cup (125 mL)	**Riesling**
4 cups (1 L)	**good-quality sauerkraut**

Heat the oil or butter in a heavy pot. Add the onion and garlic and sauté over medium-high heat until tender. The onion should brown a bit. Add the bay, coriander and juniper, then lay the sausages on top of the onions and spices. Pour in the wine and sauerkraut, cover and simmer until the sausages are cooked through, about 15–20 minutes.

SERVES 2–4

Turkey Sausage

It was my favourite Canmore-based chef, Hubert Aumeier, former partner at Valbella Meats, who taught me how to make sausages. It was no leisurely lesson, but a quick coaching session just ahead of a class I was set to teach — on making sausage. "Learn by doing" does work! What Hubert taught me is that there are no longer formal ratios of lean to fat; it is a question of using prime meats and seasoning them to taste. These saucy links or patties make a wonderful meal with a spicy salad or cold lentil salad jazzed up with fresh pineapple. Serve with good mustard and crusty rolls. Enjoy a lightly chilled rosé or a German beer.

2 lbs. (1 kg)	ground turkey (white and dark meat mixed)
4	Golden Delicious apples, peeled, diced and sautéed
2 tsp. (10 mL)	curry powder
1	lemon, zest only
~	pinch of dried lavender
2 Tbsp. (25 mL)	minced fresh thyme
2 Tbsp. (25 mL)	minced chives
~	kosher salt and freshly cracked black pepper to taste
~	hot chili flakes to taste
¼ cup (50 mL)	black beans, cooked and coarsely chopped

Combine all the ingredients, mixing thoroughly. Test for seasoning by sautéing a bit of the blend before you commit yourself to stuffing or shaping. When you are satisfied with the flavour, either shape patties or stuff sausage casings with a piping bag equipped with a plain tip, twisting the sausages as you go to whatever size you like. (See The Art of Sausage-Making, page 163.) Cook on the grill, in a hot oven or under the broiler of your oven, until the juices run clear, about 8–10 minutes, depending on the size of the sausages.

MAKES ABOUT 24 SAUSAGES

Turkey *and* Sage Sausages *with* Five Onions *and* Apple

Perfect for Christmas morning, these sausages are mild and satisfyingly dense in texture. For a lighter style, use only white meat. Serve with Prosecco or Canadian bubbly.

1	leek
1 Tbsp. (15 mL)	olive oil
½ cup (125 mL)	minced root vegetables
½	onion, minced
3	shallots, minced
4–6 cloves	garlic, minced
1	lemon, zest only
½ cup (125 mL)	chopped dried cranberries
4 Tbsp. (50 mL)	minced fresh sage
2 Tbsp. (25 mL)	minced chives
½ cup (125 mL)	minced fresh herbs, (chives, parsley, thyme, mint or any blend you like)
2 lbs. (1 kg)	ground turkey breast and dark meat
½ cup (125 mL)	apple cider or white wine, chilled
1	Gala apple, diced
~	kosher salt and freshly ground black pepper to taste

Slice the leek lengthwise, trim off the root and any tough or damaged outer green leaves, and finely mince crosswise. Transfer the sliced leek into a colander and wash very thoroughly under running water. Drain well.

Heat the oil in a sauté pan, then cook the leek, root vegetables, onion, shallot and garlic over medium heat until tender. Add the remaining ingredients and mix well. Stuff. (See the Art of Sausage-Making, page 163.) Cook and serve.

MAKES ABOUT 24 SAUSAGES

Cherry *and* Duck Sausage

This classic blend of duck and orange accented with port and cherries makes a lush link. This is wonderful in Canadian Cassoulet (see page 164), with lentils, in a crusty roll with great mustard, and *au naturel*. Try a soft Pinot Noir or Gamay.

2 lbs. (1 kg)	**duck meat, ground**
1 lb. (500 g)	**ground pork neck or shoulder**
1 Tbsp. (15 mL)	**minced fresh rosemary**
1 Tbsp. (15 mL)	**grated fresh ginger**
2 Tbsp. (25 mL)	**minced garlic**
3 Tbsp. (45 mL)	**kosher salt**
1 Tbsp. (15 mL)	**freshly cracked black pepper**
1	**orange, zest only**
½ tsp. (2 mL)	**hot chili flakes**
2 Tbsp. (25 mL)	**butter**
1	**onion, finely minced**
½ cup (125 mL)	**dried sour cherries, reyhdrated, or good cherry jam**
½ cup (125 mL)	**port, chilled**

Mix the duck and pork with the rosemary, ginger, garlic, salt, pepper, orange zest and hot chili flakes. Chill for at least 2 hours.

Melt the butter over medium heat and sauté the onion until tender and golden. Cool. Sliver the cherries. Add the onion and cherries to the meat mixture and mix thoroughly. Chill for at least 2 hours. Add the port and small amounts of ice water, mix well, and check to see if the mix is sticky. (It should be.) Stuff casings (see The Art of Sausage-Making, page 163) or shape into patties. Grill, broil, poach or sauté, and serve.

MAKES ABOUT 36 SAUSAGES

Spanish Chicken Sausage

Flamenco, mariachi bands, sunny days, long languorous evenings. Olé! This is a mild mix; jazz it up by adding the additional spices listed in the variation. Check out the new Tempranillo/Cabernet blends coming out of Spain.

2 lbs. (1 kg)	**boneless chicken meat (leg and breast), ground**
1	**orange, juice and zest**
2 Tbsp. (25 mL)	**minced sun-dried tomato**
¼ tsp. (1 mL)	**saffron**
2 Tbsp. (25 mL)	**minced fresh basil**
2 Tbsp. (25 mL)	**minced fresh oregano**
1 Tbsp. (15 mL)	**puréed garlic**
½ tsp. (2 mL)	**cracked fennel seed**
2 Tbsp. (25 mL)	**quince paste (optional)**
~	**kosher salt and hot chili flakes to taste**

Mix the chicken with the orange juice and zest, sun-dried tomato, saffron, basil, oregano, garlic, fennel and quince paste, if desired. Stir in enough cold water to make a sticky mixture, then chill for at least 2 hours. Form into patties or links (see The Art of Sausage-Making, page 163). Cook and serve.

MAKES ABOUT 24 SAUSAGES

VARIATION:

For spicier, chorizo-style flavour, add the following ingredients to the mix:

1 lb. (500 g)	**ground pork**
1 tsp. (5 mL)	**hot chili flakes**
1 tsp. (5 mL)	**Spanish chili powder**
½ tsp. (2 mL)	**smoked Spanish chili powder**
3–6 Tbsp. (45–90 mL)	**coarsely cracked black pepper**
1 tsp. (5 mL)	**sweet Hungarian paprika**
½ cup (125 mL)	**dark ale, chilled**
2 Tbsp. (25 mL)	**minced fresh mint**

North African Lamb Sausage

This subtle, spicy combination of East and West goes well with Summer Couscous, Winter Bulgur (page 125), Oregano and Lemon Potatoes (page 80) or Wilted Spinach with Shallots, Garlic and Pancetta (page 89). South Africa is producing some fabulous Syrahs, full-bodied and spicy. Pour one.

2 Tbsp. (25 mL)	olive oil
6–8 cloves	garlic, minced
2 Tbsp. (25 mL)	grated fresh ginger
1	onion, minced
½	red bell pepper, finely diced
3 lbs. (1.5 kg)	lamb shoulder or chicken legs, finely ground
4 Tbsp. (50 mL)	Ras El Hanout (see page 28) or curry powder
⅓ cup (75 mL)	dried apricots, slivered
½ cup (125 mL)	white wine, chilled
1	orange, zest only
~	kosher salt and freshly ground black pepper to taste
2 Tbsp. (25 mL)	minced cilantro

Heat the oil and sauté the garlic, ginger, onion and bell pepper over medium heat until tender. Cool. Stir in the meat, spice blend, apricots, wine and orange zest to make a sticky mixture. Season with salt and pepper, then add the cilantro. Chill for at least 2 hours. Form into patties or links (see The Art of Sausage-Making, page 163). Cook and serve.

MAKES ABOUT 45 SAUSAGES

Laureen's Italian Links

Fennel seed, coriander and garlic are key in Italian sausage. Make them "sweet" (i.e., not spicy) or hot, as you like. This recipe is from Laureen Wood, one of my favourite butchers. Italy's Piedmont region is renowned for its well-made inexpensive red wines; try an earthy Dolcetto d'Alba.

2 lbs. (1 kg)	**pork shoulder, ground**
2 Tbsp. (25 mL)	**puréed fresh garlic**
2 Tbsp. (25 mL)	**freshly cracked black or white pepper**
1	**orange, zest only**
1	**lemon, zest only**
¼ cup (50 mL)	**ice water**
1 Tbsp. (15 mL)	**cracked or ground fennel**
1 tsp. (5 mL)	**whole fennel seed**
~	**hot chili flakes to taste**
~	**kosher salt to taste**
1 tsp. (5 mL)	**cayenne**
2 tsp. (10 mL)	**coriander seed**
2 tsp. (10 mL)	**sweet Spanish or Hungarian paprika**
~	**pinch of sugar**
4 Tbsp. (50 mL)	**minced roasted red pepper**
1 tsp. (5 mL)	**minced fresh rosemary**
1 Tbsp. (15 mL)	**minced fresh thyme**

Combine the pork with the garlic, pepper and orange and lemon zest. Mix well, then stir in the ice water to make a sticky mixture. Add all the remaining ingredients. Chill for at least 2 hours. Form into patties or links (see The Art of Sausage-Making, page 163). Cook and serve.

MAKES ABOUT 24 LINKS

Venison Chorizo

If you have a hunter in your clan, you'll need some way to use up the bits and pieces after the carcass is butchered. Sausage is the perfect answer. If you don't have a hunter, substitute bison, lamb, or beef. Venison is extremely lean; add ground pork shoulder and either bacon or pork fat to restore some moisture to the mix. If you find the venison flavour too strong, increase the ratio of ground pork shoulder to venison. Your butcher will need provenance when you take the meat in for grinding. Take along your tag and license. This sausage screams for an earthy red from the Côtes du Rhône.

¾ lb. (375 g)	**smoked bacon, ground or finely chopped**
1 ¼ lbs. (625 g)	**ground pork shoulder**
4 lbs. (2 kg)	**medium-ground venison**
2	**blood oranges, juice and zest**
1 Tbsp. (15 mL)	**Hungarian sweet paprika**
2 tsp. (10 mL)	**smoked Spanish paprika**
3 oz. (90 mL)	**cognac**
1 ½ heads	**garlic, minced**
4 Tbsp. (50 mL)	**cracked black peppercorns**
1 tsp. (5 mL)	**hot chili flakes**
2 tsp. (10 mL)	**Chimayo chili powder**
¾ cup (175 mL)	**ice water**
3–4 Tbsp. (45–50 mL)	**kosher salt**

Combine all ingredients except the water and salt. Mix well. Stir in enough water to make the mixture sticky. Mix in the salt. Chill for at least 2 hours. Form into patties or links (see The Art of Sausage-Making, page 163). Cook and serve.

MAKES ABOUT 50 LINKS

Friday Fish

Ethics in the Kitchen

Making decisions about what to eat is more complicated than simply choosing what we like and avoiding foods that are bad for us. We live in a shrinking world — a beach in Bali is a mere day's flight away — but the surviving number of plant and animal species is shrinking too. Among the more glaring depletions are the ocean dwellers. Any Newfoundlander who has left Saint John's can describe in graphic detail the decline in Newfoundland since the cod disappeared from the Grand Banks.

In today's market-driven world, food is viewed as a commodity rather than as somebody's dinner. The ramifications of this are vast — including decimating fish populations, spraying poisonous chemicals on crops, monocropping and genetically engineering food so it can be shipped all over the globe. Where is "real" food in the midst of all this?

The issue of farmed versus wild fish is more tangled. Farmed fish have been blamed for environmental pollution and habitat destruction, and for the risk posed to native wild populations if the farmed fish escape. But many shellfish species — including clams, oysters and mussels — and some fish species, like tilapia, have been successfully farmed with minimal environmental damage.

Many New Age health practitioners believe an increase in disease — and the premature hormonal growth of young children — is related directly to the hormones, steroids, antibiotics and other "additives" that are fed to commercially raised animals. It always remains the consumer's choice. But if we do not make our wishes known by our shopping habits, food producers will be deprived of information — and ultimately, choices too — on what we want to buy and feed ourselves. And we won't get the quality we deserve.

ODD LOBSTER SIZES

Lobsters are called odd names to indicate their weights. Big ones over 2 lbs. (1 kg) are called "jumbos"; small ones under ¾ lb. (375 g) are called "canners." In between, there are "chickens" (about 1 lb./ 500 g) and "quarters" (about 1 ¼ – 1 ½ lb./ 625–750 g) The bigger they are, the older and tougher they are, and the longer they take to cook. They pinch harder too.

Activists say, "Think globally, act locally." Cooks can adopt the same approach to make a difference in our own corner of our shrinking world. It may sound like a small step to take, but ultimately, small actions by small committed groups are the best agent for change, according to anthropologist Margaret Mead. Put your money where your mouth is, and support local, seasonally harvested, sustainably raised food. A bit of knowledge might be dangerous, but none at all can ruin your dinner.

Oysters *au naturel with* Roasted Garlic *and* Thyme Drizzle

Choose a variety of oyster that you are partial to. I like Hama Hamas or Olympias from B.C., Washington and Oregon; Malpeques from P.E.I.; Tatamagouches, Capes or Blue Points from Atlantic Canada and the northeastern U.S. If you want to have your oysters hot and really gussied-up, make Better than Béarnaise Sauce (page 45), shuck the oysters, then broil them on the half shell topped with a spoonful of sauce. If you like them as Mother Nature made them, try this! Use your very best extra virgin olive oil. Serve Champagne. Life is good.

12	oysters in the shell
1 Tbsp. (15 mL)	Cognac
2 Tbsp. (25 mL)	berry vinegar
⅓ cup (75 mL)	extra virgin olive oil
3 Tbsp. (45 mL)	roasted garlic
1 Tbsp. (15 mL)	melted honey
1 tsp. (5 mL)	minced fresh thyme
1 tsp. (5 mL)	minced fresh chives
~	freshly cracked black pepper to taste
~	lemon juice to taste
~	kosher salt to taste

Shuck the oysters: leave them in the deep lower half of the shell but sever the muscle holding them attached. Combine the remaining ingredients, whisking well to incorporate the garlic. Drizzle over the oysters. Bottoms up.

SERVES 2—4

BERRY VINEGAR

It is easy to make your own berry vinegar. Fill a quart (1-liter) jar with fresh raspberries, blueberries or blackberries. Cover the berries with white wine vinegar. Cover snugly and put the jar away for at least a month to steep. Strain the finished vinegar through a fine mesh sieve; do not apply any pressure to the solids as you strain or the vinegar will be clouded by berry bits. Discard the berry solids and store the vinegar in clean bottles or jars. Use corks or plastic lids to avoid corrosion by the vinegar.

Summer Salad *with* New Potatoes *and* Beans (and Lobster!)

I arrived home one day to unexpectedly find a pair of coolers on my front porch. Each was jammed full of lobsters. In the face of such largesse from my friend Holly, I made a celebration salad filled with lobster. On days when the fridge's contents are a little sparser, substitute cooked monkfish, shrimp, leftover grilled halibut or poached sablefish. Serve this al fresco with a robust Viognier or buttery Chardonnay.

I arrived home one day to unexpectedly find a pair of coolers on my front porch. Each was jammed full of lobsters. In the face of such largesse from my friend Holly, I made a celebration salad filled with lobster. On days when the fridge's contents are a little sparser, substitute cooked monkfish, shrimp, leftover grilled halibut or poached sablefish. Serve this al fresco with a robust Viognier or buttery Chardonnay.

5	canner lobsters, cooked
2 lbs. (1 kg)	new Bintje potatoes
½ lb. (250 g)	green or yellow beans
4 ears	corn, cooked
¼ cup (50 mL)	finely minced red onion
4 Tbsp. (50 mL)	minced chives
1 Tbsp. (15 mL)	minced fresh lemon thyme or thyme
1 Tbsp. (15 mL)	minced fresh oregano
2 Tbsp. (25 mL)	orange-infused olive oil
4 Tbsp. (50 mL)	best-quality extra virgin olive oil
2 Tbsp. (25 mL)	Vanilla Vinegar (see page 20)
2 Tbsp. (25 mL)	Japanese rice vinegar
~	kosher salt and freshly cracked black pepper to taste
~	Caramelized Pecans (see page 41) for garnish
~	chive stalks and blossoms for garnish (optional)

Crack and shell the lobsters. Freeze the shells to make bisque (page 68) on another day. Chop the lobster meat into bite-size bits. Cut the potatoes into halves or quarters and cook in salted water until tender. Drain and keep warm.

Tip and tail the beans (or not!) and steam them until just tender. Drain and refresh with cold water to set the colour and stop the cooking process. Strip the corn kernels from the ears of corn.

Combine the shellfish and vegetables with the herbs, oils and vinegars. Season with salt and pepper. Toss gently. Arrange on plates. Garnish with a sprinkle of pecans and fresh chives, if desired.

SERVES 6–8

COOKING CRUSTACEANS

It is always easiest to ask the fishmonger to kill and cook lobster and crab. I have only accomplished the act once, and that was when my cooking school class mark was riding on the outcome. Little is as terrifying as tossing a kicking crustacean into a potful of boiling water. If you are up to murder in the kitchen, first read Alice B. Toklas for moral support, then put on a large potful of water to boil. Grasp the lobster from behind and immerse it in the water headfirst. Clap on a lid, don't wince, and immediately drink a large glass of restorative brandy or cognac. I find that sitting down promptly helps too. It is much easier to find a willing accomplice to do the deed.

Lobster for John A.

It is not every day that anyone has leftover lobster languishing in the fridge. But for those rare occasions when you do, here is a delicious way to stretch it out. Mango and lobster are one of the few happy marriages of seafood and fruit; you could use cooked crab, shrimp or salmon if some fridge raider gets to the lobster before you. Ripe papaya and halved grapes make good stand-ins for the mango. Coconut Rice (page 124) is nice. Viognier or an unoaked Chardonnay are good matches for both the tropical fruit and the rich lobster.

1 Tbsp. (15 mL)	unsalted butter
½	sweet onion, diced
2 Tbsp. (25 mL)	grated fresh ginger
1	zucchini, diced
1–2 tsp. (5–10 mL)	curry powder
¼ cup (50 mL)	dry white wine
1	lemon, juice and zest
2 Tbsp. (25 mL)	whipping cream
1 lb. (500 g)	cooked lobster tail, sliced
3	green onions, minced
1	ripe mango, peeled and diced
~	kosher salt and freshly cracked black pepper to taste
~	roasted peanuts for garnish

Melt the butter in a sauté pan. Add the onion and ginger and cook over medium heat until the onion is tender, about 5–7 minutes. Add the zucchini and curry powder and stir well, cooking for several more minutes. Add the wine and lemon juice and zest and bring to a boil. Stir in the cream and lobster. Heat thoroughly, adding a little cream or water if the pan gets too dry before the lobster is reheated. Stir in the green onions and mango, then adjust the seasoning with salt and pepper. Garnish with roasted peanuts.

SERVES 4

EAST COAST STYLE

I had a sous-chef named John A. MacDonald at my restaurant. No joke, although he took hundreds of them over his parents' patriotic naming. John A. was a Cape Breton boy, and he loved telling stories about life "back home." One of the stories that amazed me involved him trading away lobster sandwiches for peanut butter and jelly. It was beyond my comprehension until he explained that to him and many other East Coasters, lobster was a food of last resort, to be eaten when there really was nothing else. Peanut butter was a step up. This one, John A., is for you.

Mussels *in* Provençal Steam

Mussels are a mild and tender bivalve, less robust in flavour and texture than clams. Keep the flavours subtle so the mussels are not overwhelmed. Curry fanatics can always add a bit of curry powder or garam masala to the onion. Serve this simply alone with good bread to mop up the juices, or on rice, pasta tossed in olive oil or couscous. Muscadet or French Chablis with their mineral character and clean simplicity would be fabulous!

1 Tbsp. (15 mL)	olive oil
½	onion, minced
½ cup (125 mL)	minced fresh fennel
4 cloves	garlic, minced
¼ cup (50 mL)	dry white wine
½ tsp. (2 mL)	cracked fennel seeds
~	pinch of saffron
½ tsp. (2 mL)	dried basil
½ cup (125 mL)	diced fresh tomatoes
1 Tbsp. (15 mL)	honey
½	lemon, juice only
~	kosher salt and hot chili flakes to taste
2 lbs. (1 kg)	mussels
1 Tbsp. (15 mL)	minced parsley
1 Tbsp. (15 mL)	basil chiffonade

Heat the oil in a large heavy pot. Add the onion, fennel and garlic. Cook over medium heat for 5 minutes until tender. Add the wine, fennel seeds, saffron and basil. Simmer for a few minutes, then add the tomatoes. Bring to a simmer and cook until the tomatoes are as soft as you like them. Stir in the honey, lemon juice, salt and hot chili flakes. Bring to a rapid boil and add the mussels. Cover and cook for about 3 minutes without peeking. Remove the lid to check — the shells should be just cracked open, no more than ½ inch (1 cm). Serve immediately with parsley and basil sprinkled over.

SERVES 2 as a main course, or 4 as a starter

GETTING YOUR CLAMS' WORTH

Buy and cook these perishable creatures all in one day, but if you have to store them, the safest way to ensure their survival is to tear several holes in the bag before you bring them home. At home, transfer them to a colander or sieve. Suspend that over a large bowl, cover the fish with a damp cloth and add ice on top of that. Wash clams and mussels just before you plan on cooking them; they will die if they are washed too early and molluscs must be alive at the time of cooking. If the shell is closed tightly, the mollusc is living. If it is open, rap it smartly on the counter, wait to see if it closes, then toss it into the garbage if it doesn't. Once cooked, only eat molluscs with open shells.

Grilled Halibut
with Triple Citrus Salsa

The dense, meaty texture of halibut is best served by grilling, and it is enhanced by this simple seasonal salad. Use a mixture of blood oranges, grapefruit, oranges, tangerines and tangelos. For an herbal note, use a high-quality oil infused with herbs. Serve a fruity New Zealand Sauvignon Blanc.

Salsa:

4–5	mixed citrus fruits, peeled and segmented (see Cut to the Quick, page 193)
2 Tbsp. (25 mL)	fresh ginger sliced into matchsticks
1–2 Tbsp. (15–25 mL)	herb-infused olive or avocado oil
~	kosher salt and hot chili flakes to taste
1–2 Tbsp. (15–25 mL)	citrus juice

Combine all the ingredients for the salsa. Stir gently and store in the fridge until needed.

Fish:

4 5-oz. (4 150-g)	halibut steaks
1 Tbsp. (15 mL)	grated fresh ginger
½	lemon, zest only
~	hot chili flakes to taste
2 Tbsp. (25 mL)	olive oil
1 Tbsp. (15 mL)	minced fresh thyme or chives

Preheat the grill to medium-high. Sprinkle the fish with the ginger, lemon zest, hot chili flakes, oil and herbs. Place the fish on the grill and cook until just done, about 7 minutes per inch (2.5 cm), turning once. Serve with the salsa.

SERVES 4

Summertime Pan Bagnat

The best versions of these are to be had on the streets of the Left Bank in Paris or anywhere on the French Riviera. The prime requirements are juicy ripe tomatoes, great buns and a generous hand with olive oil. The rest is mostly improvisation: those with a yen for spice may layer in some hot pickled pepper rings, and those who love fish may add some good oil-packed tuna. If you have a taste for slightly bitter greens, spoon in some Arugula Pesto (page 27). The end result should be soft, ideally left to sit awhile so crust and filling meld into juicy oneness, and should involve at least 2 large napkins when consumption begins. Try a simple white or rosé from the south of France.

1	fresh crusty white bun
2–4 Tbsp. (25–50 mL)	extra virgin olive oil
1	ripe tomato, sliced
½ cup (125 mL)	oil-packed tuna
6–8 slices	Long English cucumber
2–3 strips	roasted red bell pepper
1	hard-boiled egg, sliced
2–3 fillets	anchovy
6–8	pitted Kalamata or Sicilian olives
4–5 slices	pickled hot pepper
~	kosher salt and freshly cracked black pepper

Slice the bun open horizontally. Drizzle the insides of both top and bottom with olive oil, then layer in the remaining ingredients, adding salt, more olive oil and pepper as you proceed. Let the assembled pan bagnat sit awhile before gingerly slicing it in half.

SERVES 1 greedy luncher who is unwilling to share or 2 more generous souls

Salmon *and* Fennel Pasta Sauce

Ideal for using leftovers — perhaps that pair of grilled salmon steaks or fillets from last night's dinner — this is a happy marriage of flavours. Serve hot over pasta or short-grain rice. Choose a cool Vernacchia or a lighter Sangiovese for this simple fare.

1 lb. (500 g)	**cooked salmon**
1 Tbsp. (15 mL)	**unsalted butter**
1	**fennel bulb**
1	**Belgian endive**
1 tsp. (5 mL)	**minced fresh thyme**
¼ cup (50 mL)	**dry white wine**
½ cup (125 mL)	**green Sicilian or Calabrese olives, sliced**
½ cup (125 mL)	**whipping cream**
1	**lemon, zest and juice**
~	**kosher salt and freshly cracked black pepper to taste**

Remove the salmon skin and break the fish into bite-size pieces. Set aside.

Heat the butter in a sauté pan. Trim off the stalks and tough outer layer of the fennel. Quarter the bulb and remove the core. Finely slice or dice the fennel. Toss it into the pan with the butter and sauté over medium-high heat until tender, stirring now and then.

Trim off the root of the endive. Pull the leaves apart and finely slice them lengthwise. Add the endive to the pan when the fennel is tender. Stir well and cook another minute or two until the endive wilts. Add the thyme and wine. Bring to a boil, then add the salmon pieces, olives, and cream. Boil a minute or two until everything is hot and the cream begins to thicken. Add the lemon zest, then stir in the lemon juice and season with salt and pepper.

SERVES 4

Salmon *with* Red Pepper Sauce

Some flavours are made for each other. Serve this happy partnership with grilled peppers dressed in balsamic vinaigrette and lightly dressed noodles or new potatoes. Pour an Oregon Pinot Noir.

Sauce:

1 lb. (500 g)	**red bell peppers**
¼ cup (125 mL)	**olive oil**
1	**onion, diced**
3 cloves	**garlic, minced**
3	**Roma tomatoes, peeled, seeded and diced**
~	**kosher salt and freshly ground black pepper to taste**
¾ cup (175 mL)	**whipping cream (optional)**
2 Tbsp. (25 mL)	**minced lemon thyme**
1	**lemon, zest and juice**

Grill the peppers directly on the flame of your gas range, on the grill or under the broiler until the skins are blackened on all sides. Put the peppers in a plastic bag for 5 minutes. Peel off the blackened skin and remove the seeds and membranes. Dice the peppers and set aside.

Heat the oil in a sauté pan. Add the onion and garlic and cook over medium heat until tender, about 5 minutes, without allowing the vegetables to colour. Add the tomatoes, salt, pepper and half the cream, if using. Cook until the tomatoes soften, about 15 minutes. Purée in a food processor or blender, then add the remaining cream, lemon thyme, lemon zest and juice. Stir in the roasted pepper dice. Set aside and keep warm.

Fish:

4 6-oz. fillets (4 175-g fillets)	**fresh salmon**
2 Tbsp. (25 mL)	**minced lemon thyme**
1 Tbsp. (15 mL)	**olive oil**
~	**freshly cracked black pepper to taste**

Preheat the grill to medium-high. Sprinkle the salmon fillets with thyme, oil and pepper. Grill until just cooked through, about 8 minutes per inch (2.5 cm) of thickness. Serve hot with sauce.

SERVES 4

Pan-Steamed Salmon *with* Tamarind Chutney

Pan-steaming is painless, fuss-free and so simple that even a linear thinker can do something else while the fish gently cares for itself under a lid. If time allows, sprinkle a bit of fresh minced herbs or some ground spices onto the salmon before you cook it. Purchase some German Gewürztraminer or Riesling for this dish.

4 6-oz. fillets (4 175-g fillets)	**fresh salmon**
½	**lemon, zest and juice**
1 Tbsp. (15 mL)	**minced fresh thyme or cilantro**
1 tsp. (5 mL)	**grated fresh ginger**
½ tsp. (2 mL)	**ground star anise**
~	**freshly ground black pepper to taste**
1 Tbsp. (15 mL)	**olive oil**
~	**kosher salt to taste**
½ cup (125 mL)	**tamarind chutney**

Remove any pin bones from the fish with needle-nose pliers or tweezers. Sprinkle the lemon zest, thyme or cilantro, ginger, star anise and pepper on the fish. Pour the oil into a small non-stick pan and place the fish in the pan without preheating it. Cover the fish with a lid that is too small and sits directly on top of the fish. Put the pan on the stove and cook the fish on low heat, turning several times.

When the fish is done, about 10 minutes, remove from the pan. Pour the chutney into the pan, bring briefly to a boil, and pour over the fish. Squeeze on the lemon juice and serve promptly.

SERVES 4

Poached Sole
and Salmon *in* Carrot Jus

The clean flavours and pretty colour contrast of this dish make it an ideal meal for a party. Cook this on top of the stove in a shallow pan, or on a baking sheet covered with parchment paper in the oven. Depending on your preference, you can purée the sole and stuff the salmon, or purée the salmon and stuff the sole. If the carrot juice is too sweet, tart it up with a drizzle of additional lime juice. Use caution when adding the cream to the puréed fish to avoid a curdled texture. Open a Pinot Gris from Alsace.

1 lb. (500 g)	**sole fillets**
2 Tbsp. (25 mL)	**minced fresh tarragon**
2	**limes, juice and zest**
½ cup (125 mL)	**whipping cream, or more to taste**
~	**kosher salt and freshly cracked black pepper to taste**
2 lbs. (1 kg)	**fresh salmon, in one large fillet**
¼ cup (50 mL)	**white wine**
1 cup (250 mL)	**fresh carrot juice**
1	**shallot, finely minced**
½ tsp. (2 mL)	**fennel seed, cracked**
1 Tbsp. (15 mL)	**grated fresh ginger**

Purée the sole in a food processor, then pulse in half the tarragon, half the lime juice and zest, and half the cream. Season with salt and pepper.

Check the salmon for pin bones, removing any with a pair of needle-nose pliers or tweezers. Slice the salmon into thin angle-cut pieces no more than ½ inch (1 cm) thick. Lay the pieces out flat. Pipe or spoon the sole mousse onto the salmon. Fold or roll each salmon piece and its filling into a fat package.

Heat the wine in a shallow pan. Add the juice, shallot, fennel seed and ginger. Bring to a boil. Add the filled salmon. Season with salt and pepper. Cover with a piece of parchment paper, then with a snug lid. Reduce the heat and cook over a low flame or in a gentle oven (300°F/150°C) until the fish is just cooked through, about 20 minutes. The cooking time will depend on the thickness of the fish. To check, remove one fillet and slice it open. The fish and mousse should be opaque and gently firm to the touch.

Remove the fish to a plate, cover and keep warm. Cook the poaching liquid until it is reduced by half. Season to taste with the remaining lime juice and zest, salt, pepper and cream. Garnish each serving with a dollop of sauce and a sprinkle of the remaining fresh tarragon.

SERVES 4—6

The Simplicity of Pan-Steaming

I learned this unfussy technique nearly 20 years ago in the French kitchen of Madeleine Kamman, a renowned chef and educator. It has served me well for years; I have used it on chicken breasts, thinly sliced turkey breast and fish that will withstand being turned several times — salmon, tilapia, char, trout, halibut, orange roughy, even snapper can be pan-steamed if handled carefully.

- Use a non-stick or well-seasoned sauté pan.

- Find a lid that is too small for the pan, but will sit directly on the food being cooked.

- Without preheating, add a small amount of oil to the pan.

- Immediately add the pieces of food to be cooked.

- Fill the pan: snug the pieces close to each other and cover with the lid.

- Turn the pan on to medium-low.

- Turn the food every few minutes; the low temperature will not carry through to the top surfaces. There should be no sizzling or browning, just about 7 gentle and calm minutes to produce juicy, tender chicken, fish or meat.

- Because of the low cooking temperature, it is possible to dredge the uncooked food in minced fresh herbs for added flavour and colour.

Hot-Smoked Trout Crab Cakes
with Apple Cider-Thyme Dressing

This remake of a classic leaves no room for fakery or foolish stinginess. Avoid pollock or any other not-the-real-thing. Be a purist: Dungeness crab in big chunks is best. If you cannot find crab boil spice blend, the ingredients that make up pickling spice are a very close substitute. This calls for a Germanic wine — perhaps a Riesling.

Cakes:

2 Tbsp. (25 mL)	**olive oil**
1 cup (250 mL)	**minced green onion**
¼ cup (50 mL)	**minced red bell pepper**
1 Tbsp. (15 mL)	**minced garlic**
2–3 Tbsp. (25-45 mL)	**crab boil spice blend, ground**
2	**eggs**
1 Tbsp. (15 mL)	**grainy mustard**
¼ cup (50 mL)	**bread crumbs**
½ cup (125 mL)	**grated Parmesan cheese**
1 lb. (500 g)	**crab meat, cooked**
1 lb. (500 g)	**Hot-Smoked Trout, (see page 190) broken into pieces**

Make the cakes first. Heat the oil and sauté the onion, red pepper and garlic over medium heat until tender but not browned. Transfer to a bowl, add the remaining ingredients and gently mix with your hands. Form into small patties.

Crumb crust:

2	**eggs, mixed with a little water**
½ cup (125 mL)	**all-purpose flour**
1 tsp. (5 mL)	**crab boil spice blend, ground**
1 cup (250 mL)	**panko or other fine bread crumbs**

Whisk the egg and water together in a bowl or flat tray with sides. Season the flour with salt and pepper and place on a tray or baking sheet. Put the crumbs on another tray or baking sheet. To bread the patties, dip them in the flour, then immerse them in the egg wash, then roll them in the crumbs. Chill the patties on a parchment-lined tray in a single layer.

To cook the cakes, heat a sauté pan with enough oil to lubricate the surface. Sauté the cakes, turning once. Serve with the dressing.

Dressing:

2 12-oz. bottles (2 341-mL bottles)	**hard apple cider**
1 Tbsp. (15 mL)	**minced chives**
1 Tbsp. (15 mL)	**chopped thyme or lemon thyme**
1 Tbsp. (15 mL)	**chopped parsley**
1 Tbsp. (15 mL)	**grated fresh ginger**
1	**lemon, juice and zest**
1 tsp. (5 mL)	**minced fresh thyme**
¾ cup (175 mL)	**olive oil**
~	**melted honey to taste**
~	**kosher salt and freshly ground black pepper to taste**

To make the dressing, pour the cider into a small shallow pan and boil until it is reduced to about ¼ cup (50 mL). Cool. Bring a small pot of water to a boil, add the herbs and leave them in the water for 10 seconds. Drain the herbs into a sieve, discarding the water, and immediately chill the herbs under cold running water. Pour the cooled cider into a blender, add all the remaining ingredients, and blend to purée. Adjust the seasoning — the amount of honey you add will depend on the acidity of the cider.

MAKES ABOUT 24 CAKES

THE FINE ART OF BREADING

Don't kid yourself — we're all in it for the crunch. Dipping fragile foods into a succession of flour, egg and crumbs adds a protective coating and is crisp and delicious when sautéed. Minimize mess by tossing robust food in a plastic bag of seasoned flour, shaking off all extra flour. Tender patties must be hand-dipped and gently rolled in the flour to minimize breakage. To avoid breading your fingers, use separate hands or tongs for the next stages — one hand for dipping each patty into beaten egg, and another for rolling in the crumb collection. If the food is not completely encased in crumbs, return it to the egg wash for a second dip, then re-roll in crumbs. Make sure your pan and cooking oil are hot, and that your food as it awaits breading is not stone-cold.

Hot-Smoked Trout

Smoking your own fish is more simple than it might seem. Carry your wok outside and use the grill as your heat source if your smoke detector is too efficient or your venting insufficient — or opt for the drama and risk of smoking indoors in a wok. (Hint: find the short-term "muffle" button on your smoke detector beforehand.) Choose a mild tea as a smoking agent for trout — I like experimenting with some of the green Japanese varieties, but I usually fall back on Russian Caravan. Fans of big smoke may prefer to use Lapsang Souchong.

2 Tbsp. (25 mL)	**minced fresh rosemary**
4 cloves	**garlic, minced**
1 tsp. (5 mL)	**fennel seed, cracked**
1	**orange, zest only**
2 Tbsp. (25 mL)	**white peppercorns, cracked**
2 Tbsp. (25 mL)	**olive oil**
2 lbs. (1 kg)	**trout fillets**
¼ cup (50 mL)	**sugar**
¼ cup (50 mL)	**loose black tea**
¼ cup (50 mL)	**raw white rice**

Blend the rosemary, garlic, fennel seed, orange zest, peppercorns and olive oil in a mortar and pestle or small bowl. Smear the mixture over the trout, covering all the flesh. Let stand while you ready the smoking apparatus.

To smoke the trout in a wok, line the bottom of a wok with a piece of foil about 6 inches (15 cm) square. Place the sugar, tea and rice on the foil and mix it around. Place a wire rack in the wok, and position it so that it does not touch the tea mixture. Gently lay the herbed fish on the rack in a single layer. Put the lid on, then dampen and roll up 2 kitchen towels. Lay the rolled towels in the crack between the lid and the wok, being sure to cover the gap all the way around.

Put the wok on its ring onto high heat and cook, covered, until the fish is just done, about 20 minutes. (You can turn off the heat and remove the rolled towels and lid to check whether it is done without compromising the smoking.) Once the fish is cool enough to handle, remove the skin and gently break the flesh into chunks.

If you are using an outdoor barbecue, place a shallow pan (an old battered one you don't care about is best) on top of the baffles that sit above the heat source. Add the sugar, tea and rice. Mix well. Heat the grill to medium, close the lid and wait for smoke, about 5–10 minutes. Place the fish on the grill and cook until just done, turning once if you wish.

Classic Sautéed Mountain Trout

Simplicity itself, this is the tried-and-true way to deal with fresh fish. If your offspring are budding fishers, make sure they learn how to clean their catch. That's the job of the fisher. Fresh fish does not need much help — let it taste of itself. This always tastes best cooked beside the water it was caught in, but that is not always possible. Pick a white wine with lots of fruit and a dry finish. Choices include Bordeaux, German or Alsatian Pinot Gris.

2–4	**whole fresh trout, cleaned**
4 Tbsp. (50 mL)	**melted unsalted butter**
1	**lemon, juice only**
~	**kosher salt and freshly ground black pepper to taste**
2 Tbsp. (25 mL)	**toasted chopped nuts (optional)**
~	**minced chives or fresh thyme, for garnish**

Slit the trout lengthwise along the belly and carefully slice out the backbone and attached bones, breaking the backbone free of the tail. (Small fish served on the bone are difficult to eat.) Leave the head on, or not. (Off is easier to cook.) You should end up with 2 attached fillets, skin on, that butterfly open to lie flat for fast grilling.

Heat the pan and add half the butter. When it is foaming, add the fish and cook it flesh side down. This fish is usually so thin that you needn't turn it, but watch closely, because it will cook quickly. Remove to plates, drizzle with the remaining melted butter, squeeze on the lemon juice and sprinkle with salt and pepper. Garnish with chopped nuts, if you like, and sprinkle with herbs.

SERVES 4

Poached Fresh Sablefish
with Champagne *and*
Ginger Beurre Blanc

As kids, we ate the smoked version, known then as smoked black cod. I still love its rich, buttery flavour and texture. If you do find smoked sablefish, add milk to the poaching liquid to draw out any excess salt. Fish this wonderful needs very little fussing with. A classic beurre blanc, quickly made with Champagne and spiked with ginger, is the perfect foil. To simplify, oven-roast this succulent fish and serve it with boiled new potatoes and green beans tossed in butter. Drink the rest of the Champagne and enjoy!

Fish and poaching liquid:

¼ cup (50 mL)	**Champagne**
2 cups (500 mL)	**water**
~	**several sprigs fresh thyme**
1	**bay leaf**
½ tsp. (2 mL)	**whole black peppercorns**
6–8 sprigs	**parsley stalks**
2–3 cloves	**garlic, peeled and smashed**
4 6-oz. slices (6 175-g slices)	**fresh sablefish**

Bring the wine, water, thyme, bay leaf, peppercorns, parsley stalks and garlic to a boil. Simmer for 10–15 minutes, then strain and discard the solids. Return the liquid to the pan, reduce the heat and add the fish. Cover. Poach the fish until just cooked through, about 10–15 minutes. Keep the fish in the poaching liquid until the sauce is made.

Beurre blanc:

1	**shallot, minced**
½ tsp. (2 mL)	**ground anise seed**
¼ tsp. (1 mL)	**whole anise seed**
1 Tbsp. (15 mL)	**grated fresh ginger**
1 cup (250 mL)	**Champagne**
1	**tangerine, zest only**

⅓ **cup** (75 mL)	**rice vinegar**
½ **cup** (125 mL)	**unsalted butter, cubed**
~	**cayenne to taste**
1–2 **Tbsp.** (15–25 mL)	**whipping cream**
2	**tangerines, peeled and segmented**
	(See Cut to the Quick, below)

Combine the shallot, ground and whole anise, ginger, wine, tangerine zest and vinegar. Bring to a boil and simmer until reduced by ⅔ to a syrup. Slowly add the butter, a cube at a time, whisking constantly over low heat. Stir in the cayenne and cream. Keep warm. Add the tangerine segments just before serving.

Spoon some sauce onto each of 4 warm dinner plates. Place the fish on top and serve immediately. Pass the extra sauce separately.

SERVES 4

Cut to the Quick

Oranges and other citrus fruits look prettiest when they are peeled with a knife and filleted so that no pith, the white layer under the zest, is visible. Use a cook's knife, not a paring knife, and work over a bowl to catch any juice. Cut off the top and bottom of the orange so that you can see the flesh, and set the orange on its newly created flat side on the cutting board. Use your knife to cut vertical strips of peel from the orange, cutting deeply enough to remove peel and pith. Each successive cut should begin where the previous cut ended. When you have a naked orange, hold the orange, segments horizontally positioned, in your hand; use your knife to cut a segment free of its membranes. Cut the next segment free on the edge closest to you, scraping the knife away from you so the segment is peeled from its membrane. When all the fillets have fallen away from the membrane, squeeze any remaining juices from both the membrane and the peelings into the bowl.

Potato *and* Cod Brandade *with* Olive *and* Fennel Salad

In the south of France and the north of Spain, where Basque regions overlap, there are no flavour borders. I ate this in the Languedoc, but could just as easily have had it across the border in Spain. In this amazing and complex salad, the cod contrasts with the brightly flavoured fennel salad and the pungent bite of olives. Use the olive paste on burgers, in sandwiches, on pizza, or on crackers. The confit of cod alone is good stuffed into peppers, layered in omelets, or made into cod cakes, best garnished with Olive Aïoli (page 142). Equally amazing would be a slightly chilled white from the Côteaux du Languedoc or an Alvarinho from Spain.

Confit:

2 lbs. (1 kg)	**salt cod**
4–6 cloves	**garlic**
1–2 cups (250–500 mL)	**olive oil**

To make the confit, soak the cod in enough cold water to cover. Drain after 2 hours and replace the water. Repeat 4–6 times, for 1 day, until the cod softens. Combine the garlic, oil and cod and simmer, uncovered until tender, about 20–30 minutes. Remove the fish and garlic from the pan. Break the fish into pieces. Purée the fish and garlic in a food processor with 2–3 Tbsp. (25–45 mL) oil from the pan.

Brandade:

3 cups (720mL)	**Olive Oil Mashed Potatoes (see page 80)**
~	**lemon juice to taste**

To make the brandade, heat the mashed potato, then add the cod confit and stir with a rubber spatula or wooden spoon to produce a thick, creamy texture. Stir in ½ cup (125 mL) of the oil used to simmer the cod, taste, and add lemon juice.

Olive salad:

1 cup (250 mL)	**Kalamata olives**
2 Tbsp. (25 mL)	**minced red bell pepper**
1 Tbsp. (15 mL)	**minced parsley**
2	**green onions, minced**
1 Tbsp. (15 mL)	**minced fresh basil**
½ tsp. (2 mL)	**fennel seeds, cracked**
2 Tbsp. (25 mL)	**olive oil**

Place the olives on your cutting board and flatten each olive with the heel of your hand or your thumb, then pick out and discard the pit. Chop the olives coarsely, then combine with the remaining ingredients. Set aside.

Fennel salad:

4	**Roma tomatoes, cut into ½-inch/1-cm dice (see To Seed or Not to Seed, page 71)**
¼ cup (50 mL)	**fennel dice**
1 Tbsp. (15 mL)	**finely ground fennel seed**
4 Tbsp. (50 mL)	**sun-dried tomatoes in oil, puréed**
1 Tbsp. (15 mL)	**sherry vinegar**
3 Tbsp. (45 mL)	**Spanish olive oil**
¼ tsp. (1 mL)	**smoked paprika (optional)**
~	**kosher salt and pepper to taste**

For the fennel salad, combine all the ingredients and set aside.

To serve, put the brandade in a large bowl and smooth the top. Put the 2 salads into small bowls and pass them separately, or arrange the olive salad and fennel salad around the top of the brandade in alternating spoonfuls. Serve warm.

SERVES 10–12

B IS FOR BACALAO

Salt cod in Europe is not the cardboard we get in Canada. It is a delectable, sweet and satisfying fish, unbelievably beautiful in the market, where pristine white cubes, slices and sides shimmer with salt crystals. In Canada, look for salt cod — called bacalao — in Portuguese and Spanish neighbourhoods; soak the fillets in several changes of cold water to soften and de-salt it.

Sunday Birds and Only Birds

What's Sauce For the Breast...

Cooks should think of poultry — chickens, ducks and turkeys — as two animals trapped on one skeleton. There are breasts, which get no exercise, develop no muscles and have little corresponding flavour. But they are tender and lean, which many people prefer. Thighs and drumsticks do all the locomotive work for the bird, developing muscles, tendons (mainly in the drumstick), texture — and flavour. Muscles also store higher amounts of oxygen, resulting in darker-coloured meat that is more flavourful and higher in fat. The two parts, breast and legs, are best cooked separately, using entirely different cooking methods.

Duck and goose are all dark meat, rich and filling. Both birds spend more time on the wing than chicken or turkey; as a result, these games birds have dark breast meat with higher fat content and a more defined flavour. Game birds bond well with slightly exotic ingredients, such as lavender, vanilla, ginger, sour cherries and star anise. When you make your big leap from traditional turkey or chicken and begin to eat more duck or goose, consider a contemporary sauce based on these ingredients rather than the traditional classic orange sauce. If you do opt for an orange sauce, keep it slightly acidic; a sharp edge will cut through the rich meat more effectively than something rich and cloying.

Whichever you like, consider buying a whole bird rather than parts. Not only do you get the bird, but you get the bones, too, for the stockpot. Frugal cooks will appreciate that!

Poultry in Several Parts

When you dismantle a bird, it's a bit like opening a tricky bank vault; you have to do things in the right order. It just takes practice. Your first attempts may give you a bunch of hacked-up bits instead of the sleek breasts and trim thighs you long for. Persevere. Serve slice 'n'dice instead of whole parts until you get the hang of it, but never apologize.

Use a cutting board that is big enough for the bird. I prefer to use polypropylene boards for fowl and fish and limit the use of wooden boards to vegetables and things that don't bleed. Make sure the chicken is dry, thawed, and that anything in the cavities (neck, giblets) has been removed. Keep your hands and the handle of your knife clean and dry. Be sure your boning knife or paring knife is sharp. Use only the tip of your knife. Go from point A to point B in a clean, single motion without hacking or chopping. Go back to A, then slice to B again if the first cut is incomplete. Never cut towards your hand or fingers.

Have separate containers at hand for the bones, the discard (i.e., fat and skin) and the pieces of meat. To clean up, scrub your wooden board with lots of hot soapy water, then vigorously rub a cut lemon over the surface, rinse and air-dry. Polypropylene boards are ideal candidates for the dishwasher.

1. Place the chicken breast-side down on the cutting board.

2. Make one continuous vertical cut down the centre of the back; cut from neck to tail, slicing through skin and flesh.

3. Place your knife between the two bumps just above the centre point, and slice across the back, about 2 inches (5 cm) each side of the vertical cut.

4. Turn the bird on one side and slice off the wing, placing your knife under the wing, in the deepest point of the vee where the wing and body join. Lift the bird by the wing with your other hand. Its weight will make it easier to find the natural vee; slice through the joint to sever the wing. Slice off the wing's third joint and set it aside for the stockpot.

5. Pick up the bird by one drumstick, again letting the bird's weight work in your favour. Slice the skin (only the skin, no flesh!) and any membrane in the fold between the thigh and the breast, then connect that line to the crosscut you made earlier in step 3.

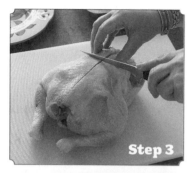

Step 3

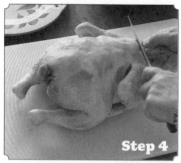

Step 4

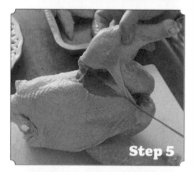

Step 5

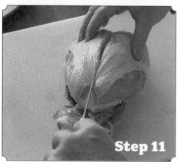

Step 11

6. Place the bird on the board breast-side down. Cut the "oyster" free, using the very tip of your knife to free the little pad of flesh from its socket. Do not sever the skin or cut the meat free from the thigh. Just "scoop" it out of the bone.

7. Set down your knife. Using just your hands, place the thumb of one hand on the hip joint and pull towards you with a fairly sharp tug, your other hand holding the leg where the drumstick and thigh meet, thumb extending down to press beside your other thumb on the hip socket. This should dislocate the entire leg in the hip socket.

8. Pick up your knife and sever the tendon or cartilage at the hip socket, freeing the leg from the body at the joint.

9. Set down your knife. Grasp the thigh firmly in one hand, the carcass in the other. In one fluid motion, pull the leg toward you and free it from the body. Cut it free if it does not pull cleanly free.

10. Repeat steps 6 through 9 on the other leg.

11. Turn the carcass breast-side up. Place your knife tip at the top of the breast bone, with your other hand pulling the skin taut. Run your knife down the length of the breast bone, cutting down to the ribcage the entire length of the breast. Your knife will fall off the keel to one side or the other of the breast and wishbone.

12. Insert your knife beside the keelbone and under the breast meat, then slide your knife toward the rear of the bird, cutting the breast free as you go.

13. Turn the bird and cut the breast meat free from the wishbone.

14. Return your knife to the top of the breast and then slice down the other side of the keel. On each slice down the keel, you should be cutting down to bone where the ribcage is. Repeat steps 12 and 13 on the other side.

15. You should now have: 2 wings, third joints removed; two boneless breasts; 2 legs, with drum and thigh attached; a carcass with very little meat attached.

16. If you wish to separate the leg into 2 pieces, hold the leg up in a vee, and place your knife in the deepest part of the vee. Slice straight down through the joint, freeing the thigh from the drumstick.

Turkey Toes

A decade or so ago, I found these kid-friendly strips at a smart Calgary restaurant that, alas, did not live long. But the turkey lived on in my memory. I was entranced by the humour of the dish. Here is my re-creation... quick, easy and sure to blow anything prefabricated out of the water! Leftovers can be frozen and reheated for a fast snack. Reheat in a single layer on a baking sheet in a hot oven; a microwave will do, although the crust on the turkey will wilt somewhat. Serve it with a tangy, acidic dipping sauce such as Hoisin Dip (page 36). Serve chocolate milk for the kids and some cold lager for the grown-ups.

1 ½ lbs. (750 g)	**boneless, skinless turkey breast**
½ cup (125 mL)	**flour or finely textured cornmeal**
1	**egg**
½ cup (125 mL)	**milk**
1 ½ cups (375 mL)	**panko (coarse Japanese bread crumbs) or other bread crumbs**
~	**kosher salt and freshly ground black pepper to taste**
~	**vegetable oil for pan-frying**

Slice the turkey across the grain into thin strips the size of fat asparagus. Put the flour or cornmeal into a shallow bowl.

Mix the egg and milk together in a second shallow bowl, blending thoroughly. Put the bread crumbs in a third shallow bowl or tray. Season the contents of each bowl lightly with salt and pepper.

Heat 2–3 inches (5–7.5 cm) of oil in a large, shallow pan over medium-high heat. (Check the temperature — it should be about 350–365°F/180–185°C to cook the turkey thoroughly. If you do not have a candy thermometer, drop a cube of bread into the fat; it should begin to colour immediately.)

Thoroughly coat each turkey strip in flour or cornmeal, then immerse in the egg-milk mixture. Roll in the bread crumbs. (See The Fine Art of Breading, page 189.) Use tongs to gently place each piece of turkey in the hot oil. Cook, turning as needed, until each turkey toe is nicely browned, about 10 minutes. To check for doneness, remove one piece to a plate or cutting board and cut it open. The meat should be white with no trace of pink. Serve hot, with your favourite dipping sauce.

SERVES 4–6

Turkey Burger Patties

This filling makes great burgers. Serve on crusty buns with the usual condiments. If your pantry does not contain dried Chinese mushrooms, simply omit them. This recipe makes very soft burgers better suited to sautéing in a pan than on the grill. For firmer patties, reduce the grated vegetables and cut the eggs back to one. A simple Beaujolais (slightly chilled) would go down well.

1	onion, finely minced
2	carrots, grated
2	parsnips, grated
1 Tbsp. (15 mL)	minced garlic
1 Tbsp. (15 mL)	grated fresh ginger
3	dried black Chinese mushrooms, rehydrated and slivered, stems discarded
1 tsp. (5 mL)	vegetable oil
1 ½ lbs. (750 g)	ground turkey
2 Tbsp. (25 mL)	minced cilantro
1 Tbsp. (15 mL)	light soy sauce
1 Tbsp. (15 mL)	fish sauce
2 Tbsp. (25 mL)	minced green onions
½ tsp. (2 mL)	hot chili paste
2	eggs

Mix the onion, carrots, parsnips, garlic, ginger, mushrooms and oil in a non-stick sauté pan. Cook until tender. Place in a mixing bowl and cool the mixture. When cool, add the remaining ingredients. Mix well. Shape into patties and sauté.

MAKES ABOUT 8 PATTIES

Panang Eggplant
with Greens *and* Turkey

One of my favourite Thai restaurants serves a dish that combines duck and eggplant in a Panang curry sauce. I fell in love with its rich, lush flavours and textures and tinker endlessly with my own variations. Here is my post-Christmas version, another wonderful way to use up dark turkey meat. Rice beer or a fruity Riesling would calm the heat in this dish.

1 Tbsp. (15 mL)	**vegetable oil**
2–3 Tbsp. (25–45 mL)	**Panang curry paste**
1	**onion, sliced**
1 Tbsp. (15 mL)	**grated fresh ginger**
4 cloves	**garlic, minced**
1	**red bell pepper, sliced**
2	**kaffir lime leaves**
2	**globe eggplants, peeled and cubed**
1 12-oz. can (1 340-mL can)	**coconut milk**
1 lb. (500 g)	**boneless cooked dark turkey meat**
1 bunch	**spinach, washed and trimmed**
1 Tbsp. (15 mL)	**brown sugar (optional)**
1 Tbsp. (15 mL)	**fish sauce**
1	**lemon, juice only**
~	**kosher salt to taste**
~	**Thai basil or mint for garnish**

Heat the oil, then add the curry paste, onion, ginger and garlic. Stir well and sauté over medium-high heat for several minutes, until the vegetables are tender. Stir in the bell pepper, lime leaves and eggplant. Add the coconut milk and turkey. Cook until the eggplant is tender, then stir in the spinach to wilt it. Add the brown sugar, fish sauce, lemon juice and salt. Garnish with basil or mint leaves.

SERVES 4–6 CURRY ENTHUSIASTS

Breast of Turkey Stuffed *with* Cranberries *and* Ginger

If you are a small household, you may already be in the habit of buying turkey breast. This is a wonderful and picturesque alternative to the whole nine yards of turkey leftovers that last forever. Any slices that remain are wonderful cold. Choose the wines of Alsace here — Pinot Gris or Riesling, perhaps.

1	**boneless turkey breast, skin attached**
1 lb. (500 g)	**ground turkey**
1	**egg**
2 Tbsp. (25 mL)	**grated fresh ginger**
2 Tbsp. (25 mL)	**minced garlic**
1–2	**grated carrots**
1 Tbsp. (15 mL)	**kejap manis (Indonesian soy sauce)**
1 Tbsp. (15 mL)	**fish sauce**
2 Tbsp. (25 mL)	**minced chives or green onion**
1 tsp. (5 mL)	**minced fresh rosemary**
2 Tbsp. (25 mL)	**chopped dried cranberries**
½ tsp. (2 mL)	**hot chili paste**
1	**lemon, juice and zest**
~	**kosher salt to taste**
~	**olive oil for drizzling**
~	**dried thyme and basil for sprinkling**

Butterfly the turkey breast so that it opens into a larger, thinner rectangle. Lay the opened piece of meat on a piece of parchment or plastic wrap. Preheat the oven to 375°F (190°C).

Combine the remaining ingredients except for the olive oil and dried thyme and basil. Mix thoroughly, then pat the mixture onto the opened turkey breast in a single layer. Using the parchment or plastic wrap as a guide, roll the meat and filling up, jelly-roll fashion, with the seam on the bottom.

Transfer to a roasting pan lined with a piece of parchment. Drizzle the turkey breast with olive oil and sprinkle with the dried herbs. Roast, uncovered, until the juices run clear when the meat is pierced with a sharp fork, 1–1 ½ hours, depending on the size of the turkey breast. (See Gauging Doneness, page 131.) Let rest 30–45 minutes before sprinkling with salt and carving in thin slices.

SERVES 4 – 6

Chicken Tandoori

Perfect for an impromptu potluck or a family dinner, this chicken dish is rounded out by a pot of basmati rice and a simple salad of cucumber and tomato in vinaigrette. If you choose a Panang curry paste, of course you might want to change the name to something more exotic! Serve this with Coconut Rice (page 124) and Fresh Peach Chutney (page 22). Try an Indian Pale Ale or a ripe, fruity American Chenin Blanc.

8	**chicken thighs, bone in**
1 cup (250 mL)	**plain yoghurt**
4 cloves	**garlic, finely minced**
1 Tbsp. (15 mL)	**grated fresh ginger**
1 - 2 Tbsp. (15 - 25 mL)	**curry powder or (Indian or Thai) paste**
1	**leek or onion, thinly sliced**

Combine the chicken, yoghurt, garlic, ginger and curry powder or paste in a large bowl. Mix well, coating each piece of chicken with the spice and yoghurt mixture. Cover and refrigerate for 30 minutes or up to 6 hours.

If using a leek, slice it lengthwise, trim off the root and any tough or damaged outer green leaves, and finely mince crosswise. Transfer the sliced leek into a colander and wash very thoroughly under running water. Drain well.

Put the leek or onion on a baking sheet or in a casserole with shallow sides. Preheat the oven to 400°F (200°C). Put the chicken on top of the leek or onion pieces. Roast uncovered for about an hour, or until the juices run clear when pierced with a fork. (See Gauging Doneness, page 131.) Serve the leek or onion with the chicken.

SERVES 4 — 6

Chicken Stuffed *with* Chèvre, Roasted Garlic *and* Herbs

Remember chicken breasts stuffed with ham and processed cheese slices? Here is what that forgettable dish can become when you use the best ingredients you can find! If you want to add a bit of ham, buy some good smoked ham and dice it finely, then add it to the stuffing mixture. The Loire Valley produces fabulous reds (Cabernet Franc), whites (Sauvignon Blanc) and rosés that would all complement this dish.

4	**free-range chicken breasts or thighs**
¼ lb. (125 g)	**chèvre**
4 Tbsp. (50 mL)	**roasted garlic**
2 Tbsp. (25 mL)	**minced herbs (rosemary, thyme, parsley and chives)**
~	**olive oil for drizzling**
~	**kosher salt and freshly cracked black pepper**

Preheat the oven to 400°F (200°C). Loosen the skin on the chicken. Combine the chèvre, garlic, and ⅔ of the herbs. Use a piping bag to fill the pocket under the skin with the stuffing. Drizzle with oil and dust with the remaining herbs, salt and pepper. Roast until the juices run clear, about 20–30 minutes, depending on the size of the breasts. (See Gauging Doneness, page 131.) To serve, slice each piece in half and serve so the filling is visible.

SERVES 4

Upside Down Roast Chicken

Roasting a chicken upside down is the most effective way to ensure the breast meat remains juicy and moist. If you do not have fresh herbs on hand for the baste, use 1 Tbsp. (15 mL) mixed dried herbs. The soft and earthy wines of Burgundy — red or white — play beautifully with roast chicken.

Baste:

2 Tbsp. (25 mL)	**olive oil**
3 cloves	**garlic, finely minced**
3 Tbsp. (45 mL)	**finely minced fresh herbs** **(tarragon, thyme, chives, parsley, sage, rosemary, basil)**
~	**freshly cracked black pepper**

Combine the baste ingredients.

Chicken:

4- to 5-lb. (1.8- to 2.2-kg)	**roasting chicken**
¼	**lemon**
¼	**onion**
3–4 cloves	**garlic**
1–2 sprigs	**fresh thyme**
1 sprig	**rosemary**
2–3 sprigs	**parsley**
~	**several sage leaves**

Preheat the oven to 400°F (200°C). Wash the bird inside and out under cold water. Drain well. Loosely stuff its cavity with the aromatics.

Use a spoon to generously spread the baste mixture over the skin of the bird, completely covering it.

Place the bird breast-side down in a roasting pan. Place the pan in the oven and roast the chicken for 45 minutes. Baste with the fats and oil from the bottom of the pan, then rotate the pan inside the oven to ensure even cooking and colouring. Roast for another 30 minutes. If you want crispy skin on the breast, turn the bird over to roast breast-side up for the last 20 minutes, basting once or twice. Test for doneness; if the bird needs more cooking, return it to the oven and roast longer. (See Gauging Doneness, page 131.)

SERVES 4—6

Roasted Chicken
with Sausage *and* Herb Stuffing

Simply classic. If you want to get fancy, you could dismantle the bird, leaving thigh and drum attached, remove all the bones and insert the stuffing under the skin of the breasts, thigh and drum. Or you could bone the bird from the back, removing all but the drum and wing, stuff and skewer it shut. On the other hand, you could simply stuff the normal cavities and let nature take its course. Classic wine for classic roast chicken is Pinot Noir.

1	leek
4- to 5-lb. (1.8- to 2.2-kg)	roasting chicken
2 links	your choice of spicy sausage
2 tsp. (10 mL)	olive oil
1	onion, minced
4 cloves	garlic, minced
4	shallots, minced
2 stalks	celery, minced
1 Tbsp. (15 mL)	fresh sage, shredded, or 1 tsp (5 mL) dried
1 tsp. (5 mL)	dried thyme
1 tsp. (5 mL)	fresh rosemary, minced
1 Tbsp. (15 mL)	fresh oregano or 1 tsp. (5 mL) dried
3 cups (750 mL)	stock or dry white wine
1 loaf	crusty bread, diced and dried
~	kosher salt and freshly cracked black pepper to taste

Preheat the oven to 375°F (190°C).

Slice the leeks lengthwise, trim off the root and any tough or damaged outer green leaves, and slice crosswise into fine shreds. Transfer the sliced leeks into a colander and wash very thoroughly under running water.

Prepare the chicken by rinsing inside and out with cold water and patting it dry.

Put the sausage in a small pot with ½ inch (1 cm) water, cover and simmer until the sausage is just cooked through, 7–10 minutes. Cool, then chop the sausage coarsely.

Heat the oil in a sauté pan, add the onion, garlic, shallots and celery and cook over medium heat until they are tender. Add the sausage, sage, thyme, rosemary, oregano, stock or wine and bring to a boil. Place the diced bread in a large bowl and add the hot mixture. Toss well and season with salt and pepper. Stuff the bird's cavities. Put any extra stuffing into an ovenproof dish, cover and set aside.

Put the chicken in the oven, breast-side down, and roast until tender, about 1 ¾ hours. (If there is extra stuffing, put it in the oven about halfway through.) Test to ensure the juices run clear before removing the bird from the oven. (See Gauging Doneness, page 131.) Let it rest for 10 minutes before carving.

SERVES A CROWD, 6—8

VARIATION:

If you want to roast vegetables along with the bird, expect to increase the cooking time substantially (by a good hour). Peel and chop root vegetables, potatoes, garlic, celery and leeks. Season with the same herbs you chose for your dressing, lightly toss the vegetables in oil and tuck them all around the raw bird. Roast uncovered, turning the vegetables occasionally as the roasting proceeds.

WHEN WE WERE VERY YOUNG

We are all influenced by what we ate as kids. If our norm was watery mass-produced chicken, odds are good we will like watery chicken with little flavour as adults. If we ate free-range birds with minimal antibiotics when we were very young, we will likely know and appreciate the "real" taste of chicken as adults. We decided to prove it. In the spirit of investigative journalism (and good eating), we decided to buy and roast several birds from different sources: one was antibiotic-free but not free-range; one was certified organic, free-range, grain and grass-fed, also antibiotic-free; the third was a commercially-raised bird purchased from a large supermarket chain store. After roasting all three breast-side down, we found that Bird "A" had the densest, meatiest texture, with a slightly sweet and pronounced chicken flavour. Bird "B had the strongest, most chicken-like flavour, with meaty and firm texture. Bird "C" had the softest texture and the mildest flavour. Our preferences reflected our palates and our upbringing. Jeff, raised in Newfoundland, accustomed to mild meat and overcooked vegetables, opted for "C"; my sons and I preferred "B."

Stir-Fried Chicken Thighs
with Hoisin *and* Ketjap Manis

Every cook needs a quickie now and then. Slot in varying veggies as the seasons change or substitute fat prawns, BBQ duck or slivered pork for the chicken. Find ketjap manis (sweet Indonesian soy sauce) in Asian markets and large supermarkets. Two grape varieties come to mind: Gewürztraminer and Viognier.

Marinade:

4	boneless, skinless chicken thighs
¼ cup (50 mL)	soy sauce
4 tsp. (20 mL)	cornstarch
¼ cup (50 mL)	rice vinegar or sake
2 Tbsp. (25 mL)	hoisin
2 Tbsp. (25 mL)	ketjap manis
½ tsp. (2 mL)	ground star anise

Cut the chicken into bite-size pieces. Mix the remaining ingredients and add the chicken pieces. Stir well and let stand for 30 minutes as you slice and dice.

The rest:

2 tsp. (10 mL)	vegetable oil
1 bunch	green onions, cut into 2-inch (5-cm) lengths
3 Tbsp. (45 mL)	grated fresh ginger
3 Tbsp. (45 mL)	minced garlic
2	red bell peppers, cut into 1-inch (2.5-cm) dice
1	onion, cut into 1-inch (2.5-cm) dice
2 cups (500 mL)	water or stock
1 Tbsp. (15 mL)	sesame oil (optional)
2 Tbsp. (25 mL)	minced cilantro
1 tsp. (5 mL)	hot chili paste
~	toasted cashews for garnish (optional)

Heat the oil in a sauté pan. Add the green onions, ginger, garlic and bell peppers. Sauté over medium-high heat until tender, about 5 minutes, adding small amounts of water as needed. Add the chicken and marinade along with the water or stock. Cook, stirring, over high heat until the chicken is cooked, about 5–8 minutes. Stir in the sesame oil, if desired, cilantro and hot chili paste. Sprinkle with the toasted nuts, if using, and serve immediately.

SERVES 4

Herbed Grilled Chicken
on Wild Mushroom Ragu

This simple dish is perfect for chilly nights. If you are not up for grilling, roast the chicken in a single layer in a hot oven for about 20 minutes instead. Open a bottle of Pinot Noir to complement the earth tones of this dish.

6–8	**small boneless chicken thighs**
4 Tbsp. (50 mL)	**minced fresh thyme**
4 Tbsp. (50 mL)	**minced fresh basil**
2 tsp. (10 mL)	**minced fresh rosemary**
6 cloves	**garlic, minced**
3 Tbsp. (45 mL)	**olive oil**
~	**freshly cracked black pepper to taste**
1 Tbsp. (15 mL)	**unsalted butter**
½	**white onion, minced**
12–15	**large brown mushrooms, sliced**
12–15	**fresh shiitake mushrooms, sliced, stems discarded**
½ cup (125 mL)	**dry white wine**
2	**Roma tomatoes, cut into ½-inch/1-cm dice (see To seed or Not to Seed, page 71)**
1	**lemon, juice only**
~	**kosher salt and freshly ground black pepper to taste**
¼ cup (50 mL)	**whipping cream (optional)**

continued...

Combine the chicken with half the thyme, basil, rosemary, garlic and olive oil. Crack pepper over the mixture and light the grill.

Melt the butter with the remaining olive oil. Cook the onion and the remaining garlic over medium-high heat until the onion is tender. Put the chicken on the hot grill and reduce the temperature to medium-high; turn the chicken once and cook until the juices run clear. Meanwhile, add the mushrooms to the sautéed onions and garlic. Cook until the mushrooms are tender. Add the wine and cook until it is reduced by half. Add the tomatoes and simmer until they begin to break down; stir in the remaining thyme, basil and rosemary. Balance the flavours with lemon juice, salt and pepper. Add the cream, if desired. Remove the cooked chicken from the grill and salt lightly.

To serve, place a spoonful of mushroom ragu on each plate. Top with 1 or 2 pieces of chicken.

SERVES 4

Duck Legs *in* White Wine

Braised legs are a cheerful way to avoid the high fat of traditional confit, and they taste just as yummy. Make lots. (Not just because it tastes better tomorrow, but because it tastes so very good now, as Winnie the Pooh might say if he ate duck.) Serve this shredded, beside a bit of tender mâche for a light lunch, on Olive Oil Mashed Potatoes (page 80), or with your favourite rice and roasted vegetables. An opulent Viognier from the USA would work well in the recipe and in the glass.

1	leek, sliced
16	duck legs, bone in and skin on
2 Tbsp. (25 mL)	ground star anise
2 Tbsp. (25 mL)	grated fresh ginger

TRIM YOUR LEGS OF UNWANTED FAT

Animal fat, including the fat of duck and goose, has been tarred with one heavy swipe of the "food police" brush as being all bad for the human body. But the fact is that duck fat is 49% monounsaturated, goose fat 57%. (Naturally produced, non-hydrogenated monounsaturated fat is one of the friendly ones that lower our LDL — the "bad" cholesterol.) Hedge your bets by eliminating as much fat as possible from either bird. Always brown duck, both breasts and legs, in a heavy pan as a precursor to any other cooking to remove as much fat as possible.

1 tsp. (5 mL)	**olive oil**
4 Tbsp. (50 mL)	**maple syrup**
2 Tbsp. (25 mL)	**finely grated tangerine zest**
1 bottle	**aromatic dry white wine**
~	**hot chili flakes to taste**
1	**carrot, sliced**
6 cloves	**garlic, sliced**
4 Tbsp. (50 mL)	**all-purpose flour**
~	**kosher salt and freshly cracked black pepper to taste**

Start a day in advance if time allows. Slice the leek lengthwise, trim off the root and any tough or damaged outer green leaves, and slice crosswise into fine shreds. Transfer the sliced leek into a colander and wash very thoroughly under running water. Combine the leek, duck legs, star anise, ginger, oil, maple syrup, tangerine zest, wine, chili flakes, carrot and garlic in a shallow non-reactive pan. Cover and refrigerate overnight.

Remove the duck legs from the marinade the next day. Sauté them in a dry pan (no fat) over medium-high heat, skin-side down, until well-browned, about 10–15 minutes. Discard any excess duck fat. Transfer the legs to a braising pan. Sprinkle the legs with the flour.

Strain the marinade, reserving the liquid. Sauté the solids in a bit of the duck fat, then add them to the braising pan. Heat the reserved marinade in the sauté pan, deglazing and scraping up any browned bits. Pour the marinade over the duck legs.

Cover the legs with parchment paper, then with a snug lid. Braise at 300°F (150°C) for 2 hours, or until the meat is tender. Season with salt and pepper to taste. Remove the meat from the pan and skim any fat from the surface of the braising liquid. Strain the liquid and reduce it by ½ to ⅔. Return the duck to the pan to reheat. Serve hot with the braising juices.

SERVES 8–12

Darl's Duck Stir-Fry
with Snow Peas

This quick and delicious stir-fry makes a little duck go a long way. Add one or two vegetables, no more, or it becomes a hodge-podge of confusing flavours! Sauce it generously and serve it over rice or noodles. Serve with a little lager or a crisp German Riesling.

1 Tbsp. (15 mL)	**vegetable oil**
4 cloves	**garlic, minced**
2 Tbsp. (25 mL)	**finely grated fresh ginger**
½ cup (125 mL)	**diced red bell pepper**
10	**field mushrooms, quartered**
½ lb. (250 g)	**barbecued duck, slivered**
¼ cup (50 mL)	**hoisin sauce**
¼ cup (50 mL)	**orange juice**
1 Tbsp. (15 mL)	**soy sauce**
2 cups (500 mL)	**snow peas, shredded**
~	**kosher salt and freshly ground black pepper to taste**
~	**lemon juice to taste**
~	**coarsely chopped cilantro for garnish**

Heat the oil in a large sauté pan. Add the garlic, ginger, bell peppers and mushrooms. Sauté over medium–high heat until tender, about 5 minutes . Add the duck, hoisin sauce, orange juice and soy sauce. Stir well and cook over high heat until the meat is heated through, about 2 minutes. Stir in the snow peas, leaving the pan on the stove just long enough to brighten their colour. Season with salt, pepper and lemon juice. Garnish with the cilantro.

SERVES 2—4

VARIATION: Endless. I like adding 5 or 6 sliced rehydrated black Chinese mushrooms for a muskier tone, or using broccoli florets and chicken for a lighter finish. Alternatively, try pork dusted with star anise and Szechuan pepper partnered with carrots and turnips.

Spanish-Style Braised Duck Legs

This is a combination of flavours common to the south of Spain, where the Moorish influence is strong. If you have no duck legs, substitute chicken legs. Serve this with Summer Couscous, Winter Bulgur (page 125.) Try a mellow Spanish Tempranillo with this one.

8–10	whole duck legs, bone in
1	onion, diced
1 Tbsp. (15 mL)	grated fresh ginger
6 cloves	garlic, sliced
2 Tbsp (25 mL)	finely ground coriander seeds
1 Tbsp. (15 mL)	green cardamom pods, cracked open in a mortar, hulls discarded
1 stick	cinnamon
~	generous pinch of saffron
5	bay leaves
½ cup (125 mL)	white wine
1	orange, juice and zest
1	lemon, juice and zest
½ cup (125 mL)	minced fresh mint
½ cup (125 mL)	minced cilantro
2 cups (500 mL)	cooked chickpeas
½ cup (125 mL)	minced dried apricots
½ cup (125 mL)	green olives, pit in
~	cayenne to taste
3 cups (750 mL)	chicken stock
~	kosher salt and freshly ground black pepper to taste
~	additional minced fresh mint and cilantro for garnish

Preheat the oven to 325°F (160°C). Heat a large ovenproof sauté pan over medium-high heat. Add the duck legs, skin-side down. Cover with a splatter guard and cook the duck for 10–15 minutes on medium-high heat, turning once, to render out most of the duck fat. Remove the duck to a plate and discard most of the fat. (Save it for something else, like confit, if you wish.)

continued...

Add the onion, ginger and garlic to the pan. Sauté on medium heat for 10 minutes, or until the vegetables are tender. Add the coriander, cardamom, cinnamon, saffron and bay leaves. Cook for several minutes, then stir in the wine, orange and lemon juice and zest, mint, cilantro, chickpeas, apricots, olives and cayenne. Mix well, then add the stock and bring to a boil.

Add the duck legs and baste with the liquid once or twice. Cover with parchment paper and a snug lid. Cook in the oven until the duck is fall-apart tender, about 3 hours. If the duck is not tender enough, cover it and cook it longer.

When the meat is cooked to your liking, remove it to a plate. Skim all the fat from the sauce. Season meat and sauce with salt and pepper, and sprinkle the fresh herbs on top. Serve hot.

SERVES 8–10

Duck Breasts *with* Rhubarb *and* Ginger Compote

For fans of duck (and who isn't?), here is a dish that balances the richness of duck with the cutting astringency of rhubarb and ginger. Play with your food by substituting pork loin or tenderloin for the duck. The recipe only calls for a little Riesling or Gewürztraminer. The rest can be enjoyed in the glass!

Duck and marinade:

4	**boneless duck breasts**
1 tsp. (5 mL)	**ground star anise**
1 Tbsp. (15 mL)	**grated fresh ginger**
1 Tbsp. (15 mL)	**olive oil**
1 Tbsp. (15 mL)	**maple syrup**
1 Tbsp. (15 mL)	**finely grated tangerine or orange zest**

Combine the duck breasts with the remaining ingredients in a shallow, non-reactive pan. Cover and refrigerate overnight if time permits. If not, half an hour is better than nothing.

At cooking time, sauté the duck breasts over medium-high heat, skin-side down, in a dry pan (no fat) until well-browned. Pour off the accumulated fat. Transfer the breasts to a grill or hot oven, or turn them and cook on the other side in the pan until medium-rare. Remove the duck from the pan, cover loosely and let stand.

Compote:

1	leek
1 cup (250 mL)	diced red rhubarb
1 Tbsp. (15 mL)	finely grated fresh ginger
½ cup (125 mL)	diced pear or tart apple
½ cup (125 mL)	Riesling, Gewürztraminer or other aromatic off-dry wine
¼ tsp. (1 mL)	ground star anise
~	hot chili flakes to taste
1 Tbsp. (15 mL)	dried cranberries
~	maple syrup to taste
~	the juice of a lemon or lime as needed
~	kosher salt to taste
4 Tbsp. (50 mL)	finely minced crystallized ginger
1 Tbsp. (15 mL)	minced fresh thyme

Slice the leek lengthwise, trim off the root and any tough or damaged outer green leaves, and slice crosswise into fine shreds. Transfer the sliced leek into a colander and wash very thoroughly under running water.

Simmer the leek, rhubarb, grated ginger, pear or apple, wine, star anise and hot chili flakes until tender. Stir in the cranberries and simmer uncovered to thicken and reduce. Add the maple syrup and lemon or lime juice to balance the tartness of the sauce. Season with salt, then add the crystallized ginger and thyme. Serve warm with the cooked duck.

SERVES 4

Roasted Ginger Duck Breast
with Curry Cream

I merged an idea by the Swiss master, Frédy Girardet, with techniques learned from my mentor, Madeleine Kamman, mistress of flavour profiles and technique. If you don't share my passion for quackers, use chicken breasts. It won't be the same, not even close, but it will still be good. If you want a meal without wings, substitute grilled or poached or pan-steamed fish or pork. This recipe calls for an aromatic wine — crisp but fruity Gewürztraminer or a Cru Beaujolais like Fleurie.

Glaze:

¼ **cup** (50 mL)	dried sour cherries
2	whole star anise pods
1 cup (250 mL)	red wine
1	lemon, zest only
2	shallots, minced
2 tsp. (10 mL)	grated fresh ginger

Combine all the ingredients and cook until the wine is reduced to a syrup. Pick out the whole star anise and discard. Set the glaze aside.

Duck and rub:

2	large boneless duck breasts, skin on
½ tsp. (2 mL)	ground star anise or curry powder
1 tsp. (5 mL)	finely grated fresh ginger
1 tsp. (5 mL)	finely grated orange or tangerine zest
1 tsp. (5 mL)	finely minced fresh thyme
	freshly ground black pepper to taste
1 tsp. (5 mL)	olive oil

Cut the whole breasts in half lengthwise. Trim each by removing most of the fat, leaving only a centre strip about ½ inch (1 cm) wide running the length of each half breast. Combine the remaining ingredients and smear the mixture on the breasts. Cover loosely and refrigerate until dinnertime, remembering to take the meat out of the fridge 10–20 minutes before cooking to take off the chill.

Heat a sauté pan with a little oil over medium-high heat and sauté the duck breasts, skin-side down, turning once, to medium-rare. Remove from the heat and let stand 10 minutes, sprinkling with kosher salt after the cooking is complete.

Sauce:

1 Tbsp. (15 mL)	**butter**
2 Tbsp. (25 mL)	**diced Gala apple**
1	**shallot, minced**
1 Tbsp. (15 mL)	**grated fresh ginger**
1 Tbsp. (15 mL)	**Ras El Hanout (see page 28)**
3 Tbsp. (45 mL)	**apple cider**
3 Tbsp. (45 mL)	**white wine**
1 cup (250 mL)	**whipping cream**
~	**kosher salt to taste**
~	**minced chives for garnish**

Melt the butter and sauté the apple, shallot and ginger until tender. Mix in the spice blend, then add the cider and wine. Continue to cook until it is reduced by half. Add the cream and reduce to a light sauce consistency. Season with salt.

To serve, slice the breast on an angle. Drizzle each plate with 1–2 Tbsp. (15–30 mL) of sauce. Place the duck beside the sauce. Garnish each portion with a drizzle of the glaze, several cherries picked from the sauce and a sprinkle of minced chives.

SERVES 4

Something Sweet Any Day

Fashionable Desserts

One of the puzzling truths of life is fashion. Not just in hemlines, but in food. Ten years ago, cakes were in; pies were out. During a short and unfortunate stint in a small mountain town as a young cook, the highlight of my work was watching a gifted baker make pie several times a week. There was art and grace in her movements as she rolled, cut and shaped. It reinforced for me just how precious is the gift of the baker's hands, and I never realized that I was watching a food falling into disuse.

In retrospect, I see the passing of an era, as cakes and pies left the domain of the home cook and became the property of restaurants. I grew up in a family that had dessert every evening, frequently home-baked cake. As a mom, especially now that I share my life with a diabetic, I rarely make dessert. But cake is still what I think of when it's a celebration, particularly of anniversaries or birthdays. In fact, in my restaurant days, cake was the special-occasion sweet of choice; a chocolate angel-food cake I called "The Queen" was my youngest son's favourite birthday cake, and a five-layer chocolate extravaganza the choice of my eldest. It is hard to get good pastry in many restaurants, and cake is no longer a simple sweet, but a part of multi-component dessert platters. Happily, I am witnessing the re-emergence of homemade tarts and pies in homemade crusts. Long live the baker-queen! Long live the pastry of careful, graceful hands!

Cookies are comforting, familiar symbols of childhood that continue to please many. North American cookies are soft, sweet, large and often filled with fruit, nuts and chocolate.

But a tuile, the fairy tutu princess of French cookiedom, is NOT soft. It is not mild, and it is not easy. Tuiles are aristocratic almond cookies, a liquid batter that rests imperiously overnight in the refrigerator, waiting for its sugar to melt. Batter, not dough. Emerging hot from the oven, the cookie is peeled off the parchment and, lightning-quick, patted around an inverted cup or rolling pin to cool.

Cool, it becomes a vessel for cream, berries, and mousse. But it is still a cookie. Crispy cookies, a continent away in style, still manage to convey comfort, *en français, bien sûr*.

Tutu Tuiles

Tuiles have a delicate crunch that is delightful as a counterpoint to any cream or fruit-based dessert, and they freeze admirably, so you never need run out. If I have time, I shape the cookies by draping them, direct from the oven, over a rolling pin or wine bottle to achieve the traditional "tile" shape. Usually, though, I am content with their flat shape, and let the cookies cool before gently lifting them from the parchment. Cookies like these lacy beauties make a gorgeous garnish for Matrimonial Bliss Mousse (page 233), Cinnamon or Star Anise Ice Cream (page 255), or any of the fruit compotes and sauces, and they are admirable afternoon nibbles all on their own with a pot of tea.

3–4	egg whites
1 cup (250 mL)	coconut or toasted hazelnuts, peeled and chopped
⅔ cup (150 mL)	sugar
3 Tbsp. (45 mL)	all-purpose flour
1 Tbsp. (15 mL)	cornstarch
3 Tbsp. (45 mL)	melted butter
2 tsp. (10 mL)	brandy or hazelnut liqueur
1	lime, zest only
½ tsp. (2 mL)	ground ginger

Combine all the ingredients, mix well and let stand overnight in the fridge to allow the sugar to dissolve. Let the batter come to room temperature before using. Set the oven at 375°F (190°C) and line baking sheets with parchment.

continued...

Spoon the batter out by the teaspoon, smoothing it with the back of a spoon dipped in cold water. Leave generous room for spreading. Bake for 7–10 minutes, watching closely, and remove from the oven when golden. Cool on the sheet before transferring to an airtight tub for freezing. Layer parchment or wax paper between each layer — these fragile cookies will stick and break if stacked directly on top of each other.

MAKES ABOUT 2 DOZEN 3-INCH (8-cm) **COOKIES**

Triple Ginger Biscotti

These are the perfect midafternoon pick-me-up with coffee. If rationalization is needed for personal reasons, consider these the best, sweetest *digestif* around. Ginger has power to soothe the savage stomach, so cookies containing ginger are sure to solve all that ails you. The fact that they are ideal "keepers" is irrelevant — who would want to keep them when they are so good to share? I have learned to love these cookies once-baked, and only rarely do I bake them a second time, but do so if you like the classic hard crunch of double-baked biscotti.

½ cup (125 mL)	**unsalted butter**
1 cup (250 mL)	**sugar**
2	**eggs**
1 cup (250 mL)	**toasted sliced almonds**
1 Tbsp. (15 mL)	**ouzo/anisette/licorice liqueur (optional)**
1 Tbsp. (15 mL)	**ground ginger**
¼ cup (50 mL)	**finely grated fresh ginger**
½ cup (125 mL)	**finely diced crystallized ginger**
1 ½ cups (375 mL)	**all-purpose flour**
½ cup (125 mL)	**cornmeal**
1 ½ tsp. (7 mL)	**baking powder**
~	**pinch of kosher salt**

Preheat the oven to 325°F (160°C). Line 1 baking sheet with parchment. Cream the butter and sugar. Add the eggs and mix well. Add the remaining ingredients and mix until blended. Divide the dough in half and shape into 2 logs, working directly on the baking sheet and flouring your hands as needed. Make each log about 1 inch (2.5 cm) shorter than the baking sheet, 2 inches (5 cm) across and 2 inches (5 cm) high. Then use the flat of your hand to flatten the logs so they are evenly wide and about ½ inch (1 cm) high. Bake for 15–20 minutes, until the dough is firm and cooked throughout. Cool, then slice into fingers on the angle, each about ½ inch (1 cm) wide. Place the cookies, cut side up, on the baking sheet and bake again for 10 minutes or until completely dry but not browned. Cool, then store in a cookie jar.

MAKES ABOUT 30 COOKIES

Triple Ginger Spice Bars

If a cookie was ever destined for breakfast, it's this one. I dare you, just once. Not quite a biscotti log, this is meant to be baked to just this side of done, sliced, and eaten slightly soft.

1 cup (250 mL)	unsalted butter, softened
2 cups (500 mL)	brown sugar
4	eggs
⅓ cup (75 mL)	molasses
4 cups (1 L)	all-purpose flour
1 ½ tsp. (7 mL)	baking powder
1 ½ tsp. (7 mL)	baking soda
1 ½ tsp. (7 mL)	ground cinnamon
1 tsp. (5 mL)	ground ginger
1 tsp. (5 mL)	ground nutmeg
¼ tsp. (1 mL)	ground cloves
~	pinch of kosher salt
4 Tbsp. (50 mL)	crystallized ginger, minced
2 Tbsp. (25 mL)	finely grated fresh ginger
1 cup (250 mL)	golden raisins
1 cup (250 mL)	Thompson raisins
½ cup (125 mL)	dried apricots, minced
½ cup (125 mL)	dried cranberries
½ cup (125 mL)	chopped dates
1 cup (250 mL)	chopped pecans or walnuts

Heat the oven to 375°F (190°C). Line 2 baking sheets with parchment.

Cream the butter, then add the sugar and mix again on high speed to blend. Add the eggs and molasses and blend well. Sift the flour, baking powder, baking soda, cinnamon, ginger, nutmeg, cloves and salt. Add to the bowl, then add all the remaining ingredients and mix well.

Form the dough into 4 logs, each as long as your baking sheets, coating your hands with small amounts of additional flour to prevent sticking. Transfer the logs to the sheets and bake 25–28 minutes. Do not overbake; they should still be soft (but baked throughout) when they come out of the oven. Cool and slice. Store in an airtight tin.

MAKES 4 LOGS, each about 10 cookies

Grandma Doris's Shortbreads

(and what I did to them)

Both my grandmothers baked cookies in their younger days. My Grandma Sarah made fat soft cookies stuffed with raisins, ideal for after school; my Grandma Doris made suave and sophisticated shortbread at Christmas, and the best chocolate chip cookies the rest of the year.

2 cups (500 mL) **unsalted butter, softened**
1 cup (250 mL) **icing sugar**
3 ½ cups (875 mL) **all-purpose flour**

Cream the butter. Add the sugar and slowly increase the mixing speed to high, then mix for 1 minute on high speed after all the sugar is incorporated. Stir in the flour. Pat into 3 large flat discs. Score each round into 12 wedges or roll out and cut into shapes. Bake at 300°F (150°C) for 20–30 minutes, until baked but pale and uncoloured. Cool thoroughly on a wire rack, then use a sharp knife to cut the wedges along the score marks. Store in an airtight tin or jar.

MAKES ABOUT 3 DOZEN COOKIES

MY VARIATIONS:

• Add ½ tsp. (2 mL) minced fresh rosemary, ½ cup (125 mL) chopped dried cranberries and 4 Tbsp. (50 mL) minced crystallized ginger.

• Add the zest of 1 orange and ½ cup (125 mL) toasted skinned chopped hazelnuts. Dip in melted dark chocolate when cool.

Pâte Brisée

This hands-on method of pastry-making requires next to no equipment beyond a good rolling pin and a clean counter. It takes a bit of attention to contain the ingredients when you add the water, but with a bit of practice, it is as easy as … pie. The end result is a tender, crisp and finely textured pastry that is entirely different from the North American flaky style.

1 cup (250 mL)	**all-purpose flour**
~	**pinch of kosher salt**
1 Tbsp. (15 mL)	**sugar (optional)**
6 Tbsp. (90 mL)	**unsalted butter, at room temperature**
4 Tbsp. (50 mL)	**ice water (approximate)**

Combine the dry ingredients on the counter. Cut the butter into pieces and combine with the dry ingredients, blending until fine and mealy in texture. Add water in small amounts until the dough just begins to hold together, blending by stiffening the fingers like the tines of a salad tosser and tossing the ingredients into the air. Don't be too exuberant; the aim is to combine while avoiding the development of gluten. Once a ball is beginning to form, smear a couple tablespoons of dough across the counter with the heel of your hand, repeating until all the dough has been smeared once or twice. This action is called *fraisage*. Gather the dough into a ball, then pat into a flat disc about 3–4 inches (8–10 cm) across. Wrap well, chill for 30 minutes, then bring the dough back to room temperature before rolling. May be frozen for up to 3 months.

MAKES PASTRY FOR 1 TART up to 12 inches (30 cm) in diameter

PASTRY TECHNIQUES

Only by using your hands (and making pastry multiple times, so you become attuned to the changes and the right feel) will you become proficient at pastry-making. The overriding rule: handle pastry as little as possible and keep everything cool while you work. Making pastry by machine is fairly high-risk. It is easy to overwork dough in a mere few seconds when using a food processor or mixer.

Gluten does not develop in flour until liquid is added. Therefore it is important to add liquid in the "right" amount. Too much makes a tough dough, too little and the dough is not cohesive. Although it is necessary to develop some gluten so your pastry will hold together, overworking the dough by mixing, kneading or rolling will develop more gluten than necessary. Keeping ingredients cool also minimizes gluten development.

Pasta Frolla

This Italian sweet pastry is rich and immensely tender. It is also hard to mess up, and can be made in a machine with no worries because of the high butter and sugar content. Instead of being rolled out, this soft pastry is patted into a pan with the hands. I learned this from Madeleine Kamman nearly 20 years ago in her French kitchen.

½ lb. (250 g)	**unsalted butter, cool and malleable**
½ cup (125 mL)	**white sugar**
½ tsp. (2 mL)	**ground cinnamon**
¼ tsp. (1 mL)	**ground ginger**
1	**orange, zest only**
2 ¼ cups (550 mL)	**all-purpose flour**

Cream the butter and sugar thoroughly. Add the remaining ingredients, mixing long enough to develop a little gluten. Turn out and pat into a fluted tart pan with removable bottom, flouring your hands to prevent sticking. Chill, then place on a baking sheet with a lip to catch any butter that drips out during baking. Bake unfilled in a preheated oven at 350°F (180°C) until golden. The pastry should be firm, crisp and evenly coloured.

MAKES 1 TART up to 16 inches (40 cm) in diameter

Resting the dough is the biggest aid in producing tender pastry. Let the dough stand (in the fridge or on the counter) to allow the gluten strands to relax and revert back to their original shape and size. If your pastry is overly elastic and bounces back into a smaller space when you roll it out, let it rest.

To blind bake (bake a pie shell unfilled), set the oven at 400–425°F (200–220°C). Roll out the pastry and fit it inside the pan. Cut a parchment paper to fit the tart shell and place on top of the pastry. Fill with dried legumes, rice or pie weights, then bake on the lowest rack of the oven for 15–20 minutes. Remove the weights and the parchment and return to the oven until the crust is just golden. Use a fork to prick holes in the pastry if bubbles form.

Almond Pâte Sucrée

This is like pasta frolla in its proportion of butter and sugar to flour. The difference lies in the addition of an egg, for a softer, more malleable, less cookie-like short dough, and ground nuts, for a different flavour and slightly grainy texture. Make it in a food processor if you wish.

2 cups (500 mL)	**all-purpose flour**
½ cup (125 mL)	**finely ground almonds**
~	**pinch of kosher salt**
½ cup (125 mL)	**sugar**
1	**large egg**
1 tsp. (5 mL)	**vanilla extract**
½ lb. (250 g)	**unsalted butter, cool and malleable**

Combine the flour, nuts, salt and sugar on the counter or in a bowl. Make a well in the centre. Combine the egg and vanilla in a bowl, then add the butter to form a paste. Add the liquid to the well. Use your fingers to mix the ingredients, working from the centre of the well outwards. When the dough just begins to hold together, smear small handfuls of it across the counter to incorporate the butter–egg mixture more thoroughly. Shape into a tidy disc, wrap and chill for at least 1 hour. Allow to soften before rolling or patting out.

MAKES 1 TART up to 16 inches (40 cm) in diameter

Apple Galette

This is an ideal entry-level dessert for the young cook looking to expand her repertoire beyond cookies. A rustic and simple free-form tart with one crust and lots of fruit, it is baked on a cookie sheet, not in a pie plate, and does not require architectural precision during rolling or assembly. You can crimp the edges to make a little retaining wall, or you can fold the pastry over the apples in a succession of pleats. Vary the final flavour by using Almond Pâte Sucrée (page 230) for a change. Serve this with Yoga Crème Anglaise (page 257) or Cinnamon or Star Anise Ice Cream (page 255).

1 recipe	**Pâte Brisée (see page 228)**
10	**tart apples (Gala, Granny Smith, Golden Delicious, Jonagold, Gravenstein)**
1–2 Tbsp. (15–25 mL)	**unsalted butter**
~	**brown sugar to taste**
1 tsp. (5 mL)	**freshly grated nutmeg**
½ tsp. (2 mL)	**ground cinnamon**
½ cup (125 mL)	**raisins (optional)**

Roll out the pastry into a 16-inch (40-cm) round. Use a piece of parchment paper to line a baking sheet with a lip. Place the pastry round on the pan. Let the pastry rest, lightly covered with plastic wrap, while you proceed with the fruit. Set the oven at 375°F (190° C), and position the rack in the centre of the oven.

Peel, core and slice the apples. Melt the butter in a sauté pan and sauté the apples until they begin to soften and brown slightly. Add the sugar, spices and raisins, if desired. Let cool, then pour onto the centre of the pastry, leaving a 1- to 3-inch (2.5- to 8-cm) border of pastry uncovered by fruit. Fold the edge of the pastry over the apples, pleating as you go and leaving a small centre section uncovered. Bake until browned, 30- 40 minutes. Serve warm.

SERVES 6 – 8

Deep Dish Apple Pie

Multiple textures add to the enjoyment of this single-crust classic. I use Pasta Frolla for this in preference to any other pastry; its rich, crisp and cookie-like nature is softened by the moist apples, and the end result is spectacular. This is best served warm, with Cinnamon or Star Anise Ice Cream (page 255). Leftovers are good for breakfast with Ginger-Spiked Yoghurt Cream (page 247.)

Streusel:

4 Tbsp. (50 mL)	all-purpose flour
2 Tbsp. (25 mL)	granulated sugar
4 Tbsp. (50 mL)	melted unsalted butter

Combine the streusel ingredients, blending with fingers or a fork until crumbly. Set aside.

Pie and filling:

1 recipe	Pasta Frolla (see page 229)
10	tart apples (Jonathan, Jonagold, Gala, Golden Delicious, Cortland, Northern Spy, Gravenstein, Granny Smith)
½ cup (125 mL)	Thompson seedless raisins
¼ cup (50 mL)	lemon juice
2 Tbsp. (25 mL)	all-purpose flour
¼ cup (50 mL)	brown sugar
1 tsp. (5 mL)	ground cinnamon
½ tsp. (2 mL)	ground allspice
¼ tsp. (1 mL)	ground cloves
¼ tsp. (1 mL)	ground nutmeg

Use your hands to pat the pastry into a 10-inch (25-cm) springform pan, fitting the pastry to the very top of the pan's sides. Chill.

Preheat the oven to 375°F (190°C).

To make the filling, peel and slice the apples. Place in a large bowl with the raisins. In a smaller bowl, combine the lemon juice, flour, sugar and spices. Add to the apples and mix well. Pour the mixture into the prepared pastry.

Cover the pie with foil, place on a baking sheet to catch any drips and bake for 50–60 minutes. Remove the foil lid and evenly distribute the streusel over the filling. Return to the oven and bake another 20–25 minutes, until crusty and brown.

SERVES 10–12

Matrimonial Bliss Mousse

This mousse is what my ex and I served our guests at our wedding. Oh well. We are still friends. Change it (no jokes, please) by changing the fruit purée. The same ingredients morph into panna cotta when poured into individual ramekins before chilling.

4 cups (1 L)	**raspberry purée, seeded**
~	**sugar to taste**
2 envelopes	**gelatin, dissolved in a small amount of warm water and chilled to syrupy consistency**
2 cups (500 mL)	**whipping cream, beaten to firm peaks**
~	**fresh berries for garnish**

Combine the purée and sugar. Stir in the gelatin once the gelatin is thick and syrupy. Fold in the cream. Turn into ramekins or a mould that has been lightly oiled. Chill until set. Serve cold, garnished with berries.

SERVES 12

Pear Frangipane *for Irene*

This is the tart I made in celebration of my German-born mother-in-law's 75th birthday celebration. I won't say what year that particular celebration was, but suffice it to say that Irene continues to celebrate robust health. This is rich, so serve small slices regardless of the occasion.

½ recipe	**Almond Pâte Sucrée (page 230)**
4	**ripe pears**
¾ cup (175 mL)	**sliced almonds**
½ cup (125 mL)	**sugar**
½ cup (125 mL)	**unsalted butter**
2	**eggs**
2 Tbsp. (25 mL)	**rum**
1 tsp. (5 mL)	**almond extract**
⅓ cup (75 mL)	**dried cranberries**
1 Tbsp. (15 mL)	**sugar**
1 Tbsp. (15 mL)	**sliced almonds**

Preheat the oven to 350°F (180°C). Roll out the pastry and carefully drape it in a 10-inch (25-cm) fluted tart pan with removable bottom. Bake the pastry to just golden, using a fork to prick the bottom if it bubbles up at all.

Peel and core the pears. Slice each pear in half. Thinly slice each half, not quite severing it at the stem end.

Finely grind the almonds with ¼ cup (50 mL) of the sugar. Remove from the food processor and set aside. Use the food processor or a mixer to cream the butter and remaining ¼ cup (50 mL) sugar, then add the eggs one at a time. Add the ground nut-sugar mixture, rum, almond extract and cranberries. Blend well and pour into the tart shell.

Arrange the sliced pear halves at regular intervals over the filling. Sprinkle the 1 Tbsp. (15 mL) sugar and 1 Tbsp. (15 mL) almonds over the exposed pear surfaces. Place the filled pan on a baking sheet with a lip to catch any drips and bake until just set, about 30 minutes. Chill. Serve cold.

SERVES 8—10

"Zebra" Summer Berry Tart *with* Espresso Ganache

This tart is beautiful and delicious, crisp and tender at once, with a hidden layer of ganache buried under the berries. Pick perfect ones. Use the best chocolate you can buy — in chocolate, as with most food, you get what you pay for. For birthday parties, make this in individual 4-inch (10-cm) rounds, using ¼ cup (50 mL) pasta frolla for each round.

1 recipe	**Pasta Frolla (see page 229)**
½ cup (125 mL)	**whipping cream**
4 oz. (125 g)	**semi-sweet chocolate (preferably Callebaut)**
1 Tbsp. (15 mL)	**espresso or coffee liqueur**
3 pints (1.5 L)	**fresh strawberries or raspberries**

Pat the pastry into a 10-inch (25-cm) fluted tart pan with a removable bottom. Chill or freeze. Bake the frozen or chilled pastry at 425°F (220°C) until golden. Cool.

To make the ganache, combine the whipping cream, chocolate and espresso or liqueur in a bowl. Melt over simmering, not boiling, water or on medium power in the microwave. Stir well. Spread ⅔ of the ganache over the base of the cooled tart shell. Arrange the berries on top of the ganache in a decorative pattern. Soften and slightly heat the remaining ganache over hot water, then dip the tines of a fork into the ganache. Use a rapid back and forth flicking motion to create "zebra" lines of ganache across the top of the tart. Chill until serving time. To serve, remove the tart from the pan and slice with a knife dipped in hot water.

SERVES 6–8

HANDLING CHOCOLATE

Store chocolate in its original wrapper at 65°F (18°C). Do not refrigerate it or wrap it in plastic. To melt chocolate, chop it finely, then heat it over simmering, not boiling, water in a stainless steel bowl to 112°F (50°C). Stir it frequently, and use a thermometer to check the temperature. If you use a microwave, use medium power, and remember to stir the melting chocolate several times. Wipe any moisture from the bottom of the bowl to prevent water drops from coming in contact with the melted chocolate. Water can make chocolate "seize" — it becomes hard and dull, impossible to rescue for chocolate-making, as intractable as a toddler.

Hot Buttered Rum Tarts

Herewith a variation of the country's best butter tarts, adapted from my southern Ontario grandmother's classic. School kids know these are the ultimate bartering tool; with butter tarts, you can trade for almost anything. For adults, they are a bittersweet memory of the disappearing past, when grandmothers baked every week and the cookie jar was always full.

1 recipe	Pâte Brisée (see page 228)
1	egg
⅜ cup (90 mL)	unsalted butter, room temperature
1 cup (250 mL)	Demerara sugar
1 oz. (25 mL)	amber rum (optional)
½ cup (125 mL)	seedless raisins, currants, dried cranberries or chopped nuts
2 Tbsp. (25 mL)	maple syrup

Preheat the oven to 450°F (230°C). Using a floured rolling pin, roll out the pastry and cut it to fit tart tins.

Combine the remaining ingredients and mix well. Spoon the filling into the pastry-lined cups to half-full and put the tart tin onto a baking sheet with a lip to catch any spills. Bake for about 10–15 minutes, until golden brown. Let cool before removing from the pan.

MAKES ABOUT 24 2-inch (5-cm) tarts

Nuts about Nuts Caramelized Nuts Tart

Nut lovers only need apply. I vaguely remember eating this for breakfast as a young cook in a mountain town. I think it might have been a hangover cure. Don't tell my sons. Serve with whipped cream or ice cream.

1 recipe	**Pâte Brisée (see page 228)**
¾ cup (175 mL)	**whipping cream**
¾ cup (175 mL)	**brown sugar**
1 cup (250 mL)	**mixed nuts, chopped**
2 Tbsp. (25 mL)	**Kahlua**
½ tsp. (2 mL)	**vanilla extract**

Roll out the pastry and fit it into a 9-inch (23-cm) fluted ring. Chill. Bake blind (see Pastry Techniques, page 228) at 400°F (200°C) until just golden. Remove and reduce the oven temperature to 350°F (175°C).

Mix the remaining ingredients well. Pour into the tart shell and put the tart pan onto a baking sheet with a lip to catch any drips. Bake about 20–30 minutes, or until bubbles on the surface are small and tight, and the caramel is a satisfactory brown. Cool at room temperature.

MAKES 1 9-INCH (23-cm) **TART**

Far-Out Filo Napoleons *with* Orange-Lime Mousse *and* **Fresh Berries**

This is the most spectacular, simplest style of serving filo. Use berries in season, and switch to poached apples and pear slices in winter, with a bit of colour from rehydrated dried cranberries when fresh berries are no longer prime. Filo squares sprinkled with sugar and cinnamon provide a simple solution to the time-consuming methods of making traditional puff pastry in Napoleon-style sweets. If you are out of filo, layer the mousse and fruit in tall wine glasses and chill before serving.

Mousse:

5	eggs
1 cup (250 mL)	granulated sugar
¼ cup (50 mL)	melted unsalted butter
½ cup (125 mL)	fresh lime juice
½ cup (125 mL)	fresh orange juice
~	finely grated zest of 1 lime
~	finely grated zest of 1 orange
2 Tbsp. (25 mL)	finely grated fresh ginger
2 cups (500 mL)	whipping cream
1 Tbsp. (15 mL)	icing sugar

Whisk the eggs and sugar in a non-reactive bowl. Add the butter, juices, zests and ginger. Mix well. Transfer to a heavy pot and continue whisking. Cook over medium-high heat, whisking constantly. When thick but not yet boiling, strain through a sieve into a clean bowl. Cover snugly with plastic, putting the plastic directly onto the surface of the mixture so a skin doesn't form. Poke several holes in the film to allow steam to escape. Cool, then chill.

Whip the cream and icing sugar to firm peaks. Fold into the cold mixture. Chill.

Pastry:

3 sheets	**filo**
¼ cup (50 mL)	**melted unsalted butter**
~	**granulated sugar for sprinkling**
~	**ground cinnamon for sprinkling**

Preheat the oven to 375°F (190°C). Lay a sheet of filo on a flat surface. Brush it with butter, then sprinkle it with sugar and cinnamon. Lay a second sheet on top and repeat the process. Add a third sheet. Slice the layered sheets into 12 squares. Bake the squares for about 5 minutes, or until golden. Cool to room temperature.

Fruit filling:

1 cup (250 mL)	**strawberries, sliced**
1 cup (250 mL)	**blueberries**
1 cup (250 mL)	**blackberries**
1 cup (250 mL)	**raspberries**
¼ cup (50 mL)	**orange juice or late harvest wine**

Combine the fruit and juice or wine. Mix gently and macerate at least 15 minutes.

Assembly:

~	**icing sugar for garnish**
~	**fresh mint leaves for garnish**

Centre ¼ cup (50 mL) mousse on a plate. Arrange fruit in a flat single layer on the mousse. Place a filo square on the berries. Add a spoonful of mousse on the top surface of the square. Arrange a layer of fruit over the mousse. Spoon a bit of mousse onto the berries, and add a second filo square on top of that. Spoon a bit of mousse onto the filo square and arrange a layer of berries on top of the mousse. Dust each serving with icing sugar and garnish with a mint leaf. Serve immediately with knife, fork and spoon.

SERVES 12 GENEROUSLY

Double Chocolate Mocha Bread Pudding

This is ideally made from leftover cake, but who ever has leftover chocolate cake? If you have none, use leftover brioche, brownies, pound cake, pannetone, sweet bread, even baguette. This is baked custard topped with stirred custard. It has a smooth, unctuous texture that brings to mind all the wonderfully sensual egg-based dishes of classic French cooking, but bread pudding is as North American as apple pie. Make this in one big soufflé dish for a casual dessert or in individual ramekins for a more formal presentation.

2 cups (500 mL)	**leftover cake, preferably chocolate**
4 cups (1 L)	**milk or cereal cream**
3	**egg yolks**
6	**whole eggs**
2 tsp. (10 mL)	**vanilla extract**
½ cup (125 mL)	**sugar**
¼ cup (50 mL)	**espresso or very strong coffee**
1 cup (250 mL)	**Espresso Ganache (see page 235)**
1 recipe	**Yoga Crème Anglaise (see page 251) or Espresso Crème Anglaise (see page 252)**

Preheat the oven to 325°F (160°C).

Slice the cake into pieces that match the size of the serving dish, larger for a big pan, smaller for individual ramekins. Divide evenly among the dishes or place it all in the big soufflé dish. Scald the milk or cream. Whisk together the egg yolks and whole eggs with the vanilla and sugar. Slowly whisk in the hot milk or cream, tempering the eggs. Add the coffee and mix well. Stir in half the ganache, then pour the mixture over the cake pieces.

Cover with parchment and bake until set, 20 minutes or so for ramekins, 30–45 minutes for the single dish. Check for doneness by inserting a small knife into the centre; it should emerge almost clean.

Serve warm with the remaining ganache and the anglaise.

SERVES 8–10

Coffee Chocolate Velvet Pâté

Thin slices, with Cinnamon or Star Anise Ice Cream (page 255) or Espresso Crème Anglaise (page 252), are ideal accompaniments to a demi-tasse of espresso when lingering at the table. "Straight up" is pretty wonderful too, especially if you pour each guest a tiny glass of grappa as a *digestif*.

1 lb. (500 g)	**dark chocolate**
½ lb. (250 g)	**unsalted butter**
2 Tbsp. (25 mL)	**instant coffee**
2 Tbsp. (25 mL)	**Kahlua**
7	**eggs, separated**
2 Tbsp. (25 mL)	**sugar**
~	**fresh berries for garnish**
~	**mint leaves for garnish**

Melt the chocolate and butter in a double boiler over simmering water or in a microwave on medium power, stirring several times. Dissolve the instant coffee in the Kahlua. Add to the egg yolks and mix vigourously with a whisk until tripled in volume. Fold the coffee-yolk mixture into the melted chocolate. Whisk the whites to medium peaks and add the sugar. Fold the whites into the chocolate mixture. Gently spoon the mixture into a terrine or pate mould lined with plastic wrap. Cover and chill for at least 8 hours. Unmould when set and serve in small slices, using a thin-bladed knife and cleaning the knife in hot water for each cut (best done beside the sink). Garnish with fresh berries and mint leaves.

SERVES ABOUT 16

Shakeh's Baklava

Crisp, crunchy, nutty, these honey-laced classics are so much better than store-bought. They freeze admirably, so don't try to eat all of them at one go... in fact, a little goes a long and sticky way. This recipe is a generous gift from my friend Shakeh Dayal, a caterer and food genius of Armenian descent. Choose baking sheets with a lip to contain the syrup. Serve with espresso or mint tea. All these filo sweets freeze well. Thaw on the counter and serve cold.

Syrup:

4 cups (1 L)	**cold water**
8 cups (2 L)	**sugar**
4 Tbsp. (50 mL)	**lemon juice**
1 cup (250 mL)	**honey**
3 sticks	**cinnamon**
1	**vanilla bean, split lengthwise**
1 tsp. (5 mL)	**whole allspice berries**
½ tsp. (2 mL)	**whole cloves**
~	**zest of 1 orange, pith removed**
2-3	**geranium leaves (optional)**
1 Tbsp. (15 mL)	**rose water or orange flower water (optional)**

Bring the water, sugar and lemon juice to a boil. Add the honey, cinnamon, vanilla bean, allspice, cloves, orange zest and optional geranium leaves, rose water or orange flower water. Simmer 10 minutes. Cool and store in the fridge. Strain through a sieve when you use it.

For each shape:

1 lb. (500 g)	**filo, defrosted**
1 lb. (500 g)	**melted butter**
1 lb. (500 g)	**chopped pecans**

Rosettes Spread 1 sheet of filo out on a cutting board, short end closest to you. Brush sparingly with butter, cover with a second sheet, and use a spoon to splash the sheet with a tablespoon (15 mL) of melted butter, more or less evenly distributed across the sheet. Place a thin dowel at the bottom of the sheet and roll the filo up around the dowel. Brush with butter on the outer surface. Lightly grasp the dowel at each end and use your hands to push the filo together, scrunching it into a wrinkled tube about 6 inches (15 cm) long. Pull the dowel free, and coil the scrunched filo length into a rosette of about 3 inches (8 cm) in diameter. Place on a baking sheet. Repeat to fill the sheet, placing the rosettes so they are just touching.

Stars Lay 9 sheets of unbuttered filo on a cutting board, stacked one on top of the other. Slice into 20 squares, 5 across and 4 down. Place a spoonful of chopped nuts into the centre of each square. Dip your fingers in the melted butter and use the butter to hold the filo edges in place as you draw together the diagonal corners to meet on top. Transfer the stars to a baking sheet. Repeat until filo and filling are used up.

Rolls Lay a sheet of filo on the board, short end closest to you. Splash with melted butter, add a second sheet and splash it. Sprinkle nuts thinly along the close short edge, fold over enough filo so that the dowel won't come in contact with the nuts, place a thin dowel along the fold and roll up snugly. Butter the outside surface, lightly grasp the dowel with both hands at opposing ends, and move your hands closer together, lightly scrunching the filo as you go to wrinkle it. Lay the roll on the counter, gently pull out the dowel, slice the filo roll into 4 equal lengths and transfer to a baking sheet. Repeat with remaining ingredients.

Bake at 350°F (190°C) for 20 minutes. Turn the pan end for end to ensure even baking, and bake for another 15–20 minutes. Drench the baked pastry with cold syrup as soon as the pan is removed from the oven, using about 3 cups (750 mL) of syrup. Garnish rosettes with chopped nuts. Chill and serve cold.

MAKES 18–20 ROSETTES, or 40 rolls or 40 stars

Stampede Shortcake
with Seasonal Fruit *and* Ginger-Spiked Yoghurt Cream

Shortcake fans fall into two distinct camps — those who like cake and those who prefer biscuits. I am firmly in the biscuit camp, trained by my southern Ontario grandmother's finest efforts. Choose your filling by the seasons.

Biscuits:

4 cups (1 L)	**all-purpose flour**
½ cup (125 mL)	**sugar**
⅔ cup (150 mL)	**butter**
4 tsp. (20 mL)	**baking powder**
3	**whole eggs**
1 cup (250 mL)	**raisins**
1 cup (250 mL)	**sour cream or yoghurt**
~	**pinch of kosher salt**
2 Tbsp. (25 mL)	**milk or cream**
1	**egg or egg yolk**

Combine the flour, sugar, butter and baking powder in a countertop mixer. Blend together at lowest speed. Add the 3 eggs and mix well. Add the raisins. Slowly add the sour cream or yoghurt and salt. When the dough is smooth, cover and place in the refrigerator for 1–2 hours to rest.

Preheat the oven to 375°F (190°C). Dust the counter with flour. Roll out the dough with a minimum of handling, and form into a rectangle about 1 inch (2.5 cm) thick. Fold in half, pat out lightly with your palms and fold over 3 more times. This helps to create layers without developing unnecessary gluten. Roll out with a floured rolling pin to a thickness of about 1 inch (2.5 cm).

Cut out with a lightly floured 2-inch (5-cm) round cutter. Arrange on the baking sheet, fairly closely together. These biscuits rise up, not out, so ½ inch (1 cm) clearance is fine. Minimizing the spacing creates a tender, less crisp exterior, so pick your preferred texture. In a small bowl, combine the milk or cream with the egg, mixing until completely blended. Use a pastry brush to brush the top surface of the scones with the egg wash. Bake for 15 minutes.

Filling:

| 1 recipe | **fruit filling of your choice (see Susan's Winter Fruit Compote, page 24, Rhubarb Ginger Berry Compote, page 248, or Lush Peach Sauce, page 245)** |
| 1 recipe | **Ginger-Spiked Yoghurt Cream (see page 247)** |

To serve, split each biscuit horizontally. Spoon a generous amount of fruit onto the base, add a dollop of spiked yoghurt and perch the biscuit top on the heap. Serve with a spoon and a fork.

MAKES ABOUT 16 2-INCH (5-cm) **BISCUITS**

Lush Peach Sauce

This quick peach sauce is a simple and seasonal way to enjoy the fruits of the summer season. Use it on ice cream, frozen yoghurt or sorbet, in crêpes or as an accompaniment to fresh berries and cookies. Make a slightly more complicated dessert by topping the fruit sauce with the streusel topping for Deep Dish Apple Pie (page 232), baking until bubbly and serving it warm.

6	**peaches**
1 Tbsp. (15 mL)	**unsalted butter**
½ tsp. (2 mL)	**freshly grated nutmeg**
1–4 Tbsp. (15–50 mL)	**sugar**
~	**lemon juice to taste**

Using a sharp paring knife, peel and slice the peaches. Melt the butter in a sauté pan and add the peaches, nutmeg and sugar. Simmer until just tender, then sprinkle with lemon juice. Serve hot.

SERVES 4

Pavlova *with* Compote *and* Yoghurt Cream

As a kid, I loved stopping at the bakery for meringues, hard and crisp, that would crumble to dust between my teeth. I'd carry them home for dessert, even though I was the only one in a family of seven who liked meringues. Now, I prefer the crisp exterior and tender inside of Pavlova, a grown-up version. For the yoghurt cream, choose a plain yoghurt with no gelatin, so the whey can drip out.

⅜ **cup** (90 mL)	**egg whites**
⅛ **tsp.** (.5 mL)	**cream of tartar**
~	**pinch of kosher salt**
¾ **cup** (175 mL)	**superfine granulated sugar**
1 Tbsp. (15 mL)	**cornstarch**
1 tsp. (5 mL)	**Vanilla Vinegar (see page 20)**
½ **tsp.** (2 mL)	**vanilla extract**
1 recipe	**Susan's Winter Fruit Chutney (see page 24) or Pineapple and Mango Compote (see page 25)**
1 recipe	**Ginger Spiked Yoghurt Cream**

Line a baking sheet with parchment. Preheat the oven to 400°F (200°C). Combine the egg whites and cream of tartar and mix with a whisk attachment until frothy. Slowly add the salt and most of the sugar while continuing to beat the whites on high speed. Stir the cornstarch into the final 2 Tbsp. (30 mL) of the sugar. Add and continue beating until thick and glossy. Stir in the vinegar and vanilla.

Spoon the meringue onto the parchment in circles about 4 inches (10 cm) in diameter. Build up along the outer edge and make a hollow in the centre of each meringue. Place in the oven and immediately reduce the temperature to 250°F (120°C). Do not open the door for 15 minutes. Bake an additional 10–20 minutes, until set, crisp but not coloured. Cool on the sheet.

To serve, fill each meringue with chutney or compote. Top with a spoonful of yoghurt cream. Serve immediately.

MAKES ABOUT 10 INDIVIDUAL ROUNDS

Ginger-Spiked Yoghurt Cream

Use this luxurious-tasting low-fat alternative anywhere you might use a spoonful of whipped cream or sour cream to garnish a dessert. If you, like me, are not a big fan of yoghurt, this may change your mind.

3 cups (750 mL)	**yoghurt**
½ cup (125 mL)	**granulated sugar**
1	**lemon, zest only**
2 Tbsp. (25 mL)	**grated fresh ginger**
¼ tsp. (1 mL)	**ground star anise**

Drain the yoghurt for 20–45 minutes through a fine sieve lined with a damp kitchen towel. Discard the whey. In a small pan, combine the sugar, lemon zest and ginger with ¼ cup (50 mL) water. Heat gently until the sugar is melted, stirring constantly, then bring to a rapid boil. Cook for 2–3 minutes, until the syrup is slightly thickened. Stir into the yoghurt along with the star anise.

MAKES ABOUT 2 CUPS (500 mL)

Buckwheat Crêpes
with Rhubarb Strawberry Sauce

I first experienced buckwheat crêpes as walkabout food in Annecy, near the French-Swiss border. Messy, maybe, but so good! We watched the crêpe maker spoon the grey batter onto his large flat hot plate, fill the crispy crêpe with cooked apples, chocolate sauce, and whipped cream and wrap it all in a twist of stout paper.

Buckwheat crêpes:

⅓ cup (75 mL)	water
⅓ cup (75 mL)	milk
⅔ cup (150 mL)	buckwheat flour
~	pinch kosher salt
1	egg
1	egg yolk
¼ cup (50 mL)	melted butter

Combine the water, milk and flour to make a smooth paste. Whisk in the remaining ingredients. Let rest 1 hour at room temperature before using.

Lightly brush a non-stick crêpe pan with additional butter and ladle in 2 Tbsp. (25 mL) of batter. Swirl it over the bottom of the pan and cook only one side over medium-high heat. Repeat to make the rest of the crêpes, stacking them on a plate as they finish cooking. Allow to cool before serving.

Rhubarb strawberry sauce:

2 cups (500 mL)	rhubarb, diced
1 cup (250 mL)	sugar
¼ cup (50 mL)	grated fresh ginger
1 sprig	rosemary
1 stick	cinnamon
1 cup (250 mL)	white wine
¼ cup (50 mL)	sliced crystallized ginger
1 cup (250 mL)	sliced strawberries

Over medium heat, simmer the rhubarb, sugar, ginger, rosemary, cinnamon and wine until the rhubarb is soft. Remove the rosemary and cinnamon stick. Add the crystallized ginger and strawberries. Cool.

To serve, place a crêpe on a large plate. Fill half the crêpe with sauce. Fold and serve immediately.

VARIATION: If rhubarb is too edgy and you want something more comforting, use the apple filling from Deep Dish Apple Pie (page 232), and top each crêpe with Espresso Ganache (page 235). Serve warm.

MAKES: 10–12 CRÊPES

Strawberry Puff

Think Sunday morning. Think coffee in bed. Think sleepy faces and slow movements. This is not a hurry-through-the-day kind of dish. Neither a soufflé nor a crêpe, this baked pancake relies entirely on eggs to puff it into a crusty and tender case for fruits of all types. Use a well-seasoned cast iron pan or a non-stick sauté pan with an ovenproof handle. If strawberries are not in season, serve Lush Peach Sauce (page 245), Susan's Winter Fruit Chutney (page 24) or Rhubarb Strawberry Sauce (page 248).

3	large eggs
¾ cup (175 mL)	milk
¾ cup (175 mL)	all-purpose flour
½ tsp. (2 mL)	salt
2 Tbsp. (25 mL)	melted butter
4 cups (1 L)	fresh strawberries
½ cup (125 mL)	whipping cream
2 Tbsp. (25 mL)	maple syrup
½ tsp. (2 mL)	ground cinnamon or nutmeg
1–2 Tbsp. (15 -25 mL)	icing sugar

Preheat the oven to 450°F (230°C). Place 1 rack in the centre position, with no rack above it (to leave headroom for the puff as it bakes). Place an ovenproof 10- to12-inch (25- to 30-cm) sauté pan on the centre rack in the hot oven to preheat for 7–10 minutes.

Place the eggs, milk, flour and salt in a large bowl and use a wire whisk to beat into a smooth batter.

Pour the melted butter into the sauté pan, using a pastry brush or paper towel to spread the butter evenly over the bottom and sides of the pan. Return the pan to the oven for 2–3 minutes to heat the butter.

Pour the batter into the hot pan and bake for 15 minutes. Reduce the heat to 350°F (180°C) and bake another 10 minutes.

While the puff is in the oven, wash, hull and slice the strawberries. If they are not sweet enough, sprinkle a spoonful of white sugar over them and toss gently.

Using a hand or counter mixer or a whisk, whip the cream until soft peaks form. Add the maple syrup and cinnamon or nutmeg. Cover and place in the fridge.

When the puff is brown and crisp, carefully remove the pan from the oven, using thick oven mitts. Set the pan down on the stove top and carefully loosen the bottom of the puff from the pan with a metal spatula. Slide the puff onto a platter. Spoon the strawberries over half of the puff, then fold the puff in half. Using a small sieve, dust the icing sugar over the puff. Slice crosswise, topping each slice with a dollop of whipped cream.

SERVES 4-6

Yoga Crème Anglaise

A regular yoga practice, like cooking, is a wonderful way to ground the spirit in the body. This classic stirred custard is wonderful with fruit, chocolate cake, soufflé, tarts.... Increase the egg yolks and use whipping cream instead of cereal cream to turn the custard into ice cream if you wish. Make extra spice blend and toss it in the teapot with a good Darjeeling for a fine pot of chai to chase away the blues. Breathe in. Aaah. Life is simple.

2 cups (500 mL)	**cereal cream**
1	**vanilla bean**
1	**cinnamon stick**
4–6	**allspice berries**
4–6	**whole cloves**
2	**cardamom pods, cracked**
½	**nutmeg, roughly chopped**
2	**star anise pods**
½	**lemon, zest only**
4	**egg yolks**
⅓ cup (75 mL)	**sugar or to taste**
2–4 Tbsp. (25–50 mL)	**Scotch, Armagnac, brandy or Calvados (optional)**

Heat the cream. Split the vanilla bean lengthwise, scrape out the seeds with a sharp knife blade, and add both seeds and pod to the cream.

continued...

Stir well, then mix in the cinnamon, allspice, cloves, cardamom, nutmeg, star anise and lemon zest. Whisk the egg yolks and sugar together, then whisk in the scalded cream and flavourings. Pour into a clean pot. Return to the heat and stir constantly with a flat-edged implement to keep the bottom loose. DO NOT BOIL! When thickened, remove from the heat and strain. Stir in the alcohol. Cover and let cool. Serve cold.

SERVES 12

VARIATION: Make *Espresso Crème Anglaise* by adding ¼ cup (50 mL) espresso to the simmering cream and eliminating all the spices except the cinnamon and vanilla. Add coffee liqueur at the end for additional flavour.

Dailyn's Queen Cake

Twelve years is a long time to cling to a favourite food, but that is what my youngest son, Dailyn, has done. This cake starred at my restaurant, where I changed its filling and its name each time I baked it. The method of cocoa incorporation is adopted from one used by American baker Rose Levy Berenbaum. I have had tube pans in neither my restaurant nor home kitchens, so I bake this angel food cake in a 10-inch (25-cm) springform with a collar of foil around its upper edge. This magical cake is dessert redemption, low in fat, rich in the mouth and tender-crumbed. I think it needs nothing to enhance its texture and flavour, but if you, like my son, prefer berry-filled cakes and cream topping, then by all means gild this glorious lily. Invite friends over to share it.

Cake:

2 cups (500 mL)	**egg whites (about 15 extra-large eggs)**
2 tsp. (10 mL)	**cream of tartar**
1 ¾ cups (425 mL)	**granulated sugar**
½ cup (125 mL)	**cocoa powder**

½ cup (125 mL)	hot strong coffee or espresso
1 cup (250 mL)	all-purpose flour
1 Tbsp. (15 mL)	cornstarch

Set the oven at 325°F (160°C) or at 275° F (140° C) if using a convection oven. Place a baking rack on its lowest setting and remove any others from the oven.

Tear off a long length of aluminum foil, fold it in half lengthwise and use the doubled length as a collar around the top of a 10-inch (25-cm) springform pan, folding the foil along itself to hold it in place. (Or use a tube cake pan.) Do not butter or flour the pan.

Whisk the egg whites until frothy, using a countertop mixer, on high speed. Add the cream of tartar and mix well. (If using a copper bowl, omit the cream of tartar.) Continue whisking the egg whites until they triple in volume, slowly adding the sugar while the machine runs.

Stir together the cocoa and coffee in a bowl or large measuring cup. Add ½ cup (125 mL) of the egg white-sugar foam and stir well. Sift the flour and cornstarch together. Fold the coffee-chocolate mixture and half the flour into the egg whites with a large spatula. Fold in the remaining flour once the first batch has been just incorporated. Gently heap the cake batter into the pan, smoothing the top.

Bake for 40 minutes, or until done. Remove the cake from the oven and gently peel off the foil collar. Cool the cake in the pan.

Filling:

2 cups (500 mL)	berries, fresh or frozen
¼ cup (50 mL)	sugar or honey
2 Tbsp. (25 mL)	cornstarch
½ cup (125 mL)	cold orange juice
½ tsp. (2 mL)	freshly grated nutmeg
~	zest of ½ orange

continued...

While the cake bakes, combine the filling ingredients in a heavy pan, mixing well. Bring to a boil, transfer the filling to a bowl and chill the filling.

....

Topping:

1 cup (250 mL)	**semisweet chocolate, preferably Callebaut**
2 cups (500 mL)	**whipping cream**
1 Tbsp. (15 mL)	**icing sugar (optional)**
2 Tbsp. (30 mL)	**Kahlua or coffee liqueur**

Melt the chocolate in a microwave on medium power for 2–3 minutes, stirring several times. Cool it to body temperature at room temperature, not in the fridge. Whip the cream, adding the icing sugar, if desired, as soft peaks begin to form. When the cream is nearly at the firm peak stage, shut off the machine and fold in the cooled chocolate and liqueur by hand with a rubber spatula. Chill until needed.

When the cake is completely cool, unmould the springform, remove the cake, and split it in half crosswise, using a fine-bladed bread knife in a gentle sawing motion around the cake's circumference. Remove the top layer to a clean plate or tray, then use the knife to loosen the lower half of the cake from the pan. Place on a serving plate.

Spoon the berries onto the cake's bottom layer in a single thickness, saving the unused berries and all the juices for another purpose. Centre the second layer of cake on the berries. Use a pie lifter or offset spatula to smooth chocolate cream around the side of the cake. Smooth additional cream onto the top of the cake. Smooth the edges and chill.

To serve, slice the cake with a hot, wet, thin-bladed knife, cleaning the knife between each slice. Serve with ice cream.

MAKES 1 10-INCH (25-cm) **CAKE, SERVES 16**

Cinnamon *or* Star Anise Ice Cream

Easy to make, hard to beat. Sometimes Mother Nature and real-life circumstances meet in unusual ways. Recently, I was making cake and this ice cream to celebrate my son Dailyn's birthday. His favourite cake was made, but I could not find the ice cream maker. I was distracted from the hunt by Mojo, my miniature schnauzer, begging to come inside. I let him in and ruffled his coat to warm him; it was cold outside, -37°C. Colder outside than the freezer, I thought. I stopped, thought again, and froze the ice cream outdoors, in the Great Outdoors Ice Cream Maker. It took 5 hours to set.

3 cups (750 mL)	**whipping cream**
2	**cinnamon sticks, or 4 whole star anise pods**
9	**egg yolks**
½ cup (125 mL)	**sugar**

Simmer the cream and cinnamon or star anise in a heavy pot. Cool, then remove the cinnamon sticks or star anise. In a bowl, whisk together the egg yolks and sugar. Slowly pour in the slightly cooled cream, whisk well, then return to the heavy pot.

Place over medium heat and cook gently, stirring with a wooden spoon. Do not boil. Cook until lightly thickened — it should coat a spoon and leave a clear line when a finger is drawn across the back of the spoon. At this point, remove from the heat, strain, then cover with buttered parchment. Cool, then chill. Make the ice cream in your ice cream maker according to the manufacturer's instructions or outdoors if the temperature is cold enough.

MAKES ABOUT 1 QUART (1 L)

Index

D

Vinaigrette
>   Apple Cider-Thyme Dressing, 188
>   Vanilla-Citrus Vinaigrette, 20
>   Gewürztraminer Vin, 21
>   Grilled New Carrots in Sherry Vinaigrette, 91

W

Warm Canadian Chevre Fondue, 42
Warm Flageolet and Borlotti Salad, 99
"Wild Child" Wild Roast Boar Kaleden Style, 135
Wilted Spinach with Shallots, Garlic and Pancetta, 89

Y

Yeast
>   Manchego and Golden Potato Pizza, 48
>   Savoyard Potato Pizza, 50

Yoghurt
>   Chicken Tandoori , 205
>   Ginger Spiked Yoghurt Cream, 247
>   Pavlova with Compote and Yoghurt Cream, 246
>   Stampede Shortcake with Seasonal Fruit and Ginger-Spiked
>   Yoghurt Cream, 244
>   Tzatziki, 37

Yoga Crème Anglaise, 251

Z

"Zebra" Summer Berry Tart with Espresso Ganache, 235